Trends and Techniques in
Modern English Literature

Trends and Techniques in Modern English Literature

Mallikarjun Patil

AUTHORSPRESS
Publishers of Scholarly Books

Worldwide Circulation through Authorspress Global Network
First Published 2011
by
Authorspress

Editorial
Q-2A Hauz Khas Enclave,
New Delhi-110 016
e-mail: authorspress@yahoo.com

Marketing
E-35/103, Jawahar Park
Laxmi Nagar, Delhi-110 092
e-mail: authorspress@yahoo.com

Trends and Techniques in Modern English Literature
ISBN 978-81-7273-595-1

Printed in India at Tarun Offset, Delhi.

Preface

Literature is a great art. It is much noble. It is a reflection of life. Along, with other arts, it teaches us culture as sciences teach us civilization. It makes our way of life strong and enduring for all times. So literature is as necessary as the very air for our breathing and becoming.

As usual, this volume, *Trends and Techniques in Modern English Literature* is a collection of articles on art, literature, religion, society and life. These nearly two dozen articles deal with English language, stylistics, the art of translation, travel literature, Greek mythology and drama, feminism, absurd theatre, existentialism, playwriting, poetry and fiction, the Bible, and cultural studies. The volume is very useful for the students and teachers of any literature, and more so for Indians.

Mallikarjun Patil

Contents

1

World Poetry: An Understanding

Poetry was basically thought of as literature which helped man to express his thoughts and feelings most imaginatively and intensively. Man used poetry as he uses literature of all forms today to speak of himself and the world. The word poetry came from the Greek word '*poien*' meaning 'to make or to create.' Man used poetry for creating an intense response in others. Poetry makes use of theme, language, sound and rhythm. Poetry uses dance and music. The early man used poetry to record the events of human existence. So poetry is the most elemental, sophisticated and subtle form of writing.

However poetry has its origin in folk literature, it is often artificial and consciously made. It is rhythmic and its subject and tones are limitless and its meaning is often obscure. Poetry expresses what is incommunicable through the use of figures of speech.

Poetry differs from prose in many ways. Of course, both employ the same kind of subject and language, poetry, unlike prose, is more intense, less direct, more suggestive and ambiguous. The rhythm in poetry is more marked and regular. The language of poetry is imagery.

Poetry-definitions are numerous and incomplete. William Wordsworth called poetry "The spontaneous overflow of powerful feelings recollected in tranquillity." Edgar Allan Poe said it is "the rhythmical creation of beauty." Edwin Arlington Robinson said "poetry is language that tells us, through a more or less emotional reaction, something that cannot be said."

The Art of Poetry

There are three major kinds of poetry – narrative, dramatic and lyrical. A narrative poem tells a story and the examples of which are ballad, epic, and metrical romance. A ballad recites a single exciting episode. It is of oral tradition. Primarily it is folk poetry depending upon dialogue, stanzaic patterns and repetitions for effect. An epic is a long narrative poem in an elevated style that recounts the story of heroic people. "The figure, often from myth, symbolises the most worthy qualities of a race or nation and the proudest moments of its history."[1] A metrical romance is a long romantic tale in verse in which the chief figures are kings or heroines who suffer under the impulse of love or religious faith and for an adventure. In the Middle Ages, such romances relating to Arthur and Charlemagne were written. Lord Byron and Sir Walter Scott wrote them. Dramatic poetry employs dramatic forms/ techniques for achieving poetic ends. Often drama makes use of such things. Robert Browning perfected dramatic monologue. Lyric that was once sung to the accompaniment of a lyre—is a brief, subjective statement, marked by strong imagination, melody and feeling and designed to create in the reader a single, unified and intense impression. It emphasis poet's personal emotions. Its forms are hymn, sonnet, ode, elegy and eclogue. Hymn is a song of praise that expresses religious emotion. The ode is an elaborate and complex construction. It is intellectual in tone. The sonnet limited to 14 lines is a fixed form of lyric. The elegy is a sustained and formal poem that sets forth a poet's meditations on death or a solemn theme. The eclogue is a form of pastoral poetry celebrating rustic life.

The Technical Elemeents of Poetry

Poetry makes use of all kinds of language. The study of poetry-writing is known as prosody. Rhythm, meter, sound structures, form, imagery and technical variations may be studied in this regard. Rhythm is the most important technical element. It is a regular recurrence of similar units of a pattern of sound. Rhythms can be quantitative, accentual, syllabic and accentual-syllabic. In the accentual-syllabic poetry, meter refers to the type and number of rhythmic units in a line. Determining meter is known as scansion. The rhythmic units, called feet, are iambic, trochaic, anapestic and dactylic. Poetry consists interlocking word sounds within a line. This is known as rhyme with three types — masculine, feminine and triple rhyme. Rhyme usually occurs at the end of lines. It may be even in the initial and internal position. Other interlockings are alliteration (ex: fancy free) and assonance. The fitting together of lines of like structure and length that are tied to other lines by end-rhyme is the usual means of creating poetic form. The stanza is an important element of form in terms of length, meter and rhyme scheme. Among the common types of stanzas are the couplet (two lines), tercet (three lines) and quatrain (four lines). Other types of stanzas are rhyme royal (seven lines), Spenserian stanza (eight lines) and a nine line of iambic hexameter. Possible stanzaic variations are endless and have been almost endlessly explored by poets. Another essential element of poetry is imagery. An image is a verbal representation of a sensory experience or of an object that can be known by one or more of the senses. An imagery is a portion of the essence of the meaning of a poem. Images may be either literal or figurative (metophorical).

Poetry has technical variations. Freedom is exercised in the sound forms of poem that is written in traditional stanzaic patterns. Variations occur within poems as we see in Emily Dickinson's poetry. In modern poetry a poem is based on irregular cadence with recurrence of images, phrases and syntactical patterns, replacing the conventional use of meter. However, the essence of poetry resides in a skillful, flexible and subtle use of the qualities of language as sound as well as meaning. In a good poem, both sound and meaning are melded into a single unit. Therefore, poetry is said to be a highly abstract art and as so very near to music.

Interpretation and Evaluation of Poetry

For example, a Frost's poem is as follows:

> Nature's first green is gold,
> Her hardest hue to hold.

Her early leaf's a flower;
But only so an hour.
Then leaf subsides to leaf,
So Eden sank to grief,
So dawn goes down to day
Nothing gold can stay.

We see Frost's meditation on nature here. How 'the gold grows into green' is explicit. Frost recalls how Eden's joy changed to sorrow. Frost uses the images of leaves, flowers, dawn and daylight. Ultimately the language is inseparable from his thought. Therefore, poetry cannot be translated or paraphrased. In fact, Frost defines poetry as something that cannot be translated.

Western Poetry

The vast body of world's poetic literature is divided into ancient (the classical Greek and Latin), medieval (from the 4th century Christian times) and modern (from Renaissance and Humanism).

Ancient Poetry

Homer's *Iliad* and *Odyssey* are the first ever classical Greek epics composed in the eighth century BC. Hesiod's *Works and Days* offers guidance. Archilochus (7th century) was a great lyric poet. Sappho of Lesbos, Alcaeus and Anacreon of Teos gracefully sang of wine, women and song. The seventh century choral odes of Terphander and Alcman reached its perfection in Pinder in the fifth century. Poetry was excellent in the dramatic works of Aeschylus, Sophocles, Euripides and Aristophanes. Theognis of Megara and Simonides of Ceos wrote fine elegies. In the Hellenistic age (320-150 BC) Theocritus introduced pastoral poetry. Moschus, Bion and Meleager of Cadara wrote fine poetry. Saint Romanos (6th century) wrote a new kind of religious poetry called *kontakia* (metrical hymns). St Andrew of Crete and St John Damascene introduced *kanon* (hymn).

Livius Andronicus translated *Odyssey* into Latin. Ennius founded classical Latin poetry in his *Annals*. Plautus and

Terence wrote dramatic poetry. Lucretius (AD1st c) wrote a philosophical poem *Dererum*. Virgil's *Aeneid* is a great work. The elegies of Catullus and Ovid, the verse of Tibullus, the Odes of Horace are well-known. Latin satire of the Silver Age (AD18-130) as produced by Persius and Juvenal, the tragedies of Seneca and the fables of Phaedrus are still read with interest.

Medieval Poetry

St Ambrose of the fourth century established the Ambrosian stanza of hymns. The medieval poetry is rich in vernacular forms of religious narratives, lyrics and allegorical poetry. Significant Old English religious poets are Caedmon and Cynewulf. Their French counterparts were St. Francis of Assisi and Jacopone Todi. *Beowulf* (AD 675) is a great masterpiece. The French *Song of Roland* (AD 1100), the Spanish *The Poem of the Cid* (1140AD), the German *Song of Hildebrand*, the Old Norse *Poetic Edda* (9-11th c), the Old English *Battle of Maldan* (10th century), the Russian *Lay of Igor's Campaign* (12th c), the Icelandic saga *Saga of Njal* are world famous. Most of these old poems dwelt with great myths, supernatural/religious figures like Arthur, Christ, Mary and others.

Amongst the early lyric and elegiac poems, the poems of the Exeter Books, of William of Aquitaine and the German *Minnesinger* are of great worth. The Italian poet Jacopo Lentino invented sonnets and it was used by Guido Guinizelli and Alighieri Dante (whose *The Divine Comedy* is a great allegory). The other significant medieval poets include the Flemish nun Hadewijch, the Welsh Dafydd Gwilym, Raymond Lully and Auzias March. Mention may be made of Chaucer (*Canterbury Tales*), Juan Ruiz, Francois Villon and Petrarch.

Renaissance was a period of brilliant creativity in all the arts. It produced a great flourishing of poetry in the vernaculars. The Italian poets Luigi Pulci, Matteo Boiardo, Ludovico Ariosto (*Orlando Furioso*, 1516) and Torquato Tasso (*Jerusalem Delivered*) were influential. Lorenzo Medici, Michelangelo and Tasso were great lyricists. In France, the best Renaissance poets were Clement Marot, Louise Labe and Maurice Sceve of Lyon School. Pierre Ronsard, Joachim Bellay were great figures of the Pleiade. In drama Robert Garnier's *Les Juives* (1583) is of great lyrical beauty. Mention may be made of Du Bartcs and Agrippa Aubigne. In England, Thomas Wyatt and Earl Surrey used the sonnet form. Edmund Spenser's *Faerie Queene* (1590) is of immense importance. So was Sir Philip Sidney. Christopher Marlowe, Machel Dryton, George Chapman and Ben Jonson wrote fine lyrical poetry. Many of these latter poets used dramatic poetry in blank verse. In Spain and Portugal, Santillana, Juan Boscan and Garcilaso Vega used fine poetry. Fray Leon and San Cruz wrote great lyrics. Luis de Camoes' *The Lusiads* is the greatest epic of the times. So is Alonso Ercilla's *Araucana*. The playwrights Lope de Vega and Pedro Calderon used poetry in drama. In Germany, Brant, Folz, Sachs and Luther wrote great poetry. Martin Opitz wrote a *Handbook of Poetics*. The Polish Jan Kochanowski and the Dutch Joost Vondel (1654) wrote fine plays.

Baroque and Metaphyscial Poetry

Baroque kind of poetry was written in the West between 1580 and 1680. Important Baroque poets of the continent include, in Italy: Tasso, Giambattista Marino, Alessandro Tassoni and Fransceso Redi; in Spain: Lope de Vega, Francisco Quevedo and Luis Gongora; in Germany: Simon Dach, Paul Fleming, Ahdreas Gryphius and Christian Hofmann; in Russia: Semion Polotsky and in France: D'Aubigne, St Amant, Theophile Viau, Gabriel Boisttus, Tristan Hermite and religious poets Jean de Ceppede, Jean de Sponde and Jean Chassignet. In England, the period poets were known more as Metaphysical poets. They were John Donne, Geroge Herbert, Richard Crashaw, Andrew Marvell and Henry Vaughan.

Neoclassical Poetry

The seventeenth century French poetry is predominantly neo-classical as is seen in Nicolas Bespreaux's *The Art of Poetry* (1674). Others include Jean Fortaine, Pierre Corneille, Jean Racine and Moliere. Voltaire and Andre Chenier wrote in the next century. John Milton (*Paradise Lost*), ranked second to

Shakespare, is the greatest neo-classical poet in England. Others include Samuel Butler (*Hudibras*), John Dryden and Alexander Pope. Dr Samuel Johnson was known for his criticism. Others were Edward Young, Thomas Gray, Oliver Goldsmith, William Collins and James Macpherson. The hymn writers were Isaac Watts, Chalres Wesley and Augustus Toplady. In Germany, Gottlieb Klopstock, Johann Goethe, Gottfried Burger and Friedrich Schiller were great poets of the time. The Mexican Juana Cruz, the Italian Pietra Metastasio, Giuseppe Parini, Vittorio Alfieri, the Russian Michael Lomonosov, Gavrila Derzhavin; the Finnish Gustaf Creutz, the Brazilian Tomas Gonzago, the Spanish Felix Samaiego and Tomas Triarte wrote fine neoclassical poetry.

Romantic Poetry

Romanticism is the greatest literary movement in modern times. It ushered in a great period of lyric poetry and individuality which swept all over the world. The first great English Romantic poets were William Wordsworth and Samuel Taylor Coleridge whose collaborative work *Lyrical Ballads* (1798) set a new age in literature. Sir Walter Scott collected Scottish songs and ballads. Lord Byron captured the imagination of Europe through his dazzling personality. P.B. Shelley and John Keats's fine lyrics are noteworthy. In Germany, Goethe was a great figure. Others were Clemens Brentano, Adalbert Chamisso, Ludwig Uhland, Heirich Heine, Annette Hulshoff, Eduard Morike, August Platen, Christian Hebbel and Conrad Meyer. In Italy, the three great Romantic poets were Ugo Foscolo, Alessandro Manzoni and Giocomo Leopardi. In Russia, Vasily Zhukovsky, Alessandr Pushkin, Michael Lermontov and Fydor Tyutchoo wrote fine poetry. In France, Alphonso Lamartine wrote great poetry. Others include Alfred Vigney, Victor Hugo, Alfred Musset and Gerard Nerval; in Latin America, the Cuban poet Maria Heredia, the Ecuadorian Jose Olmedo and Chilean Andre Bello are still read. In Spain, the duke of Rivas, Jose Espronceda, Jose Zorilla, Gustavo Becquer wrote finest poetry. In America, Edgar Allen Poe, Ralph Waldo Emerson, Henry Wadsworth Longfellow, William Cullen Bryant, John Greenleaf Whittier, and James

Russell Lowell were romantic poets of the time. Denmark's Adam Oehlenschlager, Swedish Erik Johan Stagnelius, Polish Adam Mickiewicz, the Dutch Willem Bilderdijk, Czech Karel Macha, Slavonic France Preseren, Norwegian Henrick Wergeland wrote lyrics of utmost beauty. In Finland, Elias Lonnrot compiled Finnish national folk epic *Kalevala* in 1849.

Modern Poetry: Poetry after 1850

Renaissance fostered poetry in the West. The events in the latter part of the 19th century gave way to Symbolism. The tragedy of I World War inspired Surrealism. In France, the Parnassians – Charles Baudelaire and Theophile Gautier—pioneered great poetry. The Parnassian poets avoided the personal element and stressed on the perfection of form. Symbolism which had its roots in English and German philosophy created new spokesmen like Paul Verlaine, Arthur Rembaud, Stephane Mallarme, Jules Laforgue and Jean Moreas. Paul Valery was another great symbolist. Frederic Mistrel, through his group Felibrige, made an effort to promote Provencal languages. Charles Peguy was a mystic poet. Emile Uerhaeren and Maurice Maeterlinck were Belgian symbolists. Guillarme Apollinaire heralded Surrealism and Dadaism. Surrealism was 'pure psychic antomatism' which emphasized on love, revolt, black humour, the marvelous and the inner life as reveled in dreams, madness and subconscousness and the world of hallucinations and drugs. Andre Bredon created its *Manifesto* in 1924. Other surrealists include Paul Eluard, Louis Aragon, Philippe Soupault, Benjamin Peret, Rene Char, Raymond Queneau and Aime Cesaire. Non-surrealists poets were Jean Joure, St John Perse and Francis Ponge.

In Germany and Austria, symbolists were Stefan George, Viennese Hugo and Rainer Rilke. The Expressionist poets were Gottfried Benn, Georg Trakl, and Franz Werfel. Bertolt Brecht was another. In Italy, Giosue Carducci, D'Annunzio and Giovanni Pascali wrote symbolist poetry. Hermetics were Giusepp Ungaretti, Eugenio Montale and Salvatore Quasimodo. One of the finest later poets was Umberto Saba. In Russia, the modern period was a golden age. It is the age of Fyodor Sologub,

Konstantin Balmont, Zinaida Gippius, Valeri Bryusov Aleksanr Blok and Andrei Bely. The movement Acmeism flourished between 1912 and 1917 as represented by Nikolai Gumiev, Anna Gumilev and Osip Mandelshtan. Russian futurists include Victor Khlebnikov and Vladimir Mayakovsky. Boris Pasternak, George Ivanov and Yevgeni Yevtushenko are the 1920's great poets. In Latin America, the Cuban poet Julian Casal, the Columbian Josa Silva, the Nicaraguan Ruben Dario and the Uruguayan Julio Reissig were modern poets. Latin America's other poets were Cesar Vallejo of Peru, Pablo Neruda and Vicente Huidobro of Chile, Octavio Paz and Manuela Najera of Mexico, Jose Hernadez of Argentina, Antonio Alves of Brazilia, Nicolas Guillen of Cuba, Jorge Andrade of Ecuador and Luis Aragon of Guatemala.

In Spain, Antonio Machdo was a popular poet of Andalusia. Juan Jimenez was a modern poet. Federico Lorca was a surrealistic poet. In the British Isles, the poetry of the nineteenth century was rich. Edward Fitzgerald adapted the *Rubaiyat of Omar Khayyam*. Alfred Tennyson was a Poet-Laureate. His rival Robert Browning wrote rich dramatic monologues. Others were Browning's wife Elizabeth Browning, George Meredith and Dante Gabriel Rossetti. Matthew Arnold's *Dover Beech* (1867) mirrored the growing religious insecurity of the age. A..C. Swinburne brought poetry close to music. James Thomson offered a nightmarish vision of man's lonely isolation in the modern city. Rudyard Kipling was a 'poet of Empire.' In the 1890's fine lyricism was apparent in the fashioned verses of A.E. Housman, Ernest Dowson and Lionel Johnson. Thomas Hardy's *The Dynasts* won him recognition as a major poet. G.M. Hopkin's remarkable poetry with 'sprung rhythm' was published posthumously in 1918. In the twentieth century, the major British poets are an Irishman W.B. Yeats. Yeats was influenced by William Blake, occultism and Indian philosophy and he was steeped in Irish culture. The American-born T.S. Eliot and the Welshman Dylan Thomas engage our attention. Other gifted poets of the age were 'AE' (George Russell), T. Surge Moore, Walter de la Mare, John Mansfield (the Poet-Laureate after Robert Bridges), D.H. Lawrence,

Edward Thomas, Rupert Brooke, Wilfred Owen, Robert Graves, Roy Campbell, Edith Sitwell, C.D. Lewis and Louis MacNeice.

In America between 1850 and 1900 Walt Whitman's *Leaves of Grass* and Emily Dickinson's poems were landmarks. The twentieth 20th century witnessed a flowering of gifted writers in a variety of moods and forms. Ezra Pound founded Imagism. Carl Sandburg and Vachel Lindsay had large audience. In the South the 'Fugitives'—Allen Tate, John Crowe Ransom, Donald Davidson and Robert Penn Warren were active in the 1920's. Others were Robinson Jeffers, Marianne Moore, Hart Crane, E.E. Cummings and Archibald MacLeish. T.S. Eliot, the expatriate was the most influential poet and critic of the age. W.H. Auden may be ranked with Eliot and Pound. Robert Frost stands as a major figure. Other important poets include Wallace Stevens, William Carlos Williams, Richard Eberhart, Theodore Roethke, Randall Jarrell and John Berryman. The gifted black poets were Paul Lawrence Dunbar, Arna Bontemps, Langston Hughes, Countee Cullen, Robert Hayden, Margaret Walker and the Jamaican-born Claude McKay. There were African-American spirituals and Fisk Jubilee singers.

Among the many other poets of the West since 1950, some notable have been, from Canada: Archbald Lampman; from Gatalonia: Joan Margall; from Greece: Constantine Cavafy, Nikos Kazantzakis and George Seferis; from Haiti: Oswald Durand; from the Netherlands: Jan Hendrik Leopold; from Norway: Henrik Ibsen and Bjornson; from Portugal: Eugenio de Castro; and from Sweden: August Strindberg, Guslaf Fording and Erik Karlfeldt.

Non-Western Poetry

The non-western poetry differs from the western in so far: (1) in the use of forms, (2) in the preference for certain kinds of metaphors and symbols, and (3) in its use of syntax and diction. In the non-Western poetry folklore and popular poetry are different from the written. But since the nineteenth century Western poetry has been influential all over the world.

Hebrew Poetry

The Old Testament is enough to evidence the nature of Hebrew literature. An example can be Solomon's love songs. Hebrew literature has biblical style. It does not have rhetorics as Greek and Latin poetry have. The poetry is simple. Rhyme is little used.

Persian and Arabic Poetry

Persian is an Indo-European language with a long tradition before Islam but the Arab conquest introduced new forms in it. Post-Islamic Persian poetry has a variety of meters common to Arabic as well. *Shah Namah* (11th century) is a great Persian epic of Firdausi. The Persian *Qasida* (ode) runs to 100 couplets and *Ghazal* (lyric) deals with love. The earliest Arab poems are in the *Maullaqat* (Golden odes) of the eighth century. *Maullaqat* are epic lays. Arabic poetry is in simple style.

Indian Poetry

Sanskrit is an Indo-European language imported into India by European Aryans. The indegeneous people called Dravidians used their own languages, often being influenced by the Aryans. The earliest Sanskrit writings are *Vedas* (composed between 2000 and 1000 BC). They are characterised by quantitative syllable counting which provided an effect just like that of Greek and Latin. The Sanskrit hymns are about gods, cosmos and seasons. There is nature imagery. A middle stage of Sanskrit poetry is of the two epics—the *Ramayana* (500 BC) and the *Mahabharata* (400 BC). Metaphors are often taken form nature and common life, and the erotic is popular.

Chinese Poetry

Chinese, a Sino-Tibetan language, is monosyllabic with syntax. It has tone. The earliest Chinese poetry is in the *Shih Ching* (Book of Odes, 10th century). It includes a diversity of materials from folk songs to court poems. It deals with love, war, old age and friendship. The *shish* form is still used. Another is *fu* (rhymed prose)

The Japanese Poetry

The origin of Japani language is unknown. The Japanese poetry contains imperial anthologies and an example of it is *Man Yoshu,* collection of Ten Thousand Leaves (7th c).

Reference

1. C. Hugh Holman "Poetry," *Encyclopedia Americana*, Vol. 22, p. 277.

2

Greek Drama: An Understanding

Critics trace the rise of Greek tragedy to the fifth century BC. The ancient tragedy of Greece is known as Attic drama. As F.L. Lucas says the ancient Greeks' life was close to tragedy. This was attributed to their bloody battles with enemy kings and foreigners like Persians. The Athenians had their share of aggressiveness and slavery. They had their magnificence and unhappiness.

The patron deity of Athenian tragedy was Dionysus. He was the symbol of their irrationality in life. The themes for the tragedies were from the heroic age of the past. Dionysus was adored as 'God of Trees,' Lord of Flowers' and 'Fair of Fruits.' He was associated with animals and birth and death. Above all he was a giver of ecstasy. He was the icon for man's last happiness. Dionysus was a God of Unreason as is described in Euripides's *Bacchae*.

Dorians had a role in the growth of tragedy. 'Tragedy' comes from the word 'goat-skin.' Probably it is because the chorus wore a goatskin, or because they sacrificed a goat or they had a goat prize. In the sixth century Thespis invented an actor in plays. He used masks and iambic meter for dialogues. Plutarch says, the lawgiver Solon after seeing Thespis acting in plays chided him, for such acting would pass in real life. Phrynichus (510-470 BC) is said to have originated women characters. Aeschylus added a second character and Sophocles added a third character. Greeks took themes from the heroic legends, real life and from the epics.

The tragedians wrote tragedies. Those who wrote for competition had to write three plays and often they had themselves to produce the plays during festivals such as Dionysian (in March) and Lenaean (in January). Stage preparations were simple and flexible. The first stone-seated theatre was built in the third century. There would be wooden seats. All kinds of audiences were allowed to see. The stage had a little infrastructure. Even music was unelaborated. Finally the chorus was an indivisible part of Athenian tragedy.

Tragedy

The term is broadly applied to literary, and especially to dramatic, representations of serious actions which eventuate in a disastrous conclusion for the protagonist (the main character). More precise and detailed discussions of the tragic form properly begin-although they should not end-with Aristotle's classic analysis in the *Poetics* (fourth century B.C.). Aristotle based his theory on induction from the only examples available to him, the tragedies of Greek dramatists such as Aeschylus, Sophocles, and Euripides. In the subsequent two thousand years and more, various new types of serious plots ending in a catastrophe have been developed — types that Aristotle had no way of foreseeing. The many attempts to stretch Aristotle's analysis to apply to later tragic forms serve merely to blur his critical categories and to obscure important differences among a diversity of plays, all of which have proved to be dramatically effective. When flexibly managed, however, Aristotle's discussions apply in some part to many tragic plots, and his analytic concepts serve as a suggestive starting point for identifying the differentiae of various non-Aristotelian modes of tragic construction.

Aeschylus

Aeschylus is the first of the three ancient Greek tragedians. He wrote ninety tragedies and just seven of them survive. In fact, he created the form of tragedy with a second character. Sophocles and Euripides were the other two.

Aeschylus was born of an aristocratic family at Elensis near Athens in 499 BC some thirty years after the birth of tragedy. He made his writing debut entering a group of tragedies in the contest of the annual festival of Dionysus. His two rivals at it were Choerilus and Pratinas, the leading dramatists of the day. In 484 Aeschylus received the highest award for his dramatic achievements. He also participated in the Persian wars and he died at Gela in Sicily about 456. His earliest play *The Persians* (472) deals with the Persian king Xerxes's invasion of Greece. His play *The Seven Against Thebes* deals with the misfortunes of the Lais family because of Pepus curse. The play is about Oedipus's two sons Eteocles and Polynices killing each other in a bloody war. *The Suppliants* is about the Danaus's 50 daughters acting as chorus. They run away to Argos in Greece to forestall a forced marriage with their cousins, the sons of Aegyptus.

Aeschylus's celebrated Oresteian Trilogy consists of *Agamemnon, Choephori* and *Oresteia*. This is a great Greek trilogy extant today. The first play is about Agamemnon's triumphant return from the war of Try to Argos and his getting murdered by his wife Clytemnestra with her lover Aegisthus. The second play is about Agamemnon's son Orestes's revenging his mother and her lover for their murder of his father. The last play is about Orestes's trial at Athens where due to Athena's help he is absolved of his sin. *Orestia* is the best kind of trilogy for which Aeschylus got the first prize in the drama contest of 458.

Richmond Hathorn writes, "*The Orestia* is generally acknowledged to be the most impressive monument in all dramatic literature—for its scope and complexity, for the careful elaboration of its symbolic myth, for its reinforcement by an unusually rich system of imagery, and for its weightily ethical and theological themes." It is observed: "It broaches for the first time in the history of human thought such themes as the meaning of suffering (*Pathei mathos*, "man learns by suffering.)."[1] *Prometheus Bound* is one (the other two are lost) of the extant trilogy of that name. This is about Titan Prometheus's getting punished by Zeus for his helping of mankind by bringing fire from the heaven. The play ends with reconciliation between Prometheus (mankind) and Zeus (God). The Romantic poets took Prometheus for revolt against the tyranny of rule and the theme finds a place of pride in Shelley's *Prometheus Unbound* (1822). *The Aetnaeans* and *Niobe* are his last plays.

The first critical appreciation of Aeschylus is found in Aristophanes' *Frogs*, in which the latter says Aeschylus was a source of moral improvement for Athenians. The Romans admired Aeschylus. The Romantic age found in his *Prometheus* an inspiration for revolt. Marx found *Prometheus* to be a symbol for the communist movement. In twentieth century Aeschylus is appreciated for his profundity of religious thought, largeness of dramatic structure and mastery of poetic imagery.

Sophocles

Sophocles, the Athenian was born in 496 B.C. and he lived for ninety years. Sophocles grew in a homely atmosphere and got well educated. In his times, it is said, Athens was making a good start in international politics. There were its wars with Persia. Young Sophocles made a name in the city's wars over Salamis. Sophocles died when in prime old age and that was the time of Athens' war with the Peloponnesian countries. Athens' history is seen in the works of Herodotus and Thucydides, the historians; Aeschylus, Sophocles and Euripides, the tragedians and Aristophanes, the comedian. Athenian theatre was an art and entertainment arena. The tragedy with which we are here concerned touched the deepest centers of man's individual and corporate consciousness. Tragedies were presented in the Athenian theatre annually. Competition was the order of the day. Writers wrote tragedy for expressing human instinct for ritualistic interpretation. By the bye, the elements of dance and song were essential to it. The two characteristic features—the choric element and the religious note—survive throughout the great period of Greek tragedy. Chorus was an important feature so much so that sometimes a play was called a 'chorus.' Sophocles stands midway between Aeschylus and Euripides. For him the dramatic action is vital. He uses chorus as an actor and commentator. Then there is lyric interspersed for the sake of speaking of religion.

Then Sophocles wrote over a hundred plays and only seven of them survive now. One of them is *Oedipus Tyrrannus*. *Oedipus Tyrrannus* is Sophocles's masterpiece and many consider it the greatest of classic Greek tragedies. Aristotle referred to it continually in his *Poetics*, pointing out features of the ideal tragic work. Character and action are in nearly perfect harmony. The fall of the king is made doubly horrifying by Sophocles's extremely effective use of dramatic irony. The play probably was written for production at one of the periodic drama competitions held in Athens.

Euripides

Euripides is one of the last three greatest Greek dramatists. The other two are Aeschylus and Sophocles. Euripides is a modern dramatist compared to the other two. He is a kind of avant-garde writer. He had a sense of contemporaneity in his attitude when he projected his characters. Likewise, the sufferings of his characters stem more from their minds and moods rather than from the ill-will of gods and goddesses. Here lies Euripides's invention of a new style of dramaturgy.

Euripides (480-406 BC), the youngest and most 'modern-minded' of the three great Attic tragedians, said to have been born at Salamis on the day of the defeat of the Persians in the naval battle off that island. The characteristics of his plays are their human quality (men and women are represented in them as they are in everyday life), poignant realism and the like. His extant plays, the survivals of some ninety that he is said to have written, are the following: 'Alcestis,' 'Media,' 'Hippolytus,' 'Hecuba,' 'Andromache,' 'Ion,' ' Suppliants,' 'Heracleidae,' 'Mad Heracles,' 'Iphiginia,' 'Trojan Women,' 'Helen,' 'Phoenissae,' 'Electra,' 'Orestes,' 'Iphiginia at Aulis,' 'Bacchae' and 'Cyclops.' It is said Euripides was made much fun of by the comic poet Aristophanes.

Euripides was born in 480. His father Mnesarchus was a shopkeeper and his mother Clito was a greengrocer. Euripides's early life was passed in Salamis in reading and writing. Later he moved to Athens. It is said he served in an embassy to Syracuse. He married possibly twice and had three sons. One of his sons staged his plays for long. Euripides is said to have associated with sophists like Prodicus, Protagoras, Anaxagoras and Socrates. Euripides left Athens in 408 for the court of king Archelaus of Macedonia. There he continued to compose plays including one of his last and greatest *The Bacchae*.

Euripides is said to have written 92 plays including 8 satyr plays. But only 19 of them exist today. Some of them were trilogies. The existing plays include: *Cyclops* (438), *Alcestis* (430), *Media* (431), *The Children of Heracles* (430), *Hecuba* (424), *The Suppliants* (422), *Heracles* (418), *Electra* (413), *Helen* (412), *Iphigenia Among the Taurians* (411), *Ion* (412), *The Phoenician Women* (411), *Orestes* (408), *The Bacchae* (406) and *Iphigenia in Aulis* (406). The date of the extant *Rhesus* is as uncertain as its authorship.

Euripides's early works include his plays based on folktales. His *Alcestis* is based on a primitive folktale in which a young king escapes his fated death by letting his wife die in his place. In his *Media*, a witch, a figure of folk origin, is given tragic stature as she struggles between love for her children and hatred for her faithless husband until, "passion overcoming reason"—she murders her children to take vengeance on her betrayer.

In his second phase of writing (430-410) Euripides produced *The Children of Heracles* and *The Suppliants*, both plays in which Athens is presented as the defender of the weak against tyrannical states. The theme of Athens is prevalent in his later plays *Hippolytus* and *Heracles*. In his third phase (415-408) Euripides wrote *The Trojan Woman*, which is about Greeks' indictment of cruelties upon the victimised Trojan women and children. *Electra* is perhaps the best example of the new realism—a strong psychological realism—of Euripedian tragedy. Unlike other plays on Electra, Euripides's Electra is a strong willed, frustrated virago. Her homicidal hatred for her mother, Clytemnestra and for Aegisthus, her lover, springs more from the murder of her father, Agamemnon, though it is that murder that she and her brother Orestes determine to avenge. *Orestes* is about Orestes's vengeance on society in a series of ever more outrageous deeds. *Helen* is rather a fantasy. *The Bacchae* and *Hippolytus* deal with myths. Here goddesses take vengeance upon their mortals for their neglect of them. In *The Bacchae*, the hero Pentheus, the puritanical king of Thebes, refuses to acknowledge the godhead and permits the wild orgiastic worship of the new god, Dionysus, son of Zeus and of a Theban princess Semele. Dionysus takes vengeance against the king. D.J. Conacher observes, "It used to be fashionable to regard Euripides simply as a sophistic iconoclast, bent on destroying both the grandeur of the traditional myths and of the traditional tragic structures in which their catastrophes were enshrined. Rather, his complex view of the many causes and aspects of human joy and suffering, and his appreciation of the real meaning of the great mythical archetypes, required a similarly radical and varied approach to tragic structures. It was not that he did not believe in 'gods.' Instead, he recognised that these 'gods' are within us and all around us rather than in mysterious 'outside world' of traditional mythology."[2]

Comedy

Ancient Greek comedy is a celebration of joy. It arose due to fertility cults so common in those days. The word 'komoidia' means 'the song of the revelers,'—of merry mummers for whom grossness was not merely amusing, but a religious ritual to arouse Nature's fecundity. Like the medieval Scott poets who relished in 'flytings,' the ancient Greeks indulged in abusing and parodying people. The early Greek comedy is of two types—the non-choric comedy of Sicily and the choric comedy of Athens. The first was developed by Epicharmus (c. 530- 440 BC) who like Moliere, had serious interests as well. He wrote nearly forty comedies, which are burlesques, parodies and satires of kings and commoners. The Attic comedy arose due to phallic processions and dances. Later comedy contests started at Dionysia and Lenaea at about 450 BC.

F.L. Lucas says the Old Comedy had the following features:

1. Some character has a bright idea. For instance, a man thinks of stopping the war by flying to Heaven on a beetle; or a woman by organising a women's strike.
2. There enters a chorus, sympathetic or hostile.
3. There is a set debate (*agon*) about the idea.
4. The chorus turns and addresses the audience in a parabasis—perhaps a relic of the mockeries flung at bystanders by the old phallic mummers.
5. A series of farcical episodes arises from putting the original idea into practice.

1. All ends in a revel scene—feast or wedding; a further relic of the primitive merrymaking.[3]

One unique feature of ritual comedy was that it indulged in abusing. But at the time of Samian revolt abusing was banned. Cleon retaliated Aristophanes by abusing. Pericles had to face public abusing. The fourth century comedy developed realism and romance. And hundreds of plays were written at this time though just a few like Aristophanes's *Plutus* survive.

Gradually Attic Comedy or the Old Comedy lost its stronghold and New Comedy came in its place. There were seventy playwrights of this genre. Menander and Euripides were the prominent ones. The New Comedy does not have much lyricism or heady chorus. This is a kind of comedy that stimulated Terence and Shakespeare, Moliere and Congreve, and Sheridan and Wilde.

Aristophanes

Aristophanes lived long and wrote for forty years. He wrote some forty comedies though only seven of them survive. Four of them are appeals for peace. Aristophanus's comedies are known for their satire. In *The Archarnians* (425), an Athenian farmer successfully concludes a private peace of his own; *The Knights* (424) belabours the bellicose Cleon; the hero of *Peace* (421) flies to Heaven on a beetle's back for finding peace; the heroines of *Lysistrata* (411) reached the same end by organising a Panhellenic strike of wives. The hero of *The Wasps* (422) cures his old father of a mania for sitting on juries. *The Birds* (414) is a fantasy. *The Cloud* (423) assails Socrates as the arch-sophist. Aristophanes ridiculed communism in *The Women's Assembly* (389). His plays *The Thesmophoiazusae* (411) and *The Frogs* (405) are burlesques. Aristophanus was both an entertainer and moralist.

References

1. Richmond Hathorn on Aeschylus, *Encyclopaedia Americana*, p.231.
2. D.J. Conacher on Euripides, *Encyclopedia Americana*, p. 666.
3. F.L. Lucas, *Greek Drama for the Common Reader*, Chatto and Windus, London, 1967, p. 364.

3

The Theatre of the Absurd

The term 'Absurd' was originally used to describe the disharmony in music. It was used to describe the violation of the rules of logic. Later it a wide connotation in the fields of arts, literature, philosophy and theology. The 'absurd' means man's failure or the failure of traditional values to fulfil man's material desires and spiritual needs. Danish philosopher Soren Kierkegaard used the term to describe the incongruity in Christian religion. Martin Heidegger described Christianity as absurd, for it cannot stand the test of rational principles. Jean Paul Sartre spoke of pointlessness or 'nothingness' in modern man's life. Albert Camus expressed that the disparity between man's intention and reality repeatedly checkmates the individual. In Gabriel Marcel's view the 'absurd' is the symbol of the fundamental mystery of human existence. All these thinkers are of the philosophy of Existentialism, which developed in Europe in the 1970s.

The 'absurd in life arose due to various reasons. First of all industrialisation in Europe led to urbanisation creating a massive imbalance in social life. Mass exodus led to existential crises. Industrialisation led to the creation of science and technology. The same spread to the rest of Europe. Charles Darwin's theory of evolution of species negated man's faith in the gospel and god altogether. World War I, which arose between European powers, led to the destruction. World War II led to the death of millions of men and properties. The wars affected man's isolation, frustration and dread.

Existentialism, as a philosophical trend in the twentieth century post-war Europe, is a modern school of thought. It influenced European literature widely. It spoke of man as an individual. It emphasized on man's thought, choice, action and responsibility. It held the consciousness of our own freedom as the sign of 'authentic experience,' as opposed to bad faith. The new philosophy contributed to the rise and growth of modern and post-modern ethos. Existentialism is a label for several revolts against traditional philosophy. The prominent existentialists Karl Jaspers, Martin Heidegger and Jean-Paul Sartre do not agree upon the essentials of Existentialism. The factors that bound them together are man's pre-occupation with failure, dread and death. The new philosophy speaks of man's proper choice and action culminating in his individuality. Likewise, life is absurd, evading an explanation. According to Muriel Sparks: "Existentialism speaks powerfully to the sense of the 20th century as a chaotic and even catastrophic era, in which certainties have been lost and man is faced with the abyss of nothingness. It lays stress on extreme situation, which produces dread, arising from awareness of freedom of choice (according to Sartre) or awareness of original sin (according to Kierkegaard). Extremity and existential dread are important in the works of William Golding and Patrick White, and, earlier in the century, Joseph Conrad, who in this respect as in others anticipates the 20th century zeitgeist."[1] Existentialism influenced the field of literature greatly.

The prominent leaders of existentialism have been the philosophers Martin Heidegger (1889-1976) and Karl Jaspers (1883-1969) in Germany, Jean-Paul Sartre (1905-1980) and philosopher and dramatist Gabriel Marcel (1889-1973) in France. Marcel represented the religious stream whose progenitor was the nineteenth century Danish thinker Soren Kierkegaard (1813-1855).

Jean-Paul Sartre propounded the principles of Existentialism in the 1960s. He was a great writer and thinker of modern times. Sartre was born in 1905. He graduated from the Ecole Normale Superieure in 1929. He taught philosophy in provincial high schools until he joined the army during the

World War II. Later he led a resistance movement against the Germans. After the war he began writing earnestly and did a lot of political activities. He founded a monthly review *Lex temps modernes* in 1946. He wrote several plays, novels and essays and got the Nobel Prize for literature. He died in 1980.

Jean-Paul Sartre's fame rests upon his literary works as much as upon his existential philosophy. Sartre's vision of life as nothingness is explicit in his novel *Nausea* (1949), plays *The Flies* (1946), *Dirty Hands* (1949) and *The Condemned of Altona* (1960) and essays *Being and Nothingness* (1956) and *Existentialism and Humanism* (1948). Sartre speaks of man as a 'useless passion.' He says man is terrifyingly free and a responsible being. His work *What is Literature?* is useful. *The Words* is his autobiography.

Sartre's *Nausea* depicts the life of its hero Antoine Roquentin. The hero lives in Bouville studying Marquis de Rollebon. He lives as an outsider. One day when he feels nausea he visits a picture gallery where are hung the portraits of all the town's great men who had lived, however, a bad life. Roquentin feels they lived in 'bad faith.' The novel ends in Roquentin's abandoning his research in favour of writing a work of art. Here inauthentic life is termed as 'bad faith.' 'Bad faith' means evasion of responsibility, in fact. It is nausea. Sartre's play *The Flies* depicts the life of a Greek hero Orestes's returning to Argoes for avenging the murder of his father, Agamemnon, by killing his mother Clytemnestra and her paramour Aegisthus. This is an allegory reminding the German occupation of France.

The next prominent writer is Albert Camus. He is a great existentialist writer and thinker. Camus was born in Mandovi in 1913. In the 1930's Camus committed to politics, theatre and writing. He was a non-doctrinal socialist. He travelled Europe widely. Then he began writing novels and plays. His works include his novels *The Outsider* (1946), *The Fall* (1957), *The Plague* (1958); plays *Caligula* (1938), *Cross Purpose* (1944), and a book of essays *The Myth of Sisyphus* (1955). Camus, in his *Myth of Sisyphus*, speaks of man's absurd life. The work is a critique of existentialism. The feeling of absurdity, Camus says, can strike any man in the face of any street corner. So absurdity is a universal phenomenon.

1. The mechanical nature of many people's lives may lead them to question the value and purpose of their existence; this is an intimation of absurdity.
2. An acute sense of time passing, of the recognition that time is a destructive force.
3. A sense of being left in an alien world. Camus suggests that a world, which can be explained even with bad reasons, is a familiar world. But in a world from which illusions and insight have been suddenly removed, man feels himself a stranger. As it is most intense his sense of alienation is carried to the point of nausea, when familiar objects normally 'domesticated' by names – such as stone or tree – are also robbed of their familiarity.
4. A sense of isolation from other beings.

The absurd, for Camus, is an absence of correspondence between the mind's need for unity and the chaos of the world the mind experiences, and the obvious response is either suicide or, in the opposite direction, a leap of faith.[2]

Andre Malraux is another important playwright who, in fact, lived earlier than Sartre and Camus. He lived in the beginning of the twentieth century and wrote several good plays. His works *The Consequences* (1928), *The Royal Way* (1930) and *Man's Estate* (1933) show the seeds of the absurd. In his *The Temptation of the West* Europe figures as a 'great cemetery.' Sixty-five pages of the book is full of letters supposedly written between two young men: five by A.D. — a young European traveling in the East, and the rest by Ling W. —T., a young Chinese travelling in Europe. "The more this young man sees of Europe the more convinced he becomes that European thought and culture are based on confusion and a wrong notion of reality... A.D. agrees that western man is a creature of the absurd, and uses the rest of the book to provide added reasons, and warns that the disease is spreading to the Orient. Obviously, for A. D., it is not merely God who is dead, but man also: standing alone under an empty heaven without remedy."[3] Malraux's works are about death, solitude, defeat and suffering. This theme recurs in many of his Malraux's works and is seen in the works of Jean–Paul Sartre and Albert Camus.

The 'absurd' means out of harmony with reason or property: incongruous, unreasonable and illogical. Eugene Ionesco defined it as follows: "Absurd is that which is deprived of purpose...cut off from his religious, metaphysical and transcendental roots, man is lost; all his actions become senseless, absurd, useless."[4] The absurd involves the existentialists' purposelessness, angst and dread. It is Sartre's 'bad faith.' In Martin Esslin's view it is the inevitable devaluation of ideas, purity and purpose. For Camus the absurd springs from the confrontation between man's conscience, his thirst for rationality and the inert irrational unknowable world. Still man strives for his own ethical and material system. So he achieves his own human dignity in the face of absurdity. Sharada Iyer observes, "Clearly the idea that man is absurd is by no means new. An awareness of the essential absurdity of human behaviour has been inherent in the works of many writers. Aristophanes, Plautus, Terence, Chaucer, Erasmus, Cervantes, Moliere, Swift, Pope, Butler, Anatole France, Balzac, Dickens, Chesterton, Belloc – to cite only a few they have all shown an acute sense of man's comicality."[5] According to OED "Absurd' means: (1) (of an idea, suggestion etc.,) wildly unreasonable, illogical, or inappropriate. (2) (of a person) unreasonable or ridiculous in manner. (3) (of a thing) ludicrous, incongruous."[6]

In *The Penguin Dictionary of Theatre* (1966) John Russell Taylor writes: "Absurd, Theatre of the Term applied to a group of dramatists in the 1950s who did not regard themselves as a school but who all seemed to share certain attitudes towards the predicament of man in the universe: essentially those summarised by ALBERT CAMUS in his essay *The Myth of Sisyphus* (1942). This diagnoses humanity's plight as purposelessness in an existence out of harmony with its surroundings (absurd literally means out of harmony). Awareness of this lack of purpose in all we do...produces a state of metaphysical anguish which is the central theme of the writers in the Theatre of the Absurd, most notably Samuel Beckett, Eugene Ionesco, Arthur Adamov, Jean Genet, and Harold Pinter. What distinguishes these and other, lesser figures (Robert Pinget, N. F. Simpson, Edward Albee, Fernando Arrabal, Gunter Grass) from earlier dramatists who have mirrored a similar concern in their work is that the ideas are allowed to shape the form as well as the content: all semblance of logical construction, of the rational linking of idea with idea in an intellectually viable argument, is abandoned, and instead the irrationality of experience is transferred to the stage. The procedure has both its advantages and its limitations. Most dramatists of the absurd have found it difficult to sustain a whole evening in the theatre without compromising somewhat...Indeed, by 1962 the movement seemed to have spent its force, though as a liberating influence on the conventional theatre its effects continue to be felt."[7]

The absurd is irrational and illogical. It is expressed in art and literature right from the beginning. The absurd is as old as man's ignorance. Shakespeare and T. S. Eliot have written about it finely. Malraux, Sartre and Camus, have, in their works, depicted what is the absurd in life. But all these playwrights wrote of the absurd making use of traditional literary devices like plot, characterisation, dialogue and description. They fully made use of human language.

In Martin Esslin's view: "If Camus argued that in our disillusioned age the world has ceased to make sense, he did so in the elegantly rationalistic and discursive style of an eighteenth-century moralist, in well-constructed and polished plays. If Sartre argues that existence comes before essence and that human personality can be reduced to pure potentiality and the freedom to choose itself anew at any moment, characters who remain wholly consistent and thus reflect the old convention that each human being has a core of immutable, unchanging essence — in fact, an immortal soul. And the beautiful phrasing and argumentative brilliance of both Sartre and Camus in their relentless probing still, by implication, proclaim a tacit conviction that logical discourse can offer valid solutions, that the analysis of language will lead to the uncovering of basic concepts—Platonic ideas."[8] The so-called modern absurd playwrights, on the other hand, go a step further and achieve a unity between their ends and means. The Theatre of the Absurd does not make use of plot, characterisation, dialogue and description. It just depicts a situation in man's life and establishes the absurd lying therein. Here language and style are devalued. Here poetry and symbols are employed. Esslin says, "The Theatre of the Absurd is thus part of the 'anti-literary movement' of our time, which has found its expression in abstract painting, with its rejection of 'literary' elements in pictures; or in the 'new novel' in France, with its reliance on the description of objects and its rejection of empathy and anthropomorphism."[9]

The 1920's is known for its general drama in Europe, particularly in Paris. This school is also known as 'The School of Paris" which attracted a wide range of writers and audience from across the continent. The new school was based on the existential philosophy of Sartre and Camus.

Samuel Beckett is one of the main exponents of the Theatre of the Absurd. Beckett is so famous that he is called the 'father of absurd theatre.' His plays *Waiting for Godot* and *Endgame* have established a new trend in drama. In a long series of strange works Beckett wrote fable after fable of persons trapped by perfectly logical, demoralising absurdity.

Samuel Beckett is an Irish writer. He was born in Dublin in 1906. He studied modern languages at Trinity College, Dublin. He taught at Ecole Normale Superieure in Paris. He taught French at Trinity College at Dublin. He travelled Europe writing stories and articles for magazines. Then he settled down in Paris in 1937. When he took part in the French resistance against the Germans during the World War II, he was caught. Soon he and his wife escaped to Roussillion in France. Once the war was over he settled down in Paris and began writing novels and plays.

His novels include *Murphy* (1938), *Watt* (1942), *Molly, Malone Dies* and *The Unnameable* (1947-49). Beckett's plays are *Waiting for Godot, Endgame* and *Krapp's Last Tape.* He has written numerous short plays for radio and TV. His works deal with the absurd in life. They boggle the readers' mind. Hugh Kenner observes, "In Beckett's world, readers are clearly told everything except the things they are used to knowing."[10]

The next important absurd playwright is Eugene Ionesco, a Romanian born French playwright. Ionesco tries to dramatise the absurdity of human experience and aspirations, the emptiness of bourgeois conventions, and the failure of communication.

Eugene Ionesco was born in Slatina, Romania in 1909. His father was a Romanian and mother, a French. As a child he lived in Paris. He studied at the University of Bucharest and later at Sorbonne in France. His first staged work *La cantatrice chauve* (1948) was a failure, whereas his later plays *Les Chaises* and *L'Rhinoceros* became classics of the Theatre of the Absurd. Ionesco was made a member of the French Academy in 1970. He died in Paris in 1994.

Eugene Ionesco is concerned with the tragedy of the western man. He thinks absurd theatre best shows the mechanic life of the modern man. His *La cantatrice chauve* (*The Bald Soprano*) depicts the banality of life. *Les Chaises* (*The Chairs*) is a tragic farce in which two old people living on a remote island prepare for a great gathering. But the people do not come there. The stage is filled with just chairs and a deaf narrator addresses them. Ionesco's other important plays include *The Lesson* (1958), *The Killer* (1960), *Rhinoceros* (1984), *Macbeth* (1973) and *Journey among the Dead* (1984). Ionesco wrote his *La cantatrice chauve (The Bald Prima Donna* in England, and *The Bald Soprano* in America) in 1938. He gained some popularity with *Amedee* (1954). The famous controversy with Kenneth Tynan in 1958 shows the seriousness of Ionesco's commitment to drama. R.N. Coe has called Ionesco "the most characteristic protagonist of the absurd."[11] In Arnold P. Hinchliffe's view as Ionesco's work progresses the nightmarish quality asserts very strongly the basic theme of death. Ionesco observes, "I have no other images of the world, aside from those which express evanescence and hardness, vanity and anger, nothingness or hideous and useless hate. Everything has only confirmed what I have seen, what I have understood in my childhood."[12]

Jean Genet, another absurd playwright, was a French writer. He was a versatile figure—a novelist, playwright and poet. Jean Genet was born in 1910 in Paris. When young, Genet was abandoned and he grew up in a family in the Moravan. His childhood records are bleak, often Genet getting into troubles. In fact, he began writing in prison. He detested the bourgeois society. By 1947 his work had drawn the attention of such writers as Andre Gide, Jean-Paul Sartre, and Cocteau. Between 1942 and 1948 he wrote several autobiographical works celebrating thievery and homosexuality. His prose is erotic, scatological and intensely religious, and his novels resemble extended prose poems. In David Galloway's words, "Genet's theatre is a world of illusions, a dance of death between appearance and reality. Traditional concepts of character, plot and motivation are abandoned in favour of concentration on states of mind, rituals and the fertile search for reality as in *The Maids* (1946), *The Balcony* (1957), *The Blacks* (1959) and *The Screens* (1961), in which illusion and impersonation are both major dramatic devices and central themes."[13]

Arthur Adamov is a Russian-born French playwright. He was one of the leading exponents of the avant-garde theatre in France. Adamov was born in Kislovodst, Russia in 1908. Yet he was brought up in France and Germany. He settled down in Paris in 1924. He edited a literary review *L'heure nouvelle*. Adamov began to write for the stage in the mid-1940's and he produced his important works in the next decade. His early plays *La parody, L'invasion, Le professeur taranne* and *Le ping-pong* are absurd plays as they deal with futility in man's life. Adamov wrote plays of epic theatre later. He died in 1970.

Adamov's work *The Confession* (1938) deals with the absurd. In Esslin's view: "It is a brilliant statement of the metaphysical anguish that forms the basis of the absurd."[14] In his play *La Parodie* (1945) Adamov avoids the subtleties of plot, characterisation, producing a theatre of gesture. His *L'Invasion* (1951) is about human strife. But while *Le Ping-Pong* merely asserted that whatever you do, in the end you die. *Le Ping-Pong* provides a powerful and closely integrated argument to back that proposition—it also shows how so much of human endeavour becomes futile, and why.

Herold Pinter is an English actor and playwright and acted as a director. His plays are remarkable for their combination of the commonplace and the bizarre and their preoccupation with the alienation of the individual, both from himself and from his fellowmen.

Harold Pinter was born in London in 1930. He studied at the Royal Academy of Dramatic Art, London. He joined The Royal Shakespeare Company and performed several plays in England and Ireland. He began writing plays in the 1950s. Pinter's plays are *The Birthday Party* (1957), *The Caretaker* (1959), *The Lover* (1963), *The Homecoming* (1965), *Old Times* (1971), *The Collection* (1962) and *No Man's Land* (1975). He wrote many one-actors like *The Dumbwaiter* and *The Room.* His screenplays include *The Servant* (1963), *Accident* (1967) and *The Go-Between* (1969). He directed plays like *The Man in the Gloss Booth* (1967) and *Butley* (1971).

Pinter followed Beckett. So he is pre-occupied with self—his basic questions being: who or what am I? His quest is Socratician. Pinter focuses on situations rather than events for his theme. He thinks language is inadequate for a proper communication in theatre. John Bowen thinks, "Mr Pinter's buses really run; his observation may be appalled, but it is exact. His characters do not use language to show that language does not work; they use it as a cover for fear and loneliness."[15] John Russell Taylor describes Pinter's method as orchestrated/naturalism and it is a style which excluded cosmic disorders and grotesque fantasy of the kind we associate with the Theatre of the Absurd. Pinter's plays speak of modern man's anguish and dread. His *Birthday Party* is about some unknown terror lurking in us. Esslin thinks the play has been interpreted as an allegory of the pressures of conformity with Stanley, the pianist as the artist who is forced into respectability and pin-stripe trousers by the emissaries of the bourgeois world. *The Caretaker* depicts misuse of positions.

Jean Tardieu (b. 1903), a pre-World War poet, is known for his wide range of experiment in absurd theatre. He was a staff of the French radio and TV. Tardieu's dramatic experiments are published in *Theatre de Chambre* (1955) that contains a similar kind of literature in which language loses all conceptual content and merges into music. Tardieu's play *Qui Est La?* (1947) is like Ionesco's *The Bald Prima Donna*. Here we find a family of father, mother and son seated around a dinner table. The father enquires his wife and son over certain things but he answers himself. Tardieu's *La Politesse Inutile* (1947) is about a nightmare. His *Le Meuble* depicts the absurd of a machine-furniture. *La Serrue* has the overtones of Genet. A similar motif appears in *Faust et Yorick*. His *Le guichet* is about Kafkaesque bureaucracy. His *Les Amants du Metro* has rhythmic language. Tardieu describes his play *A, B, C of Our Life* as a 'poem for acting.' It is a concerto. His play *Une Voix Sans personae* has no characters.

Ionesco has influenced Boris Vian. Vian's *L'equarrissager Pour Tous* (1949) is a comic farce. His *Les batisseurs d' Empire* is described as a poetic image of mortality. In act I of the play, father, mother, daughter Zenobie and their maid, Cruche are shown taking possession of a two-room apartment. In act II they are one floor higher, in a one-room apartment. The maid leaves them, and their daughter, who has gone to the landing, cannot return to them when the door closes. Only the father and mother are left. The world becomes narrower for them. In the third act the father is seen entering a tiny attic room, so terrified of the noise that he barricades the entrance before his wife can get to him. He is alone. But the noise, the terrifying noise of the approach of death, cannot be excluded. And now there is nowhere the father can escape to. He dies. The play has a half human being called a Schmurz (meaning pain in German); "covered in bandages, dressed in rags, one arm in a sling, he holds a walking stick in the other. He limps bleeds, one is ugly to look at."[16]

Dino Buzzati's His *Un Verme al Ministero* (*A Warm at the Ministry*) is a political satire on a totalitarian revolution. It reminds George Orwell's *1984*. If in *Les batisseurs d' Empire* the flight from death takes the form of trying to escape upwards, the same appears in the opposite direction in Buzzati's *Un Caso Clinico* (1953). Albert Camus adapted it for stage in Paris in 1955. The play is about a businessman hospitalised for his ill health. The hospital has seven floors, the floors downward showing hellish atmosphere. Buzzati shows his hero Giovanni Corte's descent. The play depicts the death of a rich man; his gradual loss of contact with reality; and, above all, the imperceptible manner of his descent and its sudden revelation to him. The hospital is a miniature society as if in conspiracy with an individual. If Boris Vian's *Les batisseurs d' Empire* shows man in active flight from death, *Un Caso Clinico* depicts him gradually overtaken by old age and illness, while totally unaware of what is happening.

Ezio D' Errico's plays display the absurd in man's life. His play *Il Formicaio* (The Anthill) depicts a dehumanised place in which Casimiro loses his identity. His *Temp de cavallette* (Times of the Locusts) shows post war Italy as a ruined village. When Joe, the Italo-American, arrives to share his wealth with the people of his homeland, a pair of juvenile delinquents murder him. He appears as a Christ-like figure, but the inhabitants are destroyed in a holocaust—of locusts—which is nothing but the destruction of the village. Only a boy survives as the hope of the new world. His next play *La Foresta (The Forest)* symbolises the modern mechanical civilisation.

If D' Errico's is a dreamland, Manuel De Pedrolo depicts a kind of geometrical austerity. His one-actor *Cruma* (1957) studies human isolation. 'Cruma' is an Etruscan measuring instrument. A resident measures the walls of an empty corridor and a visitor helps him. But his tape is blank. The resident is as mysterious as the tramps in *Waiting for Godot.* He is unaware of the outside world. De Pedrolo's second play *Homes I No* (Humans and No, 1958) is described as 'an investigation in two acts.'

Fernando Arrabal's first play, *Pique-nique en campagne* may be translated as 'a picnic in the country' depicts a soldier, Zapo in isolation of the front line of the fighting. His parents come to visit him. Soon Zapo captures an enemy and the latter is invited for a picnic. When all go for a picnic, a machine-gun explodes wiping them all. As a Chaplinesque comedy it does not have a happy ending. The play has a strange mixture of innocence and cruelty. Arrabal's *Les Deux Bourreaux* (*The Two Executioners*) holds conventional morality as self-contradictory. Here a woman Françoise denounces her husband to two executioners and she lives with her two sons Benoit and Marice. Arrabal's *Fando et Lis* is about Fando's love and hate relationship with Lis. His *L' Architecte et l'Emper eur d' Assyrie* (1967) is a classic.

Max Firish writes about contemporary problems in a vein of disillusion and tragic comedy. His play *Biedermann und die Bradistifer* (1958) is labelled a 'didactic play without a lesson.' It is a critique of bourgeois society. 'Biedermann' means bourgeois. The Biedermann is a manufacturer of hair lotion whose house is invaded by a trio of shady characters. Many guests come to his house and village. But they are incendiaries and one of them sums up their situation: "Jocularity is the third-best kind of camouflage; the second-best is sentimentality...But the best and safest camouflage is still the pure, naked truth. Funnily enough, no one believes it..."[17] The play is about destruction. The epilogue depicts Biederman in hell. It is a political satire.

Critics think Hitler's rise and fall gave way to the Theatre of the Absurd. This is more so in Germany. So Germany produced more absurd plays than any other country. Wolfgang Hildesheimer (b. 1910) is one of the first generation absurd playwrights from Germany. He spent his war years abroad. He lived in Israel today. Originally a painter he started writing fantastic radio plays—picaresque tales of forgers and grotesque oriental romances. Later he switched over to absurd plays. Hildesheimer compares the Theatre of the Absurd to a theatre of parables. He observes, "The story of the prodigal son is also a parable. But it is a parable of a different kind. Let us analyse the difference – the story of the prodigal son is a parable deliberately conceived to allow an indirect statement (that is, to give the opportunity to reach a conclusion by analogy), while the 'absurd' play becomes a parable of life precisely through the intentional omission of any statement. For life, too, makes no statement."[18] Hildesheimer's volume of plays *Spiele in denen es dunkel wird (Plays in which darkness Falls*) focuses on human absurdity. In *Pastorale oder Die Zeit fur kakao (Pastoral or Time for Cocoa*), some elderly characters disport themselves in a strange syncopation of dialogue concerned with business matters and stock-exchange deals. In *Lands chaft mit Figuren* (*Landscape with Figures*), an artist paints portraits of some pretentious characters.

If Hildesheimer's theatre is smooth, Gunter Grass's is rough. As a painter-playwright, his plays are like the canvases of Bosch brought to life. They are violent and grotesque. In *Onkel, Onkel* (Uncle, Uncle) Bollin is shown as a murderer. He tries to kill a little girl, a gamekeeper and a film star. But he cannot. Finally two children shoot him. Gaunter Grass's most interesting play *Die Bosen Koche* (*The Wicked Cooks*) transmutes a religious subject into poetic tragicomedy.

Robert Pinget's play *Lettre Morte* is based on his novel *Le Fiston* (1959) which is epistolary addressed by an abandoned father to his prodigal son. The father writes letters to his son though he does not know where he has gone to. *Lette Morte* puts the character Monsieur Levert on the stage. We see Monsieur Levert in two situations – in the bar, opening his heart to the bartender, and in the post office, trying to persuade the clerk to have another good look to see whether there is a letter from his lost son. The old man waits in unhope. Pinget's radio play la *Manivelle* (*The Old Tune)* translated by Beckett depicts an absurd situation. Pinget's full length play *Ici ou Ailleurs* depicts an astrologer Clope. *L'Hypothese* is about a man composing a hypothesis about a drown manuscript.

N. F. Simpson's plays are philosophical. His first play *A Resounding Tinkle* (1957) is based on the English class system. If Pinter's world is one of tramps and junior clerks, Simpson's is unmistakably suburban. The action of the play involving the Paradocks takes place in a suburban lower middle class. The Paradocks purchase a snake toy for an elephant toy and invite some comedians to entertain them at home. Their son Don comes home but has turned into a young woman. Simpson's second play *The Hole* (1957) portrays a group of people reacting differently about a hole in a street. The discussion around the hole becomes a survey of the fantasy life of an English village. *The Hole* is a philosophical fable. In his third play *One Way Pendulum* a nonsense world is delineated.

Jack Gelber's *The Connection* (1959) blends jazz with Beckett's theme of waiting. The image of the drug addicts waiting for the arrival of a messenger carrying their drug is a powerful conception. The dialogue explicates pointlessness. Gelbir's *The Apple* (1961) is but slightly different.

Arthur Kopit's play *Oh Dad, Poor Dad, Mamma's Hung You in the Closet and I am Feeling So Sad* takes an oblique approach of parody. Described as 'A pseudo-classical tragifarce in a bustard French tradition,' the play projects a young man's feelings about a dominating mother who tries to deprive him of contact with the outside world. The horrible woman travels with the stuffed body of her husband and the retarded son who strangles a loving girl projects a Freudian aspect of fantasy.

Once the Theatre of the Absurd established itself in the Western Europe, its influence began to spread to other parts of the world. Soviet bloc and its neighbours are prominent among them. Kafka's fiction which spread the theme of degeneration made it clear. Kafka criticised the tyranny of totalitarianism in Europe. Beckett's *Waiting for Godot,* when staged in Poland in 1956, convinced the people about frustration in man's life. Poland, a free nation for artists and writers created a new climate for the absurd theatre.

The following is about the theatre of the absurd in Eastern Europe. Slawomir Mrozek's first play *Policja (The Police*, 1958) is a Kafkaesque parable. *Policja* describes a situation in a mythical country where police crush the opposition to the tyrannical rule. There remains only one suspect without confiding with the police. When he joins the ruling regime the police lose its *raison d'etre.* The police chief, to see the police forces remain in their jobs, stimulates a police to commit a political crime. In *Na Pelnym Morzu* (*Out at Sea*, 1961) three men are shipwrecked. Now one of them is forced to be eaten. The three try to decide the victim fairly. Yet the weakest of them emerges as the victim. But he refuses to accept his fate. A fat man convinces of his heroic death. By chance a tin of beans is found and the man can survive. But the fat man refuses to eat beans. Mrozek's short plays *The Martyrdom of Peter Ohey, Charlie* and *Enchanted Night* are political allegories.

Tadeusz Rozewicz began his literary career as a lyrical poet. He began to write plays later. An atmosphere of dream and nightmare pervades his plays. Rozewicz is conscious of the threat to man in our times. His first play *Kartoteka (The Card Index*, 1960) presents the life of its hero changing his memory lane constantly.

Rozewicz's *Grupa Laokoona* (*The Laocoon Group*, 1962) satirizes Eastern Europe's taste for holidaying in Western Europe. *The Witness* is like his first one in its lyrical vein. Rozewicz is an experimenter.

Vaclav Havel is a famous Czech playwright and political leader. Havel was born to a well-off parents in 1936 in Prague. First he worked in a lab and then got admitted to a technical college where he studied economics. After some service in army he worked in a Prague theatre and became a playwright. Though Czechoslovakia Government did not allow the production and publication of his plays, they were published and staged abroad, bringing him fame. His plays *The Garden Party, The Memorandum, Audience* and *Protest* are absurdist-parables of life under totalitarianism. In the 1960s Havel involved in a dissident movement. He was a staff of the monthly *Tvar* and served as chairman of the club of independent writers. He was a spokesperson for the Charter 77 human rights movement in 1977. Of course, he was tortured in his own country. When Communist regime fell in 1989, Havel became a negotiator of the Civic Forum. His leadership brought in democracy to power. The parliament elected him president of the republic in 1989. He resigned in 1992. He regained power in 1998. Havel's *Zahradni Slavnost* (*The Garden Party*, 1963) displays a mixture of a hard satire. Schweykian humour and Kafkaesque depths are characteristic of his work. Havel's second play *Vyrozumeny* (*The Memorandum*, 1965) deals with cruel bureaucracy. Havel, and other Czech playwrights like Pavel Kohout, Ivan Klima and Frantisek Pavlicek, as protest writers, remained resistant against the neo-Stalinist regime imposed by Russia.

The trend of the Theatre of the Absurd is explicit in France, Italy, Spain, Germany, Switzerland and Great Britain. This Theatre is also there in other parts, especially in America. Esslin observes, "the convention of the absurd springs from a feeling of deep disillusionment, the draining away of the sense of meaning and purpose in life, which has been characteristic of countries like France and Britain in the years after the Second World War. In the United States there has been no corresponding loss of meaning and purpose. The American Dream of the good life is still very strong. In the United States the belief in progress that characterised Europe in the nineteenth century has been maintained into the middle of the twentieth. It is only since the events of the 1970's – Watergate and defeat in Vietnam – that this optimism has received some sharp shocks."[19]

Edward Albee, the famous American absurd playwright, was born in Washington, D.C., in 1928. When a child, he was adopted by Reid Albee, the son of a vaudeville producer. Albee grew up in New York and graduated from Choate in 1946. He settled down in New York City and held various posts in the 1950's. Albee wrote poetry and novels. His *The Zoo Story*, a one-act drama, about a psychopathic homosexual who induces an innocent stranger to kill him, won the 1960 Veron Rice award. His next three one-actors are *The Death of Bessie Smith, The Sandbox* and *The American Dream* (1961). The first depicts tensions between the races and the sexes of Memphis; and the second and the third plays ridicule American middle class values. Albee's best play *Who's Afraid of Virginia Woolf?* (1964) is a savage but witty dissection of two marriages in an academic setting. His *A Delicate Balance* and *Seascape* won him Pulitzer Prizes. He attempted several novels for the stage. Albee attacks the very foundations of American optimism. His plays focus upon man's tendency to torment others and destroy himself.

Interestingly the Theatre of the Absurd is as old as the drama. Today's absurd theatre is a combination of the absurd elements prevalent earlier. Esslin says, "Its novelty lies in its somewhat unusual combination of such antecedents, and a survey of these will show that what may strike the unprepared spectator as iconoclastic and incomprehensible innovation is in fact merely an expression, revaluation, and development of procedures that are familiar and completely acceptable in only slightly different contexts. "Pure' theatre, i.e. abstract scenic effects as they are familiar in the circus or revue, in the work of jugglers, acrobats, bullfighters, or mimes, clowning, following and mad-scene verbal nonsense. The literature of dream and fantasy, which often has a strong allegorical component."[20]

Pure or abstract scenic effects include some anti-literary attitudes like rituals and non-verbal forms. An example can be Beckett's use of music hall routine with hats, Genet's use of stylised action and Tardieu's use of sound effects. As we know a play is more than language. It is manifest in performance. Jugglery, acrobatics, bullfighting and mimes have abstract theatrical effects. They are mathematical. As William Hazlit says actions effect strong things. Nietzsche remarks stage has always drawn some strength from clowns. Mimes right from the beginning added much sublime to drama. Plays will have animal imitations, dances, singing and juggling tricks. With all its realism, the mimus not infrequently contained curious dreams and hallucinations, as in the plays of Aristophanes. In a gloss to Juvenal, the mimes are called paradox. And in fact everything fantastic is paradoxical, as are also the mimicae ineptiae, clowning and foolery. The expression probably refers to both these aspects.

Secondly, Italian *commedia dell'arte* with its Zanni and Arlecchini in Italy is used in the Theatre of the Absurd. There is a deep affinity between the Roman mime and Italian *commedia dell'arte*. The Italian art uses simpletons and illogicity. Moliere and Marivaux in France and Grimaldi in England have kept the tradition of *commedia dell'arte* alive. A part of the *harlequinale* merged into the tradition of the English music hall and American vaudeville with its cross talk, comedians, tap-dancers and comic songs. Dan Leno kind of theatre personalities have improved it.

Much of the Roman mime and medieval *commedia dell'arte* have come down in the twentieth century silent comedy of the Keystone Cops, Charlie Chaplin and Buster Keaton. Esslin thinks the silent film comedy as one of the decisive influences on the Theatre of the Absurd. It has the quality of absurdity, staging wordless and purposeless action. The talkie era however changed this opening a vista for the old vaudeville tradition. Laurel and Hardy, W.C. Field and the Marx Brothers influenced Absurd Theatre. Ionesco himself told to the audience at the American premiere of *The Shepherd's Chameleon* that "the French Surrealists had 'nourished' him but that the three biggest influences on his work had been Croucho, Chico and Harp Marx."[21] Interestingly, the Marx Brothers and W.C. Field are brilliant Surrealist comedians, skilled jugglers and musicians. Jacques Tatis Monsieur Hulot is a great figure in modern cinema.

Esslin says the tradition of the *commedia dell'arte* reappears in a number of other guises. Puppet theatre and the Punch and Judy shows are two examples. Europe's Pickelherrings and Hans Wursts who dominated the seventeenth and eighteenth centuries folk theatre are another instance of the Absurd Theatre. Folk theatre in Australia and Vienne are very rich. Ferdinand Raimund (1813-1837) and Christian Dietrich Grabbe (1801-1836) were pioneers of projecting the absurd of life. Later antecedents of the absurd include Wedekind, the Dadaists, German Expressionism and the early Brecht.

The literature of verbal nonsense is 'another offshoot of the absurd. "Delight in nonsense,"[22] says Sigmund Freud in his study of the sources of the comic. Lewis Carroll, though a mathematics don, was a great master of English nonsense verse.

Next to this Jarry, Apollinaire, the Dadaists, some of the German Expressionists, the Surrealists and the prophets of a wild and ruthless theatre, like Artaud and Vitrac matter. Jarry's *Ubu Roi* (1896) created a furore. His is a revolt against the rational well made play of the *fin de siecle.* His Ubu Roi was originally a prank aimed at a teacher. He is a savage seen through the cruel eyes of a schoolboy. Ubu becomes a king of Poland, kills and tortures all and sundry, is finally chased out of the country. The play is about man's cruelty and ruthlessness.

Guillaume Apollinaire's *Les Mamelles de Tiresias (Tiresuas's Breasts*, 1917) is a grotesque vaudeville. His *Couleur du temps (The Colour of Time)* is a verse play in which a group of aviators escape from the war; arrive at the south pole, where they want to find eternal peace; discover a beautiful woman frozen into ice; and kill each other fighting for her. It is an allegorical dream.

The Dada movement which began in Zurich merged with a central European tradition. It involved writers, painters and sculptors. The founder-members included Tristan Tzara (1896-1963), Romanian poet Hugo Ball (1892-1974) and his wife Emmy Hennings (1885-1948), Richard Huelsenbeck (1892-1974), Hans Arp (1887-1966) and Marcel Janco (b. 1895). The movement owed its name to a lucky dip into a French dictionary. The Dadaists destroyed the conventional bourgeois art. Tzara noted in his diary: "The performance decided the role of our theatre, which will leave the direction to the subtle invention of the explosive wind (of spontaneity), with the scenario in the auditorium, visible direction, and grotesque means – the Dadaist theatre."[23] But Dada art was essentially destructive. Its theatre has nonsensical business and decorated with bizarre and costumes. Its immediate parishioners are Ribemont-Dessaignes, Paul Dermee and Tzara. Tzara's *Le Coeur a Gaz* (*The Gas Heart*) was the most successful play. Tzara himself called it "the biggest swindle of the century, in three acts. Ribemont-Dessaignes's *L'Empereur de chine,* (*The Emperor of China*) depicts a ridiculous situation of Chinese politics.

The German Expressionism has its own contribution to the rise and growth of the Theatre of the Absurd. Yvan Goll (1891-1950), as a Jew, made use of the grotesque to attack the bourgeois. Goll's *Der Unsterbliche* depicts a musician who loses his mistress to a tycoon and sells his soul to him for a large sum. Bertolt Brecht followed Goll, calling him a Corteline of expressionism. Brecht's plays range from anarchic poetic drama to Marxist didacticism. He makes use of clowning and music hall humour for depicting modern man's problem of identity crisis. *Im Dickicht de stadte (In the Jungle of Cities*, 1921) depicts a fight to the death between two men, Garda and Shlink, who are old friends with a strange relationship of love and hatred. *Dickicht der stadte* presents the problems of communication between human beings which preoccupies Beckett, Adamov and Ionesco. Actually Shlink and Garga fight for a contact. Brecht's *Mann ist mann* (*Man Equals Man*) anticipates the absurd in its thesis that human nature is not a constant. Esslin observes: "Brecht's personality contained a strong element of anarchy and despair. Hence even in his politically committed period, the picture he presented of the capitalist world was essentially negative and absurd: the universe of *The Good Woman of Setzuan* is ruled by imbecile gods, that of *Puntila* is modelled on a Chaplinesque formula of slapstick and in *Then Caucasian Chalk Circle* justice is done only by the unlikeliest of accidents."[24]

Once German expressionism ceased and Dadaism became weak the Surrealist movement took off. But Surrealism was positive. Andre Breton says, "Surrealism was a pure psychic automatism by which it is proposed to express, verbally, in writing or in any other way, the real functioning of thought."[25] Two good Surrealists to influence the Theatre of the Absurd are Roger Vitrac (1899-1952) and Antonian Artaud (1896-1948). Vitrac's *Les Mysteres de l'Amour (The Mysteries of Love)*. It has lovers' sadistic fantasies. Here past, present and future merge in a dreamlike fashion. Vitrac's *Victor, ou Les Enfants au Paouvoir (Victor, or Power to the Children*, 1924) has a boy hero Victor who loves Esther. Victor's father loved Esther's mother. When the young lovers expose their parents' adultery, Esther's father hangs himself. When nine years old Victor dies, his parents commit suicide. Antonin Artaud directed Vitrac's Surrealist plays. Artaud was an actor, director and even a madman. He was a great stage genius. Artaud made use of myth and magic to expose the indepth of man's mind. His theatre is known as Theatre of Cruelty. Artaud thinks man has dormant conflicts in his mind.

Esslin thinks Artaud formulated the basic tenets of the Theatre of the Absurd. Louis Aragon's *L' Armoire a Glace un Beau Soir (The Mirror-Wardrobe one Beautiful Evening*) is a fine sketch. Here a soldier meets a nude-woman, the President of the republic appears with a Negro general and Siamese twin sisters appeal to the President for permission to marry separately. And fairies are introduced. Aragon's *An Pied duMur (At the Foot of the Walls*) uses the same method. Another poet Robert Desnos (1900-1945) wrote a Surrealist play *La Placede l'Etiole* (1927) which refers to a starfish as the symbol of the dreams and desires of its hero. Raymond Radiguet's (1903-1923) *Les Pelicans (The Pelicans*, 1921) anticipated Ionesco's onslaught on the bourgeois. Rene Daumal (1908-1944) and Roger Gilbert Lecomte (1907-1943) wrote equally nonsensical plays in Jarryesque spirit. Julien Torma (1902-1933) wrote nonsensical plays. The hero of his play *Coupures* (Cuts) is presented as fate. His *Le Betroy* begins in disaster. This kind of nonsense is found in Lewis Carroll, Edward Lear and Christian Morgenstern. Raymond Roussel (1877-1933) who travelled the world was quite undramatic. From Apollinaire to the Surrealists and beyond, there appeared many painters and sculptors who wrote haunting plays. For example, Kokoschka and Ernst Barlach (1870-1938) made use of mythical feature of the Theatre of the Absurd. So did Picasso. Stanislaw Witkiewicz's (1885-1939) plays are full of dream, madness and parody. Another Polish novelist Witold Gombrowicz's (1904-1969) *Iwona* (1935) takes us to the fairy world of Hans Christian Andersen. His *Slub* (1963) is a dream play. The Spanish writer Ramon del Valle-Inclan (1866-1936) wrote *Las Galas del Wefunto The Gala of Death*) and *Los Cuernos de Don friolera (The Horns of Don Friolera*), both caricatures. The plays of Federico Garcia Lorca have a similar approach.

In the English speaking American theatre Gertrude Stein understood of Dadaism and Surrealism and wrote the play *Four Saints in Three Acts*. F. Scott Fitzegerald's *The Vegetable* (1922), as a grotesque nonsense, is an early example of the absurd. So is E.E. Cumming's *him* (1927).

When Nietzsche's Zaratustra descended from his mountains to preach mankind he met a saint. The latter said he could stay with him, praising God. But Zaratustra refused it as he believed that God was already dead. Since Nietzsche's *Zaratustra* which appeared in 1883, the number of atheists has increased manifold. So now religion is not so strong a force in the world. So is the case with God. And the things in the world are falling apart.

The Theatre of the Absurd is an expression of world's disintegration. It says since the art forms of yore, of a religious era have lost their validity, one must try for new ways. The absurd theatre tries to convince man the ultimate realities of his condition.

So man has his own predilections: waiting for a saviour as in Beckett's plays, rebelling against death in Ionesco's *Tueur sans gages*, or hiding reality in Genet's plays, or trying to establish his position or break out into freedom. The Theatre makes man aware of his precarious and mysterious position in the universe. In the absence of metaphysical value system, it depicts man's confrontation in the depth of his personality, his dreams, fantasies and nightmares.

The Theatre of the Absurd does not depict any ideological proposition or man's problems. Nor does it tell a story. It communicates a pattern of poetic images being undramatic that way. For example, the happenings do not constitute a plot in Beckett's *Waiting for Godot.* Brecht, Ibsen and others have made use of dramatic, narrative and lyrical properties to drive home a point, whereas the Theatre of the Absurd does not. In the conspicuous absence of psychology, subtlety of characterisation and plot, it uses lyrical inserts giving it great emphasis. Ibsen, Stindberg and James Joyce with the help of language, tried to explore the psyche of man, whereas the Theatre of the Absurd makes use of language economically. As George Steiner thinks language is reduced in theatre. Here language is devalued. Communication is often shown in a state of breakdown. Likewise, characters are often ununderstandable, for they speak less. So they appear comic. Yet the Theatre of the Absurd transcends the category of comedy and tragedy and combines laughter with horror. It presents a picture of the disintegrating world. Most of the actions are mysterious and insensible. The absurd plays have psychological motifs. Therefore the absurd is not historical, but universal. It is an ever happening phenomenon. In a play like *Waiting for Godot* waiting is not just the event. The act of waiting is omnipresent. Here we are confronted with the projection of a psychological reality and human archetypes shrouded in perpetual mystery.

So there is some difference between realistic theatre and the Theatre of the Absurd. The former deals with the objective external realities whereas the latter deals with the psychological realities. Yet both theatres are equally realistic though concerned with different aspects of reality in its vast complexity. The Theatre of the Absurd is seen as an attempt to communicate the metaphysical experience. It expresses the view that man is in a world of uncertainties.

Often literature needs innovation and new approaches to plot-construction, characterisation and language. If Brecht contributed a valid vocabulary for presenting the external reality of the world, the Theatre of the Absurd contributed an internal psychological reality.

The Theatre of the Absurd has enriched the mainstream drama. Most of the post Theatre of the Absurd has been written in the vein of Beckett and Ionesco. In fact, Brecht's epic tradition and the absurdist elements characterise the younger generation playwrights. For example, Edward Bond's *Lear* (1971) has the epic sweep of a Brechtian parable play but its treatment is of the absurd tradition. The plays of Tom Stoppard show the impact of the Theatre of the Absurd. His *Rosencrantz and Guldenstern are Dead* (1966) uses structural elements of *Waiting for Godot.* In America Sam Shepard writes absurd plays. In France Romain Weingarten and Roland Dubillard and in Germany Peter Handke, Wolfgang Bauer and Thomas Bernahard follow the same tradition today.

References

1. Marion Wynne-Davies, *Guide to English Literature*, Bloomsbury Publishing Limited, London, 1989, pp. 214-215.

2. Albert Camus, *The Myth of Sisyphus,* qt by Arnold P. Hinchliffe, *The Absurd,* Methuen and Co Ltd, Norfolk, 1969, p. 36.
3. Andre Malraux, *The Temptation of the West,* qt by Arnold Hinchliffe, *The Absurd*, p. 16.
4. Eugene Ionesco, *Dans les armes de la ville,' Cahiers de la Compaignie* Madeleine Renaud-Jean-Louis Barrault, Paris, no. 20, October 1957.
5. Sharada Iyer, "Theatre of the Absurd," *Studies in Literature in English*, ed by Mohit K. Ray, Atlantic Publishers, New Delhi, 2005, p. 101.
6. *Concise Oxford Dictionary*, OUP, New Delhi, 1990, p. 6.
7. John Russell Taylor, *The Penguin Dictionary of Theatre*, London, 1966.
8. Martin Esslin, *The Theatre of the Absurd,* Penguin, London, 1991, pp. 24-25.
9. Ibid., p. 26
10. Hugh Kenner on Samuel Beckett, *Encyclopaedia America*, p. 427.
11. R. N. Coe, 'Eugene Ionesco: "The Meaning of Unmeaning," *Aspects of Drama and the Theatre*, Edinburg, 1951, p. 15.
12. Eugene Ionesco, qt by L. C. Pronko, *Avant-Garde,* University of California Press, 1902.
13. David Galloway on Jenet Genet, *American Encyclopedia*, p. 392.
14. Martin Esslin, op.cit., p. 89.
15. John Bowen, "Accepting the Illusion," *Twentieth Century*, February, 1961, p. 162.) (16Boris Vian, *Les batisseurs d' Empire*, Paris, L'Arche, 1959, p. 8.
16. Max Firisch, *Biedermann und die Brandstifter,* Berlin and Frankfurt, Suhrkamp, 1958, p. 78.
17. Wolfgang Hildesheimer, *'Erlanger Rede uber das absurde theatre,* Akzente, Munich, no. 6, 1960.
18. Martin Esslin, op.cit., p. 311
19. Ibid., p. 328.
20. Ionesco, *Time,* New York, 12 December 1960.
21. Ibid.
22. Sigmund Freud, *Der Witz und seine Beziehung zum Unbewussten* 1905, Frankfurt: Fischer, 158, p. 101.
23. Tristan Tzara, *Chronique Zurichoise, Die Geburt des dada*, p. 173.
24. Martin Esslin, op.cit., p. 378.
25. Andre Breton, qt by Martin Esslin, *The Theatre of the Absurd*, p. 378.

4

Social Realism in Indian English Drama

The British ruled India, and accordingly they influenced us in art as in life. English (partly Western), and American literatures have been influencing modern Indian life and art.

The present essay is about Realism in Modern Indian English drama.

First let us understand what is this drama, and what is this realism in the drama. As we know, a drama is a form of composition designed for performance in the theatre, in which actors take the roles of the characters, perform the indicated actions, and utter the written dialogue.

Another word for drama is play.

Aristotle defined tragedy as "the imitation of an action that is serious and also, as having magnitude, complete in itself, in the medium of poetic language and in the manner of dramatic rather than of narrative presentation, involving 'incidents arousing pity and fear, wherewith to accomplish the catharsis of such emotions."

Drama has been a very effective and powerful genre in the world of literature. "It is a mimetic representation of life combining in itself the real and the fictional art and reality and presenting the events and characters within a dimension of space and time. It combines the quality of narrative poetry with those of visual arts. It is a narrative made visible." (Martin Esslin, *The Field of Drama*, Methuen, London, 1987, p. 56)

The forms of drama are tragedy, comedy, farce, opera, mosque, heroic drama, poetic drama, closet drama, social drama, absurd play, sitcom, streetplay, full length play, once-act play, folk play, epic drama and the like. Dramatic art first began in ancient Greece, with Aeschylus, Sophocles and Euripides and Aristotle's *Poetics* is the best document on the art of drama. So is our Bharata's *Natyashastra*. Indian drama much of which is idealistic, and symbolic is quite plentiful. We have Bhasa, Kalidas, Sudraka, Srhi Harsha, Bhavabhuti and others.

Drama is the great art in the West. India lacks it. The medieval India lacked this art. Because of the British influence, we have dramatic activities in the twentieth century.

In literature, we have what we can call a trend of attitudes and perspectives, and that is called realism. According to M.H. Abrahms this realism is a "recurrent mode, in various eras and literary forms of representing human life and experience in literature."[1]

Realism is applied by literary critics in two diverse ways: (1) to identify a movement in literature during the nineteenth century that included Honoré de Balzac in France, George Eliot in England, and William Dean Howells in America, and (2) to designate a recurrent mode, in various eras and literary forms, of representing human life and experience in literature. Chris Baldick defines realism "as a mode of writing that gives the impression of recording or reflecting faithfully an actual way of life."[2]

Realistic writing is often opposed to romantic writing. The *romance* is said to present life as we would have it be-more picturesque, fantastic, adventurous, or heroic than actuality; realism, on the other hand, is said to represent life as it really is. This distinction in terms solely of subject matter, while relevant, is clearly inadequate. It is more useful to identify realism in terms of the intended effect on the reader: realistic literature is written to give the effect that it represents life and the social world as it seems to the common reader, evoking the sense that its characters might in fact exist, and that such things might well happen. To achieve such effects, the writers we identify as realists may or may not be selective in subject matter-although most of them prefer the commonplace and the everyday, represented in minute detail, over rarer aspects of life-but they must render their materials in ways that make them seem to their readers the very stuff of ordinary experience.

Now I like to present you a brief history of realistic Indian English drama. The British who began realist literature right fro the Age of Victoria, introuduced their literature in India. Their amateur play troups, and amature British people like Kipling in India more so, staged British plays right from the beginning of the 19th century. Much of their secular playwriting was realistic, no doubt. Our secular playwriting in Bengali and Marathi began after the setting up of universities in Bombay, Calcutta, and Madras in 1861, acquainting students mainly with two streams of dramas—the Shakespearean and the Sanskrit. The newfound pride of Indians, both in themselves and in their culture, spurred them to emulate and translate Shakespeare in their own languages. At the same time translations of the classical Sanskrit plays of Kalidasa, Bhavabhuti, and Narayanabhatta were being done in Marathi, Bengali, Assamese, Oriya, Kannada, Telugu and other languages.

Though Krishna Mohan Banerjea's *The Persecuted,* or *Dramatic Scenes Illustrative of the Present State of Hindoo Society in Calcutta* (1831) was the first play in English written by an Indian, it was less a play and more a dramatised debate of the conflict between orthodox Hindu customs and the new ideas introduced by Western education.

The first play in Bengali to emulate Shakespearean tragedy was Jogendrachandra Gupta's *Kritivilas*, produced in 1852. The first original Marathi play, again, took its theme and form from Shakespeare's history plays. It was Vinayak Janardan Keertane's *Thode Madhavarao Peshwe*, produced in 1851.

Shanta Gokhale observes, "In two epilogues written in English for their production in Bombay and Poona, we see the double-edged vision with which students looked upon the dramatic culture they had inherited from the British. The first is by B. E. Modie, a student of Elphinstone College, Bombay. It follows a college performance of *The Taming of the Shrew* and was published in *Native Opinion*, 3 March 1867. It suggested, apologetically, that given time Indians too would speak English as well as the English themselves."[3]

This represents the attitude of the educated, Westernised, urban elite towards the English language and towards 'native' culture.

The Kannada playwright T.P. Kailasam (1885-1946), on the other hand, had his education for six years in England, aad he wrote both in Kannada and English. His plays dealt with contemporary themes, and were written in the everyday language. A geologist by training, T.P. Kailasam was a sportsman, actor, bohemian, and wit, given to composing and reciting plays to his friends extempore. Five of his plays have been published. His stage directions in these plays clearly show his strong sense of theatre. In this he was unlike most of his contemporaries and immediate successors. Many of his plays are realistic plays.

T.P. Kailasam's English plays unlike his Kannada plays are inspired by Puranic themes, but he renders them brilliantly in the intellectual idiom of our own day. *The Burden* and *Fulfilment* (1933) are short poignant pieces. *The Burden* handles the theme that Bhasa dramatised in his Statue Play, but Kailasam's play has a power and beauty of its own. Bharata, returning from his grandfather's place to Ayodhya, slowly gropes his way to the terrible truth that Dasaratha, his father, is dead. Like Oedipus, Bharata too learns the truth last of all, even Satrugna's eyes being opened a little earlier; and Kailasam has shown in the play that he can make prose a fit vehicle for the expression of tragic emotion. *Fulfilment* is a longer, and a more lacerating play; it bites and stabs. Ekalavya, Drona's unique pupil in archery, is about to join the Kauravas on the eve of the Kurukshetra war. Krishna tries to dissuade Ekalavya from making common cause with the human-wolves, the Kauravas, but Drona's pupil is adamant. Ekalavya and Krishna debate about 'first and last' things, about man's duty, about good and evil, about courage and cowardice. Krishna is driven at last to stab Ekalavya on the sly, and is further compelled to assure the dying, archer that his mother will not grieve on account of his death. To carry out his promise, Krishna is forced to commit one more murder—he kills the mother too, lest she should learn about Ekalayya's death and grieve for him. A terrible play—as terrible in its sheer horror as Lord Dunsany's *Night at an Inn—Fulfilment* is almost the crown of Kailasam's dramatic art. Krishna remains divine-human in spite of his ruthlessness, for his words to Ekalavya have already prepared us for the double tragedy and the pre-ordained 'fulfilment.' *The Purpose* (1944) chronologicaily a later play, unfolds Ekalavya's youthful idealism during his discipleship in archery. A more sustained dramatic adventure was Kailasam's *Karna*: *the Brahmin's Curse*, which although written much earlier was published as a book only in 1946. Kailasam's rendering of puranic characters like Bharata, Krishna, Ekalavya, Rama, Droupadi, Kunti and others has a touch of iconoclasm.

Among other writers of verse plays, a reference may be made here to Dhan Gopal Mukherji who wrote a musical play *Laylaa-Majnu*, Dilip Kumar Roy who has dramatised the life of Chaitanya, and B.S. Mardhekar, author of Prometheus Rebound, an audacious new rendering of the andent Greek myth, already handled fruitfully-though in widely different ways-by Aeschylus, Shelley and Andre Gide.

There is also Bharati Sarabhai, the most distinguished of the women dramatists. Her first play *The Well of the People* (1943), was a poetic pageant more than a play. Her more recent play *Two Women*, is in prose but often packed with thought. The tension at the heart of Hindustan, the opposing pulls of tradition, and revolt, the paralysis that makes the impulse to move forward in so futile a gesture—this tension, these pulls, and this paralysis are the soul of the play.

It is a far cry from Kailasam or Bharati Sarabhai to V.V. Srinivasa Iyengar, for the latter was mainly a master of social comedy, delighting in the incongruous and droll elements in the lives of the sophisticated middle-class people in cities.

Considering that nowhere except Bombay has English-language theatre been commercially viable, and given that everywhere amateur groups, rather than risk their scarce funds on untried Indian playwrights, have depended heavily on successful plays from the West to attract audiences. An astoundingly large number of plays have been written. More than 200 plays, all written since Independence, are mentioned by S. Krishna Bhatta in the bibliography to his book, *Indian English Drama: A Critical Study* (1987). Most of them have not been performed, many are not even performable, and few are available in print.

In the beginnings of the twentieth century we have had a host of playwrights, who wrote about Indina myths and history.

Rabindranath Tagore (1861-1941) was the grandson of Prince Dwarakanath Tagore, and the son of spiritually inclined father Maharshi Debendranath Tagore. The Togores were the most intellectual family of the time. Tagore's *Gitanjali* fetched him the Nobel Prize for literature. Tagore wrote many plays as well as poetry and novels. His plays include *The King and the Dark Chamber, The Post Office, Sacrifice, The Cycle of Spring, The Curse at Farewell, Red Oleanders, Mukta Dhar, Chandalika, The Court Dancer, Devouring Love*, and others. He has dealt with mythic, historica and social themes in his plays.

Sri Aurobindo wrote many plays in verse and his plays are in the Eligebathan manner. He wrote *Perseus the Deliverer, Vasavadatta, Rodogune, The Viziers of Bassora* and *Eric*. *Perseus the Deliverer, Rodogune* and *Eric* take us to Syria and Norway of long ago, while *Vasavadatta* and *The Viziers* are about the ancient Indian themes. All the plays have Aurobindovian undertones.

Sri Aurobindo was a 'prophet and a recluse' and he stood apart in unique solitariness, and anyhow his five plays were but a small fraction of his phenomenal literary output. The verse dramatic form has, attracted other writers too, thanks mainly, to the potent spell of Shakespeare and the Elizabethans. For example, there appeared in 1928 a play in five Acts and 27 Scenes entitled *Nala and Damayanti* by Vasudeva Rao. It is a *tour-de-force*. Another unusual verse play is *The Flute of Krishna* by P.A. Krishnaswamy (1950). The girl Vidyaratna has a vague thirst for the infinite, and dreams of Krishna's flute which is really the Indian bhakta's perennial food.

A far more important writer than either Vasudeva Rao or Krshnaswamy, Harindranath Chattopadhyaya has always been noted for his fecundity and versatility, and he is not only a commendable poet, he has a number of plays and playlets also to his credit. *Five Plays* (1937) contains some of his characteristic work as a playwright revealing his social consciousness, flair for realism, and the bite in his prose writing. *The Window* (dedicated to the Brave Textile Workers of Parel, Bombay) gives a lacerating account of the slum life of the workers, and ends with the Worker protesting against the proposal to tax light, smashing the window-panes, and rushing out with the words: 'Light, Light in the worker's home-for ever.' 'The Parrot' is dedicated 'to all those whose morality is not a parrot's; cage." In *The Sentry's Lantern,* Chattopadhyaya probes into the consciousness of a bourgeois poet: a merchant and a worker, all three awaiting the dawn when they are to be hanged. The Worker says: 'The Revolution will come, the Revolution will come, red like this dawn, red like this dawn. 'The Coffin' is another satire on the bourgeois artist and his make-believe world. The last play 'The Evening Lamp' is dedicated to those who may be able to light it towards the new Dawn of Realism. K.R.S. Iyengar comments, "Harindranath's plays and playlets on the lives of the saints are, perhaps, less dramatically effective than his plays of social protest, but they have their individuality too."[4]

Dilip Kumar Roy wrote *Sri Chaitanya* (1850), and Indira Devei wrote *The Begger Princess* (1956) on Mirabai and V.S. Aiyangar (1871-1954) wrote *Rama Rajya,* all on India's past. Swami Avyaktanand's *India Through the Ages* (1947) is a collection of ten plays and the last of the bunch *All Prophets' Day* is about national integration and secularism.

A.S.P. Ayyar and J. M. Lobo-Prabhu are two other dramatists of some distinction. In *Slaves of Ideas and Other Plays*, Ayyar handles the prose medium effectively, and he is seen to be a vigorous critic of contemporary life. His *Trial of Science for the Murder of Humanity* is both good dialectic and good drama.

The six plays of Joseph Mathias Lobo-Prabhu (1954) deal with social realities like inter-caste marriage, marital incompatibility and women's education. Unfortunately, these paywrights had little practical knowledge in theatre and could not write better plays as in the west.

Lobo-Prabhu's *Collected Plays* includes *Apes in the Parlour*, a long skit on our sophisticated life, *The Family Cage* is an attempt to present the plight of a widowed sister in a joint family, *Flags of the Heart* is a sentimental piece. Lobo-Prabbu's energy is obvious, he can write dialogues with facility, he can devise situations but his characters are rarely alive, and his denouements are seldom wholly convincing.

There is, then, S. Fyzee-Rahamin's *Daughter of Ind* (1940. Its theme is the love of the untouchable girl, Malti, for her master, an idealistic Englishman.

Suryadutt J. Bhatt's *The Trial Celestial* (1940) is too heavily weighted with purpose to be a good play.

An entirely different kind of play is *Hali* (1950) by G.V. Desani. It is known for its originality, symbolism and the richness of its imagery.

Lakhan Deb's *Tiger-Claw* (1967) is a three-act play in verse on the controversial killing of Afzal Khan by Shivaji.

However, four plays written by Asif Currimbhoy (1928-94) during this period deserve serious attention. They are *The Doldrummers* (1960), *The Dumb Dancer* (1961), *Goa* (1964), and *The Hungry Ones* (1965). Born into an illustrious Khoja family of Bombay, Currimbhoy was educated in the United States and for much of his life worked in a multinational oil company. His plays, of which there are twenty-nine in all, are substantial in content and rich in theatrical devices. He uses monologues, choruses, chants, songs, slide projections, sound effects, mime, anything in fact that furthers the dramatic purpose. Despite its importance, his work has yet to be the subject of a full-length study.

The Doldrummers revolves around the lives of four young people, Tony, Joe, Rita, and Liza—the Doldrummers of the title-who have not worked in a year of Sundays. Joe, who is doing his Ph.D., is disillusioned with what the country's freedom has brought him. His life goes on as before, without much purpose.

Tony lies in a hammock all day, drinking and playing the guitar, grateful to have a friend who is doing a Ph.D. Rita loves Tony passsionately, with an innocence which Joe corrupts by pointing out that if her aim is to ensure that Tony gets everything he wants, and if Tony wants the good life, her only choice is to sell her body. Liza, who is brash, amoral, and gossipy, comes and goes, sometimes as catalyst, sometimes chorus-like. In the end, Joe commits suicide, leaving Rita pregnant, as though leaving in her a hope for the future.

Critics observe that 'the play moves at a brisk pace.' Currimbhoy achieves his social purpose, though not at the expense of his art. He is a deeply compassionate playwright and allows his characters to reveal themselves. Though he writes from a moral position, he never becomes a moralist. His treatment of a character like Senhora Miranda in *Goa*[5] (1965), an allegory about the liberation of Goa where neither side is to blame and neither really wins, is a case in point.

Senhora Miranda, a woman of mixed parentage who needs to pretend that she is of pure Portuguese stock, yearns to be in Lisbon about which she has heard so much. This yearnning is projected on to a Portuguese do-nothing drunk, Alphonso, for whom she harbours a sexually explicit passion. However much she may lie and pretend, her dark-skinned fourteen-year-old daughter, Rose, is a living reminder of what she really is. Currimbhoy touches upon this aspect of her situation with great sympathy.

As Peter Nazareth writes, "Asif Currimbhoy interweaves the public event with the private to create exciting drama which asks moral questions about humanity in the cataclysmic period of decolonisation."[6]

Currimbhoy was ignored in India till news of the reputation he enjoyed in the United States reached the country. The Asian theatre scholar Faubion Bowers had declared in New York's *The Village Voice* that Currimbhoy was emerging 'more and more clearly as a playwright of international stature.' *Goa* was produced at the University of Michigan in 1965. In 1968 it was staged at the Martinique Theatre on Broadway and *The Hungry Ones* was performed at the Theatre Company, Boston, and at Café La Mama. The *Doldrummers* was given a tryout at the Actors' Studio. Meanwhile, it had been banned in India. It was only in 1969, after writers like Khushwant Singh and Mulk Raj Anand wrote letters of protest to the *Times of India*, that the ban was lifted and the Little Theatre Group in Delhi staged it.

Another English play to be banned was *A Touch of Brightness* (1968) by Partap Sharma (b. 1939). The play, set in the red light district of Bombay, tells the story of a young street urchin, Pidku, and the attachment he forms for a beggar girl, Prema, who has recently turned up in the neighbourhood. Jealous of the attachment is Benarsi Baba, a pavement-dweller passionate about chess. Pidku is his adopted son. Benarsi Baba sells the girl into a brothel, and Pidku vows to buy her freedom, but by the time he manages to earn enough money to do so, she is dying of venereal disease. The language of the play is inflected with Hindustani words and expressions like *aiye, bapre baap,* and *kya baat hai*, and these lend authenticity to the speech. The play raised the hackles of India's image-makers, who banned it from going to the first Commonwealth Arts Festival. An editorial in one newspaper asked whether India's image would be enhanced by letting drama-lovers in London know the heartening fact of the existence of brothels in this country. The author filed a writ petition in the Bombay High Court in 1966, challenging the ban.

The announcement in 1968 by Theatre Group, Bombay, of the Sultan Padmasee Award for Indian plays in English gave much needed encouragement to a floundering genre. The award was won by Gurcharan Das for *Larins Sahib*, but also in the competition were Gieve Patel's *Princes* and Dina Mehta's *Myth-makers*.

Until 1968, Theatre Group had staged only European and American plays, with the avowed aim of acquainting Indians with Western theatre techniques. Towards the end of the 1960s, however, a strong back-to-the-village movement had started amongst the urban elite, affecting social and cultural attitudes in important way. The announcement of the award for Indian plays in English could have been Theatre Group's response to this change.

Gurcharan Das (b. 1943) took recourse in history to cull from it a character and a story that had the potential of being turned into a colourful romantic tale. Set in Lahore in 1846-7, *Larins Sahib* (1970) deals with the crisis that overtook the Punjab seven years after the death of Maharaja Ranjit Singh, when the East India Company routed the Sikhs. His *Larins Saheb* deals with Ranjit Singh's queen's affair with the Resident Henry Lawrence. Das colours his language according to the race and class of the speaker. While he gives Hardinge the characteristic idiom of the English upper classes—'Damn these bloody tribes! Damn this bloody country! Damn the whole world... This brandy's no good'—he creates, for some of the exchanges between Lawrence and the Rani, a courtly, allusive idiom. Evidently, he did not wish to be seen as interpreting history, but as breathing life into facts. *Larins Sahib* is, as a consequence, a well-crafted piece of colourful dramatic entertainment rather than an attempt to relate the past to the present. Das has written two other plays, *Mira* (acted 1970) and *9, Jakhoo Hill* (acted 1996, though written in 1974). These have been collected in *Three Plays* (2001).

Nissim Ezekiel (b. 1924) wrote his plays years after his mentor, Ebrahim Alkazi, had left Bombay for Delhi in 1961 to become the first director of the National School of Drama. Ezekiel had worked closely with Alkazi in Theatre Unit during the latter's years in Bombay, and this stood him in good stead when he came to write his own plays.

It would not be wrong to say that Alkazi's was the single most powerful and enduring influence on theatre in Bombay in the 1950s. Trained in London at the Royal Academy of Dramatic Art, Alkazi conceived theatre as a totality. During his fourteen years in Bombay, Alkazi directed plays ranging from Greek tragedies to Shakespeare, and from Ibsen to Samuel Beckett and John Osborne.

In Ezekiel's *Three Plays* (1969) are collected *Nalini, Marriage-Poem*, and *Sleepwalkers*. *Nalini*, described as a comedy, is generally considered the most successful, as also the more important play, while *Marriage-Poem* shines like a polished gem, but in a very small setting. It explores an upper-middle-class marriage in which the homebound wife craves the attention and love of a husband who, if he ever loved her, is now indifferent. The insecurity of her position drives her to alternate between nagging him and trying to seduce him. He on the other hand is trapped between his dreams of another woman and his feelings of tenderness towards his lonely wife. *Nalini* concerns itself with precisely that class of westernised Indians who were then beginning to express their guilt about being without roots. *Sleepwalkers* is a one-act satire in a minor key on the Indian habit of always looking up to the United States.

Like Ezekiel, Gieve Patel (b. 1940) was also inducted into theatre by Ebrahim Alkazi. The apprenticeship began in 1958 while Patel was still an undergraduate. During this period he helped backstage in Alkazi's Theatre Unit productions, and did a minor role in one of them. Patel has written three full-length plays. They are set in South Gujarat, the place where his parents come from. His chief protagonists are Parsis, Iranian Zoroastrian refugees who settled in the west coast of India 1200 years ago, fleeing Islamic persecution. This sect, to which he belongs, has carved a cultural niche for itself.

The desire to possess and control—people, thought, property— is a leitmotif that runs through Patel's plays. *Princes* (acted 1970) deals with the waning fortunes of Parsi land-owning families shortly after Independence, when the Land Ceiling Act and prohibition began to erode their sources of income. Patel believes that theatre language is a constructed artifice. The English language is uniquely handled in all his plays, and in each play towards a specific end.

In *Savaksa*, a play set in a 'large village working its way towards becoming a small town,' the provincial characters continue to use this inventive speech. *Savaksa*, aged sixty years, is a wealthy provincial landowner and political leader who aspires to marry an eighteen-year-old girl from an impoverished Bombay family. The girl appears interested. Savaksa is an unusual lover to say the least. As part of his wooing he shows her a patch of chronic eczema on his arm, and speaks of it as a pleasurable symbol of power and possession.

City and village, poverty and wealth, woman versus man, Patel holds these contradictions in a prism.

Mister Behram (1988), Patel's third play, was produced by Stage Two Theatre Society for the Bombay Arts Festival in 1987. Behram, a brilliant lawyer and reformist in the nineteenth-century Gujarat, adopts an orphaned tribal boy into his own family, educates him to become a lawyer like himself, and consents to his marriage with his daughter. The play charts the course of Behram's desire to possess and control the young man, Naval, an obsession that destroys all the positive values he has lived by.

Cyrus Mistry (b. 1956) entered his first play, *Doongaji House* (1991), for the second Sultan Padamsee Award in 1978. It won the award but was not produced until 1990. In the publisher's note to the book, Adil Jussawalla states that the reasons why the play had to wait for twelve years to be staged would provide an accurate picture of the conditions in which the English-language theatre had been functioning since the mid-1970s.

In 1972, Pesi Khandalawala produced *Ah! Norman*, which turned out to be a commercial hit and is credited with having created a new theatre-going audience in Bombay. Unfortunately, it was an audience which seemed to want only more slick revues full of *double entendre*. In such a situation, it is no surprise that a play about the crumbling fortunes of a Parsi family, such as Mistry's *Doongaji House,* would have problems finding a producer.

Whether on stage or in films, Bombay's Parsis had always been portrayed in a stereotypical way for comic effect. With *Doongaji House* (as also with Mistry's stories, particularly Percy which was made into an award-winning film in 1990), this small community was at last being taken seriously. The production of the play by Stage Two Theatre Society was a huge success.

Using the conventions of traditional Parsi farce, Mistry brings to his play themes that are universal and existential: the common human desire for happiness, which is often thwarted by forces beyond the individual's comprehension, and the ultimate loneliness and vulnerability of all human beings. A striking feature of the play is its language.

A year after Mistry won the Sultan Padamsee Award, another Parsi writer, Dina Mehta (b. 1928), won the playwriting competition sponsored by the BBC. Her play *Brides Are Not for Burning* (1993) was broadcast on BBC World Service and its stage version performed in several Indian cities. Mehta's play takes its inspiration from a social problem, the killing of brides who do not bring enough dowry. The success of Mehta's play depends less on character and language than on her ability to reveal a social situation in its many-sidedness. Laxmi's death has been declared an accident, but no investigation is made into its causes.

Girish Karnad is a great playright today. His *Yayati* (1961) is based on the *Mahabharata*. His play *Tughalak* (1964) is an absurd historical play. *Hayavadana* (1971) makes use of folk theatre. So is *Nagamandala. Anjumallige* is a social play. *Taledanda* is about Basava. Lankesh's *Sankranti* and H.S. Shivaprakash's *Mahachaitra* also deal with Basava-theme.

In recent years, Bangalore has also emerged as a centre for Indian plays in English, the most visible playwright there being Mahesh Dattani (b. 1958). Dattani's *Where There's a Will* was first performed by his group, Playpen, in the *Deccan Herald* Theatre Festival in 1988, the same festival at which his *Dance Like a Man* was also performed the following year. The production travelled to Bombay where it was seen by Alyque Padamsee, who offered tc direct Dattani's next play *Tara* (1990). He also invited Dattani to write a play on communalism, and the result was *Final Solution*. Dattani shows that communal attitudes have evolved over a period of time and are often based on ignorance. At the centre of Dattani's work is the Gujarati joint family settled in Bangalore. *Where There's a Will* is a comment on the role of money in family relationships. The problems faced by a male Bharatanatyam dancer belonging to an illustrious family is the theme of *Dance Like a Man*. Amritlal Parekh is strongly opposed to his son choosing dance as a profession. A woman in a man's world may be considered progressive. But a man in a woman's world is-pathetic, he says to his wife, Ratna, who is an ambitious dancer herself.

Zubin Driver from Bombay and Vijay Padake from Bangalore whose plays have been staged and won critical acclaim but are as yet unpublished. R. Raj Rao (b. 1955), who teaches at the University of Pune, is yet to write a full-length play, but has brought out a collection of three one-acters and a monologue, *The Wisest Fool on Earth and Other Plays* (1996). His plays are memorable for their brutal candour and scatological wit.

Short plays and one-act plays of varying quality appear in journals and magazines, and it is impossible to keep track of them; it is likely a few good playlets, along with numberless bad ones, have been covered up by oblivion. It is very seldom that plays appear in book form. And of the plays lying buried in old books and magazines, few seem to have had a chance on the stage. Some of the poets of yesterday tried verse dramas too, more poems than dramas, in fact: Uma Maheswer's *Buddha and Sita in Her Sorrows*; V. Saranathan's *Indrajit*; B.N. Saletore's *Savitri*; V.N. Bhushan's *Samyukta and Anklet Bells*; Manjeri Isvaran's *Hira Bai* and *Yama and Yami*. Of full-length plays, K.S. Ramaswami Sastri's *Droupadi* is a retelling of the epic story, while D.M. Borgaonkar's *Image Breakers* is a problem play on the institution of marriage. Amarendra's English version of V. Chandrasekharam's *Kanchananamala* portrays the Phedre-like Tishyarakshita, Emperor Asoka's wife, whose incestuous love for her step-son brings about the tragedy. Krishna Gorowara has published a number of short plays in journals: *The Way Up,* and *A-Mourning Do We Go, Call It a Day, Refineries Unlimited*, and *Indo-Anglians in Anglia*. Gorowara has an eye for comedy and satire, and he specialises in urban sophistication, its poses, quirks, negations and self-deceptions.

Now we shall understand that the broad socio-political themes of modern Indian English drama can be anything related to society and politics. Often it is mythology and history too. Indian plays are about nation and secularism (Swami Avyaktanand's *All Prophets Day*), marriage, marital incompatibility and women's education (Joseph Lobo-Prabhu's plays like *Apes in the Parlouri*), workers issues (Harindranath's

The Window), liberation, the passion of love/sex (Currimbhoy's *The Doldrummers* and *Goa*), untouchability (Pratap Sharma's *A Touch of Brightness*), refugees (Gieve Patel's and Khandalwala's plays), love as passion, rootlessness and American dream (Ezekiel's plays), human desire for happiness (Cyrus Mistry's *Doongaji House*), women's exploitation (Dina Mehta's *Brides are not for Burning*) money-matters (Dattani's *Where There a Will*) and history and myth (Karnad's *Tughlak* and *Nagamandal*).

If Indian drama in English is still in its infancy, the publication of plays is even more so. Publishers will take plays seriously only if they have been produced, but producers will touch plays only if they are commercially viable. And there are not many of these. In short, few plays get published.

References

1. M. H. Abrahms, *A Glossoray to Literary Terms*, Wadsworth, New Delhi, 2005, p. 269.
2. Chris Baldick, *Oxford Dictionary of Literary Terms,* OUP, 2008, p. 281.
3. Shanta Gokhale, *The Dramatists*, rept in *An Illustrated History of Indian Literature in English,* ed by A. K. Mehrotra, Permanent Black, New Delhi, 2008, p. 338.
4. K. R. S. Iyengar, *Indian Writing in English,* Sterling, New Delhi, 2006, p. 233.
5. Asif Asif Currimbhoy's *Goa.*
6. Peter Nazareth, qt by Bayapa Reddy, *Studies in Indian Writing in English*, Prestige, New Delhi, p. 37.

5

Trends and Techniques in Modern and Post-Modern Indian English Fiction

The 1930s is the take-off decade for the Indian English novel. Of course, Indian English novel has had many examples of fiction in the past, and due to Indians' negligence of their literary history, much damage is done to our heritage. The early English novels in India appeared at a time when the genre was still in a malleable stage. Yet pre-novel forms existed in Indian vernaculars. For example, Kylas Chandra Dutt's *A Journal of Forty-Eight Hours of the Year 1845* is about Indian confrontation with the British. These tracts do not have a proper generic structure. Indian writers then read British and some other European writers like Wilkie Collins and Benjamin Disraeli—and made use of British literature epigrams from Byron, Scott, Shakespeare and Coleridge. For example, Madhavaiah writes "Carlyle has said somewhere—perhaps in that huge hotchpotch of facts and fancies—*Sartor Resartus*—that religion is the bond of society.' K.K. Sinha evokes Scott when he wants to defend purdah.

As the author appreciated the English literature or culture his works were greatly read. In fact, readers in Britain believed that S.K. Ghosh was an 'Englishman in masquerade!' English influence is felt heavily, for example, Fielding's famous bull-of-fare metaphor at the beginning of *Tom Jones* is replicated on the first page of *Govinda Samanta*. The convention of closure as found in the Victorian novel is found in Indian novels. Bankimchandra Chattopadhyaya's (1838-94)

Rajmohan's Wife ends thus: "And now, good reader I have brought my story to a close. Lest, however, you fall to censuring me for leaving your curiosity unsatisfied, I will tell you what happened to the other persons who figured in this tale." *Rajmohan's Wife* serialised in *The Indian Field* in 1864 possibly the first Indian English novel, appeared at a time when romance was the acceptable narrative mode and there was no precedent as yet of mimetic rendering of contemporary domestic life in fiction. The novel is known for its traditional Indian country life. Yet its realism is modified by other narrative conventions: of Sanskrit *kavya*, of Vaishnava love poetry, of the English Gothic novel in its evocation of terror. Then the novel dwelt with the middle class life.

The only woman novelist Krupabai Satthianadhan (1862-94) wrote two novels—*Kamala* (1894) and *Saguna* (1895)—about women. What strikes us is the author's concern with gender, caste, ethnicity and cultural identity—issues which were not important then as now. The two novels deal with the predicament of women.

Modernism and the 1930s and 40s Fiction

The 1930s and 40s is the time when modernism was triumphant in Europe. The nature of European modernism which has somehow influenced Indian fiction of the big three is as follows: "The term 'modernism' is for an international tendency in the arts brought about by a creative renaissance during the last decade of the nineteenth century and lasting into the postwar years. Strictly speaking, modernism cannot be described as a 'movement' or reliably characterised by a uniform style. Indeed it may be said to have embraced a wide range of artistic movements (including symbolism, impressionism, post-impressionism, futurism, constructivism, imagism, vorticism, expressionism, data and surrealism) and to have originated in cosmopolitan circles in Berlin, Vienna, Munich, Prague, Moscow, London and Paris. At a slightly later period it spread to New York and Chicago, and became synonymous with a worldwide reaction against positivism and representational art. Its most notable landmarks in English literature are commonly understood to include Henry James's *The Ambassadors* (1903), Conrad's *Nostromo* (1904), T.S. Eliot's *The Waste Land* (1922), and Joyce's *Ulysses* (1922). One might add the work of Pound, Yeats, Ford Madox Ford, Virginia Woolf and, in America, Faulkner, to a list which is by no means exhaustive."[1]

Technically, modernism was distinguished by its opposition to traditional forms and to the aesthetic perceptions associated with those forms. It was persistently experimental. A common quality was the highly self-conscious manipulation of form, together with an awareness of pioneering studies which were contemporaneous in other disciplines. These included, in psychology, William James's *Principles of Psychology* (1890) and Freud's *The Interpretation of Dreams* (1899); in Physics, Einstein's *General Principles of Relativity* (1915); and in Anthropology, Sir James Frazer's *The Golden Bough* (1890-1915).

Herbert Read suggested that modernism is not so much a revolution, which implies a turning over, even a turning back, but rather a break-up, a devolution, some would say a dissolution. Its character is catastrophic. Much of the difficulty of modernist texts, which has intimidated some readers, stems from this attempt to 'break up' or recreate the experience of reading. Stream of Consciousness, the use of myth as a structural principle, and the primary status given to the poetic image, all challenged traditional representation.

M.A.R. Habib observes, "Modernism comprised a broad series of movements in Europe and America that came to fruition roughly between 1910 and 1930. Its major exponents and practitioners included Marcel Proust, James Joyce, Ezra Pound, T.S. Eliot, William Faulkner, Virginia Woolf, Luigi Pirandello, and Franz Kafka. These various modernisms were the results of many complex economic, political, scientific, and religious developments over the nineteenth century, which culminated in World War I (1914-1918). The vast devastation, psychological demoralisation, and economic depression left by the war intensified the already existing reactions against bourgeois modes of thought and economic practice. Rationalism underwent renewed assaults from many directions: from philosophers such as Bergson, from the sphere of psychoanalysis, from neoclassicists such as T.E. Hulme, the New Humanists in America, and neo-Thomists such as Jacques Maritain. These reactions were often underlain by a new understanding of language, as a conventional and historical construct. The modernist writer occupied a world that was often perceived as fragmented, where the old bourgeois ideologies of rationality, science, progress, civilisation, and imperialism had been somewhat discredited; where the artist was alienated from the social and political world, and where art and literature were marginalised; where populations had been subjected to processes of mass standardisation; where philosophy could no longer offer visions of unity, and where language itself was perceived to be an inadequate instrument for expression and understanding."[2]

Mulk Raj Anand attributes his novelistic negotiation of tradition and modernity to 'the double burden on my shoulders, the Alps of the European tradition and the Himalayas of my Indian past.' These novelists had the context: the social and political upheavals of the 'Gandhian whirlwind' and the era of late modernism in Europe. At home this phase marked the Indian struggle for independence culminating in Swaraj in 1947. In the 1930s Gandhi's Civil Disobedience gained a momentum. There was anti-nationalism and Gandhi became the icon of such disturbed struggle. So the 'Mahatma theme' was announced within the nationalist agitation as a uniquely imaginative, carefully symbolic and irresistibly fictionalisable way of doing politics. This resulted in poetic apotheosis in Dandi March. This was Gandhi's Satyagrah. All these events found their way in 'Mahatma Fiction' of the period, both in Indian languages and English. Premchand's *Rangabhumi* (1925) in Hindi, Ramanalal Desai's *Gram Lakshmi* (1940) in Gujarati, G. T. Madkholkar's *Muktatma* (1933) in Marathi and Satinath Bhaduri's *Jagari* (1946) in Bengali offer Gandhian themes. K. S. Venkataramani's (1891-1951) *Murugan* (1927) promotes Gandhian economics. Venkataramani's *Kandan* (1932) is about Civil Disobedience.

A recognisably Gandhian tone predominates the fiction of K.Nagarajan's (1893-1986) *Athavar House* (1937). R.K. Narayan's comic portrait of Gandhi is seen in his *Waiting for the Mahatma* (1955). Bhabani Bhattacharya (1906-88) has Gandhian education as a motif in his famous famine novel *So Many Hungers!* (1947). Many novels deal with Gandhian sub-themes: emancipation, if not empowerment of women, uplift of utouchability and Hindu-Muslim communal harmony. That is socio-economic transformation. The use of Gandhi themes or the use of Nehruvian socialism is totally new and transforming. That way Nehru's conflict with Gandhian ideology is there. This troubles Indian English fiction. There is an uneasy synthesis between the two.

The 1940's novels deal with these conflicts. Yet ironically Indian English Muslim novelists of this time Aamir Ali, K.A. Abbas and Humaun Kabir wrote more of Hindus than of Muslim characters. K.A. Abbas's *Tomorrow is Ours* (1943) explores the issues of nationalism and untouchability. Nehru's works, Gandhi's *Young India* and *Harizan* recount Indian lives and stories. For example, Anand redrafted his novel *Untouchable* after he read an article in *Young India.* Gandhi's prose is literary as much as informative. Raja Rao was particularly impressed by Gandhi's autobiography. Bhattacharya's *Gandhi, The Writer* (1969) celebrates Gandhi's autobiography as a model for novel. Bhattacharya says, "Gandhi is a writers' writer," and the best Indian writing "bears his counter signature." Because the prose writers and prison diaries of the time inspired writers. Besides, English writers wrote even in their own languages. The writers were undecided about the status of English in independent India. But Rajaji said, "English is Saraswati's gift to India." The writers, hence, thought that English is a royal medium for national communication and unification. Even Gandhi said to Anand, "The purpose of writing is to communicate, isn't it? If so, say your say in any language that comes to hand."

Leela Gandhi observes, "Thus modernism was not only well disposed to the immediate political concerns of the 1930s and '40s expatriate Indian novelists, but also instrumental—albeit accidentally—in helping them to reach cultural affiliations. Moreover, many of these novelists benefited materially from the atmosphere of literary, and sometimes economic patronage which characterised the ethos of European modernism. In particular, it was E.M. Forster who facilitated the early careers of many of the writers under discussion. Anand's *Untouchability* bears the authoritative seal of Forster's laudatory preface. Forster's preface to the Everyman's Library edition of *A Passage to India* lavishes praise upon Ahmed Ali's *Twilight in Delhi* which was published by Hogarth Press. G.V. Desani's cult novel *All About H. Hatterr* appeared to favorable reviews by, among others, T.S. Eliot, who spoke for many when saying: 'In all my experience, I have not met with anything quite like it.'"[3]

M.R. Anand dominated the 1930s and 40s fiction. When in London he took part in Virginia Woolf's Bloomsbury Circle, yet developing an interest in Indian philosophy and aesthetics. This is seen in his first novel *Untouchable* (1935), which narrates one day in the life of Bakha, like Alexander Solzhentsyn's *One Day in the Life of Ivan Denisovich* and the novel ends with solutions in conversion and flush-toilet system. His fiction makes use of north Indian linguistic flavor.

Many of Anand's literary and political preoccupations reappear in Raja Rao's fiction. Raja Rao's upbringing and education as in Anand's case, combine Indian and European influences. He adhered to Indian philosophy, yet he was an expatriate as he studied western philosophy in France. Rao's pre-independence novel *Kanthapura* (1938) is known for its Gandhi theme as well as its classic foreword which is a manifesto for the practice of Indian writing in English. The foreword begins by describing the difficulty of bridging the cultural and historical gap between the English language and the Indian tale. He observes: "One has to describe in a language that is not one's own the spirit that is one's own." This dichotomy Rao claims can only be resolved through a systematic indigenisation of English—by infusing it with the breathless and unpunctuated 'tempo of Indian life.' So also, faced with the indisputably western origins of the novel form, the Indian writer is required to undertake the rather more difficult task of generic appropriation, by relocating his narrative within the epic tradition of the *Ramayana* and the *Mahabharata*. What follows is a story about the gradual coming of Gandhianism to a small caste ridden village called Kanthapura on the Malabar coast. Narrated as the reminiscences of an old woman, its tone is informed by her preliminary invocation to the goddess Kenchamma, who functions as the presiding deity over the events of the ensuing tale. Rao is known for the formal puzzle of translating Indian modes of feeling and expression into English. The novel deftly makes use of L1 over L2. that is the influence of Kannada over English. Several of the themes which occupy *Kanthapura* are echoed in Rao's subsequent works. Rao situates his next novel *The Serpent and Rope* (1960) in Europe. At the same time, Rao shifts his focus from Gandhism to Vedanta and from nationalist narrative to metaphysical fiction. *The Serpent and the Rope*, continues his complex experiments with form and cultural translation, successfully blending elements of the European novel with those of the Indian epic.

G.V. Desani (1909-2000) is an Indian novelist by virtue of his ancestry. Born in Kenya, he lived in England and was a public lecturer. He spoke of Indians and English people's shared identities. Edward Blunden liked him. When in BBC service he wrote a long prose poem *Hali* (1950) in the style of Tagore. E. M. Forster liked it. Desani came to India in 1940 and studied yoga and occult. He studied Buddhist thought in Japan. He migrated to America to teach religion and philosophy and he was Prof Emeritus at the University of Texas, Austin. Desani's *All About H. Hatterr* (1948) is about his improbable life. It is a Joycean linguistic burlesque where Indian English—much like Joyce's Irish English—relentlessly jostles against all the known rules of grammar and diction. Shakespeare combines with Indian legalese, cockney with babuism. Anglo-India rubs up against the pompous drone of colonial club talk, and grievously unpunctuated sentences find a temporary hiatus in random and arbitrary capitalisations. Structurally, the novel is more or less a growing up story about the education of the eponymous and mad-hatterrish hero H. Hatterr, son of a European merchant seaman and a lady from Penang. Set in British India, it is rigorously organised around a set of seven episodes, involving Hatterr's attempt to find a higher truth. Leela Gandhi observes, "Desani's intensely self-conscious novel prefigures more recent books like Salman Rushdie's *Midnight Children* and Allan Sealy's *The Trotter-Nama*. Chronologically, its linguistic experimentation and irreverent handling of the Great Books of the European canon are possibly more revolutionary than those in recent Indian fiction. Desani's slightly precious and arrogant posturing is, in context, both startlingly unusual and useful in the history of the incipient Indian novel in English."[4]

As with Desani's, Sudhin Ghose's (1899-1965) novels sound idiosyncratic. He is known for a tetralogy which records in the style of a *bildungsroman*, the growing up of a nameless orphan narrator over a 20 years period. His fiction depicts urban-rural polarity and it is known for self-conscious Indianness of their narrative structure and sources.

Abrey Menen (1912-89) is another important though neglected novelist, whose complex cultural background contributes to his strikingly objective view of both Europe and India. Menen balances his thoughts about the east and west. He writes about homosexuality. His works are known for cultural hybridity. His novels like *Abode of Love* (1956) explore cultural misunderstandings between the civilised and the primitive and that way he is a critic of the west.

The 1930s and 40s Indian English fiction showcases a tremendous freedom movement in India, and a war atmosphere in Europe. This phase of fiction is a foreground for the post-colonial Indian English fiction and even diaspora novels.

R.K. Narayan was born and brought up in a rural town near Madras. He stayed in Mysore. The British rule, English language and literature, were great influence and inspiration to him. His day-dreaming helped him. He started his career as a freelancer, and then began prose pieces. That is to say 'he began somehow.' Soon in the midst of confusion and dislocation in his mind, Narayan found out a fictitious town, Malgudi as the locale for his fiction. Malgudi appears to be a colonial town with its post-office, bank, middle class suburb, small roadside shops and low caste slums and missionary schools. Grahame Greene who helped Narayan to get his first novel *Swami and Friends* (1935) published spoke of 'sadness and beauty' of its atmosphere.

Narayan's next novels *The Bachelor of Arts* (1937) and *The English Teacher,* like Chekhov's works, speak of cultural dislocation. Pankaj Misra says, "Narayan's world is a part-feudal, part-modern setting of inchoate longing and vague dissatisfactions and intellectual impotence, the confused inner life of a fragmented makeshift society that has yet to figure out its past or future."[5] But Narayan's many novels *Mr Sampath, A Tiger for Malgudi,* and *Talkative Man* are failures in style and vision. Narayan's last and best novel *The Guide* (1958) has a cinematic technique.

The Novelists of the 1950s and 1960s

Once the British left India Indian English writer felt it bad to write in English, the language of the just departed. Only the 'big three' continued to write and Narayan's *The Guide* was the first novel to notice public attention in the 1960s. Khushwant Singh (b. 1915) and Manohar Malgaonkar (b. 1913) continued to write. The 1950s was a slow period and P.M. Nityanandan (b. 1928) produced the first campus novel with his *Long, Long Days* (196). Yet many women writers Kamala Markandaya, Ruth Prawer Jhabvala, Nayantara Sahagal and Anita Desai continued to write and win western favour.

Arun Joshi (1939-93) had his education in the US. His fiction is about the encounter between the east and west. He wrote *Foreigner* (1968), *The Apprentice* (1974) and *The Last Labyrinth* (1981). The second novel resembles Arthur Miller's plot in *The Crucible.* A striking feature of his fiction is his experiment with different narrative techniques. In *The Foreigner*, the narrator moves freely across time and geographical space; *The Apprentice* is a monologue; *The Last Labyrinth* has a trope of labyrinth; and *The City and the River* is different in technique. His best novel *The Strange Case of Billy Biswas* (1971) depicts a man who alienates from society and nature. It reminds us of Conrad's *Heart of Darkness.*

Dissatisfaction with the metropolis and modernity is a recurrent feature in Anantanarayanan's (1907-81) *The Silver Pilgrimage* (1961). As A. Madhavaiah's son, he based his novel on Dandin's *Dasa-Kumar-Charite*. It is full of incidents. The narration accommodates folk tales and ballads and shifts to a dramatic arrangement of dialogue when necessary. It is known for its humour. The novel abrogates the European convention of novel.

Nayantara Sahgal is a political novelist. Her novels reveal the Indian political elite—the richest sections of Indian society. Kamala Markandaya's novels display a remarkable range of characters. The conflict between tradition and modernity and east and west runs in her works. Anita Desai (b. 1937) deals with man's inner psychology. She says, "Writing is to me a process of discovering the truth—the truth that is nine-tenths of the ice- berg that lies submerged beneath the one-tenth visible portion we call reality." Her most characters are women and traumatised people. There is breakdown of relationships, martial and familial. Ruth Prawer Jhabvala (b. 1927) is 'one of the European writers who have written about India.' Her fiction is about urban middle class in a Jane Austenish vein. Her *Heat and Dust* (1975) is a study of the interaction between India and Britain. Her satire borders on cynicism. Her work includes American and Jewish characters and settings. Jhabvala's attitude is totally Eurocentric.

The 1950s and 1960s phase of Indian English fiction did not create remarkable new trends in writing, though the women writings established a base for future.

The Indian Diaspora: 1970s and 80s

Indian diaspora writers began in the eighteenth century. We have old diaspora and new diaspora writers. The old diaspora writers are those who migrated to Fiji, Trinidad, Mauritius, South Africa, Malaysia, Surinam and Guyana long ago. The father Naipaul that is Seepersad Naipaul is an example. The old diaspora is called *girmit* (indentured) diaspora. Panic, nausea, schizophrenia, hysteria, time-lag, estrangement, violence, nostalgia, madness are some of the themes written about. Some of the old diaspora writers are Harold Ladoo (Trinidad—Canada), Subramni (Fiji), Cyril Dabydeen (Guyana-Canada), David Dabydeen (Guyana-England), K. S. Maniam (Malaysia) and Neil Bissnoondath (Trinidad—Canada). Non-girmit diaspora writers who lived in the Asian subcontinent like Menon Marath (b. 1906), Santha Rama Rau (b. 1923), Balachandra Rajan (1920) and Victor Anant (1927) write their narratives set in their motherland. For example, Marath approaches India with an insider's intimacy. But Santha Rama Rau's approache is of outsider's. She is a 'poor expatriate.' G. Vassanji, another diaspora writer was born in Kenya (b. 1950), raised in Tanzania, educated in America and presently lives in Canada. He writes novels of the Shamsi traders of Gujarat who migrated to East Africa in the last century. Likewise Ahmed Essop (b. 1931), a Gujarati in South Africa writes of African diaspora.

If the old diaspora depicts Indians' withdrawal into zones of exclusivity the new diaspora depicts life traversing gender, class, ethnicity, nation-states. Ved Mehta's (b. 1934) is a typical blind case. Masala-diaspora refers to international fictional portrayals of Bharati Mukherjee (India-US), Farrukh Dhondy (India-Britain), Rohinton Mistry (India-Canada) and Meera Syal (Britain). Bharati Mukherjee's novels depict Indians' domestic violence. She deals with sexuality, politics, crime, migrancy and nationalism. Dhondy does the same. Mistry deals with the changing fortunes of the Parsis in India.

Postmodernism and Salman Rushdie

It is said, 'Postmodernism' is an international movement, affecting all the contemporary arts, which has succeeded modernism. Opinions vary as to whether it is entirely distinct from modernism or differs from it only in degree. In literature, it has its origins in the rejection of traditional mimetic fiction in favour of a heightened sense of artifice, a delight in games and verbal pyrotechnics, a suspicion of absolute truth and a resulting inclination to stress the fictionality of fiction. All these traits, of course, are already present in modernist works like Joyce's *Finnegans Wake*. Key American texts of early postmodernism include Nabokov's *Pale Fire* (1962), Thomas Pynchon's *V* (1963) and Kurt Vonnegut's *Slaughterhouse 5* (1969).

Various reasons have been offered for these departures, including the belated availability of Kafka's work in English and the influence of Samuel Beckett and the Theatre of the Absurd. Stressing socio-historical and political conditions, the critic Larry McCaffrey has identified 22 November 1963 - the day Kennedy was shot - as the beginning of postmodernism. Later events (the Vietnam War, the proliferation of nuclear weapons) encouraged the fantasies of William Burroughs, the reclusive abstractions of Donald Barthelme and the intricate structures favoured by John Barth. Elsewhere, the incipient independence of nations like Colombia catalysed the emergence of magic realism, a central subset of postmodernism. Marquez's *One Hundred Years of Solitude* is often celebrated as the key postmodernist text. In Germany the suspicion of linguistic structures inherited from Nazism prompted the work of Gunter Grass. Literature in English outside the USA has sometimes seen postmodernist strategies adopted by writers confronting a postcolonial experience, like Salman Rushdie in *Midnight's Children* (1981).

The distrust of traditional mimetic genres, allied to the philosophical climate of structuralism and deconstruction, has encouraged postmodernism to embrace popular forms, such as detective fiction (Umbeito Eco's *The Name of the Rose,* 1983), Science Fiction (Doris Lessing's *Canopus in Argos* sequence) and fairy tale (a recurrent source in the work of Angela Carter). Equally postmodernist is the blurring of boundaries between the novel and journalism in Truman Capote's *In Cold Blood* (1966), the New Journalism of Tom Wolfe and others, and Robert Pirsig's *Zen and the Art of Motorcycle Maintenance* (1974). Recent observers have noted an abandonment of the extravagance of authors like Pynchon and the emergence—in the work of Raymond Carver or Nicholson Baker, for example—of a kind of experimental realism which ostensibly returns to mimetic structures while retaining a distinctly postmodernist bewilderment. Perhaps the most typical recent practitioner is

Don Delillo. A useful distinction to make is that between post-modernity—the period since the 1960s characterised by social, political and cultural fluidity and uncertainty - and postmodernism as the artistic response to it. This distinction makes it possible to see instances of postmodernist art as sharing some of the characteristics of postmodernity while retaining a critical distance from it.

Salman Rushdie is a 1970s spokesman for Indian English fiction. This phase of Indian English fiction is in postmodern tone. Rushdie's *Midnight Children* is a great work. Rushdie's fiction is much political. He is an erudite and conscious writer. Rushdie's problem is rootlessness as in *Grimus*. It is a kind of multiple rooting. *Shame* is a critic of Pakistan as *Midnight Children* is a critic of India. As Rushdie says in a 1995 interview, his novels *Midnight Children, Shame*, *The Satanic Verses* and *The Moor's Last Sigh* are a response to post-independence India as an age. Rushdie showed Indian English novelist a way to be 'postcolonial.' His descriptions, techniques, idiosyncratic characters help us to know how to use English for sensational effects.

The 1980s witnessed a golden age after the first with the 'big three' in the 1930s and 40s. This second renaissance in Indian English fiction was pioneered by Rushdie. This phase was, in fact, post-modern phase, in Indian fiction, as in world literature. In the fiction of this phase, we find the appearance of a certain post-modern playfulness. The turn to history, a new exuberance of language, the reinvention of allegory, the sexual frankness, even the prominent reference to Bollywood—all seem to own something to Rushdie's novel. There is magic realism. Along with Rushdie's internationalising Indian English fiction, promotion of publication in India facilitated post-modern fiction. Most abroad-published novels will have an Indian edition. Ravi Dayal's press published Stephanite College writers—Allan Sealy, Amitav Ghosh, Shashi Tharoor, Upamanya Chatterjee, Rukun Advani, Mukul Kesavan and Anurag Mathur. Penguin India, Rupa and IndiaInk have done a pioneer work in printing and marketing. The Indian middle class readership is a backbone for this boom. This fiction made use of Indian English with regional tang or masala mix of a culture. English is implicated in the polyphony of Indian languages. Now Indian English achieved a privileged status. It became one of *our* languages—an elite language, the language of getting on, of business, of identity and of modernity. Modern Indian life is well documented in the works of Stephan College writers. Amitav Ghosh is perhaps the best of them. His *The Calcutta Chromosome* is a science novel; and *The Shadow Lines* a partition novel. Ghosh, Seally and Vikram Chandra and Vikram Seth make use of history as a source material. On the other hand, Shashi Deshpande writes of urban middle class women. Arundhati Roy too did the same and Geeta Hariharan has made use of folklore in her fiction.

There are many other new novelists. The mention may be made of Rajendra Chenni from Shimoga, Basavaraj Naikar and Mallikarjun Patil from Dharwad. Of course there are many many more from the other parts of the country who need to be appreciated.

References

1. *The Cambridge Guide to Literature in English,* ed. Dominic Head, CUP, 2006, p. 756.
2. M.A.R. Habib, *A History of Literary Criticism and Theory*, Blackwell, London, 1988, p. 628.
3. Leela Gandhi, "Novelists of the 1930s and 40s," *Indian Literature in English*, ed by A. K. Mehrotra, Permanent Black, New Delhi, 2003, p. 174.
4. Leela Gandhi, "Novelists of the 1930s and 40s," *Indian Literature in English*, p. 187.
5. Pankaj Misra, "R. K. Narayan," *Indian Literature in English*, ed by A. K. Mehrotra, p. 199.
6. Ibid., p. 205.
7. *The Cambridge Guide to Literature in English,* ed Dominic Head, p. 756.

6

Indian English Women Novelists' Contribution

India has produced many women novelists who write in English as prolifically and effectively as the men. Some of them are Kamala Markandaya, Anita Desai, Ruth Prawer Jhubvala, Shobha De, Arundhati Roy and others. Some of them like Jhubvala and Roy have even won great honours for the country. The following is a brief and critical survey of the same.

I Phase: Eighteenth Century to the 1920s

Indian English literature is as old as Bankimachandra Chattopadyaya's English novel *Rajmohun's Wife* (1864). Lord Macaulay's *Minute* on English education in the 1830s and the Bengal Renaissance of the second part of the nineteenth century led to the rise of Indian English literature. The temptation of the West added its mite to the spurt of English writing in colonised countries. The status of English with the strength of being a pan-Indian language was there. Anyway English was of the superior white masters' language. The West as the Euro-centured, Christian civilisation and its imperialism were the strength of it. Many of these reasons led to the temptation of writng in English.

Another stream is the Western interest in indology. The Orientlists Sir Charles Wilkins, Nathaniel Brassey Halhed, Sir William Jones, John Gilchrist and Henry Colebroke worked in comparative philology, lexicography and translation. In his *Asiatic Researches*, Jones the laying foundation for historical linguistics, said: "Sanskrit, Greek and Latin have sprung from a common source."

Between 1866 and 1889, Nandashankar Mehta in Gujarat, Bankimachandra Chattopadhyaya ('The Scott of Bengal') in Bengal, Samuel Pillai in Tamil, M.V. Rohalkar in Marathi, K.V. Pantulu in Telugu and O.C. Menon in Malayalam published novels in their languages yet through the English support. Arvind Krishna Mehrotra says, "The exposure to English colonialism necessitated some Indian writers to discover prose, the realist novel and poetry whose grafts they inserted in their tropical languages where they have since flourished. Other writers with a similar social background and with the same Macaulayan education reversed the procedure as it were, and sought to tie and wax themselves to an English stem."[1]

The Western life influenced these novelists and they used quotations and references from the British writers. For example, A. Madhaviah used Carlyle's statement that: "Religion is a bond of society." These novels sometimes dealt with rich Indian past as in the case of K.K. Sinha's *Sanjogita* (1930) or they dealt with British encounter as in the case of A. Madhavaiah's *Thillai Govindan* (1908). Some of them dealt with peasants' life as in the case of Lal Bihari Day's *Govind Samanta* (1874). Often they dealt with middle class life as the English novels did in the West. These novels have ambivalence about Western civilisation—on the one hand as liberating and on the other as a threat to Hindu identity. This novel is known for its traditional Indian country life. Yet its realism is modified by other narrative conventions: of Sanskrit *kavya*, of Vaishnava love poetry, of the English Gothic novel in its evocation of terror. What is true of men's fiction is also true of women's fiction during this period. Interestingly these novels were more like romances, the predecessors of the novel.

Indian women began to write fiction as well as cultivate other arts. First, as in the West, they imitated the male writers, though, like the English, they did not adopt psydonyms or publish books anonymously. They simply imitated men. First they aspired for education as an emancipating and empowering power. Then, they began to fight for their rights as human rights. In fact, Indian women's fiction has its own tradition as the British women's. The latter is shown clearly in Elaine

Showalter's study *The Literature of Their Own* where she says that English women's fiction has three stages: the first stage from 1840 to 1880 (the death of George Eliot); the second stage from 1880 to 1920 (this age refers to the "Second Wave" of feminism) and the third stage from 1920 to 1960 (the time women's movements became strong). Here the first phase is marked by imitation; the second by protest and the third by self-discovery. The third phase does not have either imitation or protest, both forms of dependencey. Showalter calls these three phases as feminine, feminist and female stages. This kind of trajectory can be found in Indian women's fiction. We need to initiate more researches in this regard.

Indian women have started their feminist struggle. This is an on-going movement. As Jane Freedman says there are many feminisms of concerns with women's inferior position in society. Feminists call for changes in all fields of life for overcoming the discrimination against women. In a way, feminism refers to feminists' movements that took place in the nineteenth and twentieth centuries, as referred to the 'First Wave.' The 'Second-Wave' feminism refers to the resurgence of feminist activity in the late 1960s. Some theorists divide feminism as liberal feminism, Marxist (social) feminism and radical feminism. Liberal feminists think of social injustice based on man-woman divide; and radical theorists think of women's depending as a result of patriarchy. Recent classifications include psychoanalytical feminism, post-modern and poststructuralist feminism, black feminism, Western feminism and Eastern feminism.

It is in this background we need to understand Indian women's fiction. Yet Indian women imitated and now they are protesting against man's whisky and cigar politics. Not many of them have started to self-discover. They are likely to take many more years for it. Bessie Head in her article "Why I Write?" wrote, "I am building a stairway to the stars, I have the authority to take the whole mankind up there with me that is why I write."[2] Likewise Indian women first want emancipation and then empowerment. They are not just contented to be sadharmini with men but also sahbagini. This is what Virginia Woolf's called androgini theory.

Krupabai Sattianadhan was the earliest Indian woman to write fiction in English. Her novels *Kamala: A Story of Hindu Wife* (1894) and *Saguna: A Story of Native Christian Wife* (1895) are feminist works. The two novels deal with the theme of gender, ethnicity and culture. They speak of the predicament of women. Her novels provide textual pleasure and feminist and cultural concerns. *Saguna* is largely autobiographical. As the daughter of a Christian convert, the protagonist manages despite the odds, not only to receive formal education, but also to get admission to a medical college, and eventually meets a man who could share her life as an equal.

What Meenakshi Mukherjee tells us is that the nineteenth century Indian English novelists were less educated, timid and traditional. She observes, "To me, the most radical difference between early novels in English and those being written today lies not in thematic concerns, formal innovations, or in the texture of language—such variations would be inevitable across this span of time in any body of literature—but in the sense of an audience. The tentativeness of nineteenth-century novelists, not only about writing in an acquired colonial language but also about their readership, has been replaced by an overwhelming confidence among postcolonial writers that the English language belongs to them as much as to anyone else; a text written in a global language has potentially a global constituency, and therefore, as a corollary, a national one too. The issues are not merely literary but are informed by cultural politics and market forces. It is worth analysing the complex circumstances that made Bankimchandra shift from English to his Bengali mother tongue before he could gain national recognition as a writer, while at the end of the twentieth century one would expect the process to be reversed."[3]

II Phase: Gandian Age or the Period of Modernism of the 1930s and 1940s

The 1930s and '40s is the time when modernism was triumphant in Europe. The nature of European modernism which has somehow influenced Indian fiction of the big three is as follows: "The term 'modernism' is for an international tendency in the arts brought about by a creative renaissance during the last decade of the 19th century and lasting into the postwar years. Strictly speaking, modernism cannot be described as a 'movement' or reliably characterised by a uniform style. Indeed it may be said to have embraced a wide range of artistic movements (including symbolism, impressionism, post-impressionism, futurism, constructivism, imagism, vorticism, expressionism, data and surrealism) and to have originated in cosmopolitan circles in Berlin, Vienna, Munich, Prague, Moscow, London and Paris. At a slightly later period it spread to New York and Chicago, and became synonymous with a worldwide reaction against positivism and representational art. Its most notable landmarks in English literature are commonly understood to include Henry James's *The Ambassadors* (1903), Conrad's *Nostromo* (1904), T. S. Eliot's *The Waste Land* (1922), and Joyce's *Ulysses* (1922). One might add the work of Pound, Yeats, Ford Madox Ford, Virginia Woolf and, in America, Faulkner, to a list which is by no means exhaustive."[4]

Technically, modernism was distinguished by its opposition to traditional forms and to the aesthetic perceptions associated with those forms. It was persistently experimental. A common quality was the highly self-conscious manipulation of form, together with an awareness of pioneering studies which were contemporaneous in other disciplines. These included, in psychology, William James's *Principles of Psychology* (1890) and Freud's *The Interpretation of Dreams* (1899); in Physics, Einstein's *General Principles of Relativity* (1915); and in Anthropology, Sir James Frazer's *The Golden Bough* (1890-1915).

Herbert Read suggested that modernism is not so much a revolution, which implies a turning over, even a turning back, but rather a break-up, a devolution, some would say a dissolution. Leela Gandhi observes, "Thus modernism was not only well disposed to the immediate political concerns of the 1930s and '40s expatriate Indian novelists, but also instrumental—albeit accidentally—in helping them to reach cultural affiliations. Moreover, many of these novelists benefited materially from the atmosphere of literary, and sometimes economic patronage which characterised the ethos of European modernism. In particular, it was E.M. Forster who facilitated the early careers of many of the writers under discussion. Anand's *Untouchability* bears the authoritative seal of Forster's laudatory preface.

Forster's preface to the Everyman's Library edition of *A Passage to India* lavishes praise upon Ahmed Ali's *Twilight in Delhi* which was published by Hogarth Press. G.V. Desani's cult novel *All About H. Hatterr* appeared to favorable reviews by, among others, T.S. Eliot, who spoke for many when saying: "In all my experience, I have not met with anything quite like it."[5]

Mulk Raj Anand attributes his novelistic negotiation of tradition and modernity to 'the double burden on his shoulders, the Alps of the European tradition and the Himalayas of his Indian past.' These novelists had the context: the social and political upheavals of the 'Gandhian whirlwind' and the era of late modernism in Europe. At home this phase marked the Indian struggle for independence culminating in Swaraj in 1947. Opt to that is Raja Rao's swadeshi novel *Kanthapura* with a foreword. A statement of it reads: "One has to describe in a language that is not one's own the spirit that is one's own.' Whilst R.K. Narayana depicted of Indian life as it is even to this day: traditional, provincial and simple.

Many novels deal with Gandhian themes: freedom struggle, Hindu-Muslim discord, Harizan uplift, removal of untouchability, emancipation, if not empowerment of women and the like. This was socio-economic transformation. The use of Gandhi themes or the use of Nehruvian socialism is totally new and transforming. That way Nehru's conflict with Gandhian ideology is there. There is an uneasy synthesis between the two.

Desani's *All About H. Hatterr* (1948) is about his improbable life. It is a Joycean linguistic burlesque where Indian English—much like Joyce's Irish English—relentlessly jostles against all the known rules of grammar and diction. Structurally, the novel is more or less a growing up story about the education of the eponymous and mad-hatterrish hero H. Hatterr, son of a European merchant seaman and a lady from Penang. Set in British India, it is rigorously organised around a set of seven episodes, involving Hatterr's attempt to find a higher truth. It is said, "Desani's intensely self-conscious novel prefigures more recent books like Salman Rushdie's *Midnight Children* and Allan Sealy's *The Trotter-Nama.* Chronologically, its linguistic experimentation and irreverent handling of the Great Books of the European canon are possibly more revolutionary than those in recent Indian fiction. Desani's slightly precious and arrogant posturing is, in context, both startlingly unusual and useful in the history of the incipient Indian novel in English."[6]

Cornelia Sorabji and Sarojini Naidu, who were prominent in public life, and associated with women's causes and politics during the last period of British rule, were also acclaimed for their writing in Britain and British India. Sorabji's books about traditional women who lived in purdah, and her reflections on her life in Britain, were reviewed enthusiastically. Her pro-British and anti-nationalist sentiments were wellknown. Cornelia Sorabji was born and brought up in Nasik and Pune and she had a fellowship to Oxford in law. She knew many languages and cultures. She founded the social service league in Bengal and attempted to improve the health of mothers and infants. She was instrumental in the abolition of child-marriage. Finally she settled down in England. Cornelia Sorabji's first published work, *Love and Life Behind the Purdah* (1901), is a collection of eleven narratives. Some were fictional and others drawn from her first encounters with Indian legal life. Most of them were quite melodramatic, revealing women caught between tradition and change. Stylistically, *Love and Life Behind the Purdah* illustrates several of her mannerisms. She loved syntactic inversions such as 'garbed was she' and 'how know we' and archaic words like 'sward,' 'beseem,' 'bewraying' and 'thrid.' These recur throughout her books. She was influenced during her university years by Pateresque purple passages and overdrawn figurative prose. A typical simile compares the chatter of pilgrims to 'some mountain torrent... glittering light-imprisoned under the brilliant rays of a lingering death.'

Between the Twilight is a collection of 14 stories. Her tracts *The Purdahnashin* (1917) and Shubala (1920) speak of her concern for women. She said of Razia that she should have put aside her womanhood so that, like Queen Victoria, she would succed in politics. Sorabji said that in India people must cross religious barriers and be united in their moral ideals. Her autobiography *India Calling* (1934) speaks of her life in India. What is strange is that she never found out mistakes with the British Raj.

III Phase: The Novelist of the 1950s to 1970s or Postmodernism

In the post-independence times, Indian English fiction seemed to have a bleak future again. The triumvirate Mulk Raj Anand, R. K. Narayana and Raja Rao continued to write with diffidence. R.K. Narayana's *The Guide* (1958) won the Sahitya Academy Award. Men writers like Ruskin Bond, Manohar Malgonkar, P.M. Nityanandan and Khushwant Singh each wrote a few novels.

Shamala Narayana observes, "Perhaps the dominant concern of the literature of this period is with character development and psychological depth, often combined with a sense of the alienated individual, dissatisfied with modem life. It may be that this sense of alienation reflects the situation of the Indian writer in English in the 1950s and 1960s possessed of an education and elite status separating him from the mass, although it might just as easily be seen as an attempt to affiliate Indian writing to the dominant forms of Western fiction at the time. The theme of alienation takes on a special edge in the numerous novels published by women in the period. While they form no particular school, it is their emergence which is perhaps the most striking feature of the period. This is 'emergence of woma' theme. Writers such as Kamala Markandaya, Ruth Prawer Jhabvala, Nayantara Sahgal and Anita Desai have had an international readership ever since, a quartet of women writers joining the male trio as India's best-known writers in English until the emergence of the Rushdie generation."[7]

Khushwant Singh used history, religious discord and current affairs in his chatty, digressive narratives. Bond's forte is short story, nature descriptions and his fiction shares with Narayana a strong sense that small provincial town represents real India. Arun Joshi experimented with different narrative techniques. He uses psychological space, monologue and realistic mode. Dissatisfaction with the metropolis and modernity is a recurrent feature of the novels of this period, but there is only really one novel which consequently turned to experimenting with non-Western narrative forms: M. Anantanarayanan's *The Silver Pilgrimage* (1961). The model for his account of the adventures of Jayasurya, a prince of sixteenth-century Sri Lanka, is Dandin's *Dasa-kumara-charita* rather than the Western picaresque novel, although its resources are by no means only Indian. Excerpts arranged as a preface to the novel include lines from Shakespeare, Donne and Rilke through to Tamil poets such as Avvayar, Pattinathar and Tiruvalluvar. The most important function of this prolegomena seems to be to warn the reader against stock responses: the key epigraph is from Jalaluddin Rumi: "Sell your Cleverness and buy Bewilderment." The novel is known for its humour.

No other novelist of the period followed Anantanarayanan's deliberate abrogation of the conventions of the European novel. Innovation can however be found in the psychological depth of the experience of women characters, although that experience is almost restricted, as one would expect, to the English-educated elite and the complexities of their position in relation to traditional and modern roles for women. Not surprisingly, novels with such women are often autobiographical, and a number of women such as Venu Chitale (*In Transit*, 1951), Zeenuth Futehally (*Zohra*, 1951) and Mrinalini Sarabhai (*This Alone is True,* 1952) published single novels of self-discovery. Attia Hosain's *Sunlight on a Broken Column* (1961) has proved among the most popular of these studies of elite women's consciousness, widely admired for the lyricism of its prose style and its vivid re-creation of the distinctive Muslim culture of Lucknow before Independence. Hosain (1913-98) was born into an aristocratic Muslim family in Lucknow, and studied at the city's Isabella Thoburn College. In the 1930s she came under the influence of the nationalist movement and the Progressive Writers Group, before migrating to England in 1947, where she worked as a broadcaster and journalist. Her first book, *Phoenix Fled* (1953), was a collection of stories, and *Sunlight on a Broken Column* was to be her only novel. The novel is dominated instead by her personal struggle against the claustrophobia of family authority and, paradoxically perhaps, a nostalgia for the lost world of her childhood.

Anita Singh observes, "The contemporary literary stage of Indian English writing is agog with women writers who have made significant inroads in world literature, winning top international literary awards increasingly more and more women are giving voice to their concerns and experiences and creating a body of 'literature of their own.'"[8] This can be seen with reference to Indian women writers in the post-independence era.

One woman novelist in whose fiction the personal and the political have been less segregated is Nayantara Sahgal, perhaps unsurprisingly, given that she spent much of her childhood at Anand Bhavan in Allahabad, the ancestral home of the Nehrus. Sahgal (b. 1927) the second of the three daughters of Vijayalakshmi Pandit (Nehru's sister) and R.S. Pandit (a Sanskrit scholar and lawyer) studied in missionary schools in India, and Wellesley College, Massachusetts, where she received a BA in history. After her return to India in 1947 she stayed for some time with Nehru in Delhi, and her novels reveal a close acquaintance with the political elite. Two years later she married Gauram Sahgal, a businessman, and had three children. The marriage broke up when she met E.N. Mangat Rai, a civil servant. *Relationship* (1994), a selection of their letters, reveals something of the pressures brought to bear on a couple flouting the middle-class conventions of the time. Sahgal's novels present the life of the richest sections of Indian society, their hypocrisy and shallow values; at the same time,

Sahgal is concerned with the Indian heritage and its value for the educated Indian. Her *Rich Like Us* (1985) won the Sinclair Prize for fiction. *Plans for departure* (1985) won the Commonwealth Prize for fiction.

Kamala Markandaya (Kamala Taylor nee Purnaiya. b. 1924) is a writer who has attempted, not always successfully to look beyond the elite in her exploration of similar themes. She is a realist. Markandaya was educated at Madras University. She worked as a journalist before becoming a full-time writer. Married to an Englishman she is now settled in Britain. Her ten novels present a remarkable range of characters from Rukmini a poor peasant woman in *Nectar in a Sieve* (1954), through the urban poor of *A Handful of Rice* (1966), to the highest circles of princely life in *The Golden Honeycomb* (1977). The conflict between tradition and modernity and East and West runs through all her work. *The Coffer Dams* (1969) and *Pleasure City* (1982) are her contemporary examinations of the meaning of progress. Her *The Nowhere Man* (1972) deals with white man's maltreatment of Indians in England.

Anita Desai of the group deals with the middle calss people and she writes of people's psychology. Indeed she has often made her priorities in this respect clear: "Writing is to me a process of discovering the truth-the truth that is nine-tenths of the iceberg that lies submerged beneath the one-tenth visible portion we call Reality. Writing is my way of plunging to the depths and exploring this underlying truth... My novels are no reflection of Indian society, policies, or character." Desai's westernised, educated women appear to have the luxury of freedom of choice, but deeper analysis reveals them to be frustrated and emotionally dependent. Except in her most recent novels, her protagonists have all been women and range from the daughter and young wife (*Cry, the Peacock,* 1963) to the middle-aged wife and mother (*Where Shall We Go This Summer*?, 1975) to a grandmother and grandfather (*Fire on the Mountain*, 1977). All these women tend to be fragile introverts whose emotional traumas sometimes lead to violent death. Most of Desai's novels reveal the breakdown of relationships, marital or familial. Her novels depict the attempt of urban middle-class women to harmonise the needs of the self with the demands traditionally made of Indian women by the family. Desai's later novels seem to be an attempt to move beyond the sometimes suffocating psychological studies of her earlier work. As part of the attempt she seems to have switched, in novels such as *In Custody* (1984) and *Baumgartners Bombay* (1988), to male-centred plots. *In Custody* (made into a successful film) deals with the growing disillusionment of Deven, a young college teacher. *Journey to Ithaca* (I995) is completely Eurocentric in its vision of India as a land of heat and dust.

Mention of Ruth Prawer Jhabvala (b. J927), novelist, short-story and screenplay writer, raises an interesting problem for the historian of literature. Jhabvala wants us to consider her as a European writer who has written on India. Yet she has written about the Indian middle class and she is "the Jane Austin of India." She deals with East-West encounter, racial prejudice, fasle values and Indian social culture. Shamala Narayan and Jon Mee observe, "The 1950s and 1960s were not a period of great innovation for Indian writing in English, though they witnessed the foundation of writing careers that have lasted over several decades and which, especially for women writers, brought international acclaim. Many of the novels seem highly sceptical of the dominant forms of Indian culture and society. What these novelists did demonstrate was a command of the dominant forms of the English novel, and the right of Indian novelists to be taken seriously in terms of the criteria of Western novel-writing. Perhaps this represents a building up towards the cultural capital so conspicuously consumed by the Rushdie generation of the 1980s and 1990s."[9]

From Sugar to Masala

This is a writing by the Indian diaspora. There is a distinction to be made between the old and new Indian diasporas. This distinction is between, on the one hand, the semi-voluntary flight of indentured peasants to non-metropolitan plantation colonies such as Fiji, Trinidad, Mauritius, South Africa, Malaysia, Surinam. and Guyana, roughly between the years

1830 and 1917; and on the other the late capital or postmodern dispersal of new migrants of all classes to thriving metropolitan centres such as Australia, the United States, Canada, and Britain. Many Indians settled down abroad and they wrote of their diasporic esperience. Such writers can be Seepersad Naipaul, Harold Ladoo, David Dabydeen, Menon Marath, Balachandra Rajan and Victor Anant.

Having left it in his maturity, Marath approaches India with an insider's intimacy, while Santha Rama Rau, who has scarcely spent any time in India (save for two crucial years during World War II), approaches it with an outsider's curiosity, especially in her autobiographical novel *Home to India* (1945). This is an account of her coming to consciousness, both politically and culturally, against the backdrop of nationalistic struggles against the British Raj, resulting in the gradual weakening of her Anglophilia, her feelings of bourgeois privilege, and a growing identification with subaltern India. Santa Rama Rau has written two more novels—*Remember the House* (1956) and *The Adventurer* (1970). She herself is a poor expatriate and lives in the US. Her novel *Remember the House* (1955) draws on her exile in Japan, Philippenes and China.

Another batch of diasporic writers is G. Vassanji, Ahmed Essop, Ved Mehta and others. In his ambivalent identification with some aspects of desh and pardesh, Ved Mehra anticipates the work of many writers of the new or masala diaspora, such as Bharati Mukherjee (India-United States), Farrukh Dhondy (India-Britain), G.S. Sharat Chandra (India-United States), Agha Shahid Ali (India-United States), Saleem Peeradina (India-United States), Rohinton Mistry (India-Canada), Sujata Bhatt (India-Germany), Pico Iyer (Britain), and Meera Syal (Britain). Whereas the writers of the old diaspora tend to concentrate on the chinks within, say, the girmit enclave, the new diasporic writers are inclined to inhabit the threshold zone of intercutting subjectivities that defines the experience of migrancy.

The narratives of Bharati Mukherjee. (b. 1940) provide the best examples of this. Her novels trace the split in the diasporic subject, expressed in that sense of being here and elsewhere, of being at home and abroad. *The Tiger's Daughter* (1972) considers this feeling in relation to Tara, New York-returned and married to an American, as she attempts to reconnect with Calcutta only to find that everything has been affected by an estranging alchemy. *Wife* (1976) examines the darker side of this split when Dimple, unable to cope with the tumult of irreconcilable values and emotions that haunt those in transit between places, roles and cultures succumbs to a liberatory madness, culminating in the murder of her husband. In *Jasmine* (1989) the eponymous heroine struggles to cheat the stars by fleeing to America, a country in which personal destiny is connected to individual action rather than as in India to the fateful action of the planets. *Jasmine* describes herself as transitory as becoming as rebirthing, and her life becomes a statement on the United States. The novel is known for its theme of resistence. Mukherjee's fiction shows how immigrants are transformed by the idea of living in the US. This is what we can call the American Dream.

In her impressive novel *Anita and Me* (1996), Meera Syal, actress and script-writer for Gurinder Chadha's acclaimed film *Bhaji on the Beach* (1994), arrives at a less melancholic definition of diasporic selfhood: "The place in which I belonged was wherever I stood and there was nothing stopping me simply moving forward and claiming each resting place as home." This process of identity-formation, however, takes a long and convoluted route, littered with false starts and rash detours, over the terrain of the novel. This is world as home theme.

Jhumpa Lahiri's women have similar predicament. Lahiri writes of migration in *Nameshake*. Chitra Devikarani's *The Mistress of Spices* tells of the main character Tilo's ability to function as a healer and seller of magical spices in her Oakland community, attempting to empower its dislocated inhabitants. Uma Parameswarana points out that these diasporic writngs are articulate and intelligent. For these writers home is where their feet are.

The movement from Seepersad Naipaul to Meera Syal suggests an important rethinking of the concept of home within the diaspora especially as this occurs against the backdrop of the global shift from the centring or centripetal logic of monopoly capitalism to the decentring or centrifugal logic of transnational capitalism. Whereas for the sugar diaspora 'home' signifies an end to itinerant wandering, in the putting down of roots, 'home' for' the masala diaspora is linked to the strategic espousal of rootlessness, to the constant mantling and dismantling of the self in makeshift landscapes.

After Midnight or Postmodern Fiction (After 1970)

It is said, 'Postmodernism' is an international movement, affecting all the contemporary arts, which has succeeded modernism. Opinions vary as to whether it is entirely distinct from modernism or differs from it only in degree. In literature, it has its origins in the rejection of traditional mimetic fiction in favour of a heightened sense of artifice, a delight in games and verbal pyrotechnics, a suspicion of absolute truth and a resulting inclination to stress the fictionality of fiction. All these traits, of course, are already present in modernist works like Joyce's *Finnegans Wake.* Key American texts of the early postmodernism include Nabokov's *Pale Fire* (1962), Thomas Pynchon's *V* (1963) and Kurt Vonnegut's *Slaughterhouse 5* (1969).

Various reasons have been offered for these departures, including the belated availability of Kafka's work in English and the influence of Samuel Beckett and the Theatre of the Absurd. Stressing socio-historical and political conditions, the critic Larry McCaffrey has identi-fied 22 November 1963—the day Kennedy was shot—as the beginning of postmodernism. Later events (the Vietnam War, the proliferation of nuclear weapons) encouraged the fantasies of William Burroughs, the reclusive abstractions of Donald Barthelme and the intricate struc-tures favoured by John Barth. Elsewhere, the incipient independence of nations like Colombia catalysed the emergence of magic realism, a central subset of postmodernism. Marquez's *One Hundred Years of Solitude* is often celebrated as the key postmodernist text. In Germany, the suspicion of linguistic structures inherited from Nazism prompted the work of Gunter

Grass. Literature in English outside the USA has sometimes seen postmodernist strategies adopted by writers confronting a postcolonial experience, like Salman Rushdie in *Midnight's Children* (1981).

The distrust of traditional mimetic genres allied to the philosophical climate of structuralism and deconstruction, has encouraged postmodernism to embrace popular forms such as detective fiction (Umbeito Eco's *The Name of the Rose,* 1983), Science Fiction (Doris Lessing's *Canopus in Argos* sequence) and fairy tale (a recurrent source in the work of Angela Carter). Equally postmodernist is the blurring of boundaries between the novel and journalism in Truman Capote's *In Cold Blood* (1966), the New Journalism of Tom Wolfe and others, and Robert Pirsig's *Zen and the Art of Motorcycle Maintenance* (1974). Recent observers have noted an abandonment of the extravagance of authors like Pynchon and the emergence—in the work of Raymond Carver or Nicholson Baker, for example—of a kind of 'experimental realism' which ostensibly returns to mimetic structures while retaining a distinctly postmodernist bewilderment. Perhaps the most typical recent practitioner is Don Delillo. A useful distinction to make is that between postmodernity—the period since the 1960s characterised by social, political and cultural fluidity and uncertainty—and postmodernism as the artistic response to it. This distinction makes it possible to see instances of postmodernist art as sharing some of the characteristics of postmodernity while retaining a critical distance from it.

Salman Rushdie is a 1970s spokesman for Indian English fiction. This phase of Indian English fiction is in postmodern tone. Rushdie's *Midnight Children* is a great political novel. He is an erudite and conscious writer. Rushdie's problem is rootlessness as in *Grimus*. It is a kind of multiple rooting. *Shame* is a critic of Pakistan as *Midnight Children* is a critic of India. As Rushdie says in a 1995 interview, his novels *Midnight Children, Shame*, *The Satanic Verses* and *The Moor's Last Sigh* are a response to post-independence India as an age. Rushdie showed Indian English novelist a way to be 'post-colonial.' His descriptions, techniques, idiosyncratic characters help us to know how to use English for sensational effects.

The 1980s witnessed a second coming for the Indian novel in English. Its messiah seems to have been Salman Rushdie. The appearance of *Midnight's Children* in 1981 brought about a renaissance in Indian writing in English which has outdone that of the 1930s. Its influence acknowledged by critics and novelists alike, has been apparent in numerous ways: the appearance of a certain postmodern playfulness, the turn to history, a new exuberance of language, the reinvention of allegory, the sexual frankness, even the prominent references to Bollywood, all seem to owe something to Rushdie's novel.

Rushdie's fame may have identified an international audience for Indian writers in English, but commercial developments in English-language publishing within India have played their role in enabling a new crop of novelists to come forward. Many writers to publish abroad now also insist on a separate Indian edition of their work. Ravi Dayal's publishing house has nurtured a group of writers identified with Delhi's elite (of the St. Stephen's College). Allan Sealy, Amitav Ghosh. Shashi Tharoor, Upamanyu Chatterjee, Rukun Advani, Mukul Kesavan and Anurag Mathur were all students at this college in the early 1970s who self-consciously acknowledge each other's influence in their books.

Jon Me says, "Such views cannot simply be dismissed as reactionary traditionalism: if nothing else they alert the literary critic to the question of the relationship between the novels of the 1980s and the Indian regional languages. One of the legacies of *Midnight's Children* was a vibrant model for rewriting English in dialogue with those languages. Anita Desai has claimed that it was only after Salman Rushdie came along that Indian writers finally felt capable of using the spoken language, spoken English, the way it's spoken on Indian streets by ordinary people. However, Desai's account is not quite accurate. Contemporary novelists rarely attempt street-wise realism. More often they bring different languages into comic collision, testing the limits of communication between them, celebrating India's linguistic diversity, and taking over the English language to meet the requirements of an Indian context, a perspective."[10]

New novelists of the 1980s such as Chatterjee (b. 1959) have tried to demonstrate that, on the contrary, the Indian 'tang' is not a pure essence but the masala mix of a culture that has always been able to appropriate influences from outside the subcontinent. The English language has a privileged place in Indian culture. It is the language of the former coloniser and remains an elite language, the language of getting on, the language of buriness, the language identified, above all with modernity. Here mention may be made of new writers Ranga Rao, Amit Chaudhuri and Kiran Nagarkar. Both Rushdie and Amitav Ghosh used magic realism as well as history. Ghosh's *The Calcutta Chromosome* (1996) is something like science fiction. The year1995 saw two new novelists address the issue of translating Indian history into the novel: Mukul Kesavan (b. 1957) and Vikram Chandra (b. 1961). Vikrma Seth's *A Suitable Boy* (1993) is an allegory of nationhood. It is a metaficitonal narrative.

Shashi Deshpande (b. 1938) as perhaps the leading writer deals with the situation of women in urban, middle-class life. Deshpande's novels are *The Dark Holds no Terror* (1980), *Roots and Shadoes* (1983), *That Long Silence* (1988), *Small Remedies* (2000) and *The Binding Vine* (1992). Deshpande's women achieve personhood yet do not negate the family or society. They go beyond what Elaine Showalter calls the 'Female Phase.' They experience a kind of enlightened reintegration into the society. *The Dark Holds no Terror* creates a resistence to patriarchy.

Gita Hariharan (b. 1954) has not adopted Deshpande's realist mode, though there are thematic similarities in their fiction. Hariharan came to writing after a career as a journalist and shows an interest in literary experimentation in a less epic mode. Hariharan's *A Thousand Faces of Nights* (1992) and *The Ghosts of Vasu Master* (1994) are concerned with rewriting folk tales and children's stories. Her character Devi searches for a story of her own. Namita Gokhale's *Paro* is known for resistance to patriarchy. Shobha De's novels have often been labeled as pulp fiction. In *Socialite Evenings,* Karuna seeks to escape from her stultifying life by writing her memoirs. She presents an outrageious picture of perversion as resistence.

A similar struggle to fashion female autonomy in the context of received narratives faces Ammu, the heroine of Arundhari Roy's 1997 Booker-Prize winning novel, *The God of Small Things*. Roy (b. 1960) who was trained as an architect and has also written filmscripts, is on her mother's side from a Syrian Christian family and was brought up in South India. Her heroine, who shares Roy's regional and religious background, is a divorcee struggling against the fate laid out for her by convention: 'She was twenty-seven that year, and in the pit of her stomach she carried the cold knowledge that for her life had been lived. She had had one chance. She made a mistake.' Having already transgressed community boundaries by marrying a Hindu, she compounds the mistake by taking a chance across the boundaries of caste and falls in love with Velutha, a 'paravan.' Critics think *The God of Small Things* is a feminist text where "Ammu underscores the woman's right to her body. Ammu's act of marrying out of the Syrian Christian community itself is said to be a quite assertion of her right over her body."[11]

In Manjula Kapur's *Difficult Daughters* Virmati is Kapur's difficult daughter seeking emancipation from the business called life. In her second novel *A Married Woman* the heroine Astha struggles to keep her identity intact while seeking equal opprtunities within and without the familial threshold.

Indian English fiction by women though not fierce, has nonetheless, been significant because it has tried to question the commodification of women as bodies. An overview of contemporary Indian fiction in English reveals an incredible array of talent. Many of the novelists seem to regard India's wealth of literary and mythical tradition as freely available to rewrite in the present. A different perspective might construe this trend as the self-serving attempt by sections of the elite to represent their own modernity in terms of a continuity with India's past. It is true that many of these novelists are foreign returned or divide their lives between India and other places. It is true that marketers of the Indian novel in English have shown great concern. There has developed over the past few years, a sense that India sells abroad. Yet any assumption that recent writing is simply doing the ideological work of the globalised middle classes has to concede the complex nature of the relationship between culture and class, especially in the contemporary Indian situation. The idea of India has been subject to reassessment across the whole range of Indian culture in the past two decades. Today Indian English fiction makes us think that English is one of our own languages and we can write in it.

References

1. A.K. Mehrotra, *Indian Literature in English*, ed by A. K. Mehrotra, Permanent Black, New Delhi, 2003, p. 112.
2. Jessie Head, qt by Anita Singh, "Stairway to the Stars..." *Parnassus*, ed by N.K. Agrawal, Lucknow, vol. 1, 2009, p. 13.
3. Meenakshi Mukherjee, "The Beginnings of the Indian Novel," *Illustrated History of Indian English Literature*, p. 102.
4. *The Cambridge Guide to Literature in English,* ed Dominic Head, CUP, 2006, p. 756.
5. Leela Gandhi, "Novelists of the 1930s and 40s," *Indian Literature in English*, ed. by A. K. Mehrotra, p. 187.
6. Pankaj Misra, "R.K. Narayan," *Indian Literature in English*, ed by A.K. Mehrotra, p. 199.
7. Shamala Narayana, *Indian Literature in English,* ed by A.K. Mehrotra, pp. 218-219.
8. Anita Singh, *Indian Literature in English,* ed by A. K. Mehrotra, p. 14.
9. Shamala Narayan and Jon Mee, *Indian Literature in English*, ed by A.K. Mehrotra, pp. 130-131.
10. Jon Mee, "After Midnight," *Indian Literature in English*, ed by A. K. Mehrotra, p. 320.
11. Harish Trivedi, qt by Anita Singh, *Indian Literature in English*, ed by A. K. Mehrotra, p. 15.

7

Women's Resistance in Indian English Women's Fiction

Injustice, in any form, is a universal phenomenon. It is expressed in the form of class, caste, creed, colour, religion, regionalism, gender, language and ideology. As to injustice to women, woman is victimised in several ways. She is more oppressed than man. She is doubly oppressed, in fact. Here is an attempt to understand woman's resistance against injustice as portrayed in Indian English women's fiction.

Resistance is not just protest and defiance. It is individualistic self-assertion, the quest for identity, the question of 'control' over sexuality. Mahatma Gandhi spoke *satyagrah* (passive resistance) as a powerful kind of resistance for injustice. Usha Bande thinks resistance in turn shapes the social order by its non-confrontational, non-violent action. In time, it becomes the dreaded 'weapon' of the weak. Resistance involves re-interpretation so as to bring the marginalised into the centre. It considers the depressed. It is a stand against. It is a behavioural strategy having the potential to dislodge the dominant structure. It is non-confrontational and contestatory. It is a part of the dynamics of social life. Yet resistance is variable, complex and multivalent. Representation of resistance in women's fictional narrative articulates both the existence of the dominant power structure and the female desire to disavow and defy that structure. Besides, in the South Asian context, women's issues need to be addressed and it is culture-specific.

Resistance literature is a worldwide phenomenon today. This was made possible because of decolonisation, democratic and secular govts, Marxism, and feminist movement. To put it simply, postmodernism is an anti-authoritarian movement; post-structuralism is a critique of historicism with its emphasis on the injustice towards the marginalised; postcolonialism represents a heightened awareness of power relations between the erstwhile imperial power and the colonial subject, and post-feminism shifts its focus to the terrain of culture to resolve women's issues. In fact, resistance is the basis for all kinds of change and change is a continuous and universal process. Resistance is 'a projection of alternative truth.'[1] Foucault calls resistance a 'reverse discourse.'

Usha Bande distinguishes 'resistance literature' from 'literary resistance.' She says that "Resistance literature stands for definitive texts, which examine the relationship between literature, and Third world liberation movements whereas 'literary resistance' is contestatory in nature and it is used for a genre of oppositional writing, a writing meant not only to protest but also to materially and conceptually change the existing situation to allow for empowerment."[2]

Resistance started in India during the Indian freedom struggle against the British. This found an example in literature. Works like Khushwant Singh's *Train to Pakistan* and Bhishma Sahni's *Tamas* (on partition), Shashi Tharoor's *Riot* (on Ayodhya issue), Amrinder Kaur's *Lajo* (on 1984 riots), Bapsi Sidhwa's *Ice-Candy Man* and *The Pakistani Bride* (on Indian Partition), Taslima Nasreen's *Lajja* (about fundamentalism) and Manjushree Thapa's (of Nepal) *The Tutor of History* speak of resistance. Even Dalit literatures speak of this. The Kannada Bandaya (protest) literature and the Marathi Dalit literature speak of it amply.

Yet here my emphasis is on woman's resistance to patriarchy and other socio-political forces, more than other kinds of resistance like Dalit or African-American resistance. The paper attempts to examine Indian women novelists' depiction of woman's resistance, questioning the traditional imperatives. One thing is that many women do not resist, because they have emotional ties with patriarchy and they want to balance man-woman relations socially. Such women are more practical than ideal. Historically speaking, Indian women joined their men in their struggle against the British for independence. One of their basic issues was education. The people's concept of 'new woman' was 'one of purity, loyalty, moral security and domesticity.' A woman needed to become a good wife and a good mother. Often women themselves liked to foster the traditional virtues. Education meant to make them so. They needed less self-emancipation if not self-empowerment. Woman writers like Anandibai Joshi, Pandita Ramabai, Rokeya Sakhawat Hossain (Bangla), Sarla Devi Choudhuri and others reaped the benefits of education for social change. For example, Manganayagam Thambiah in her novel in 1914, criticised the system of arranged marriage.

These women's struggle is different from protest, dissent and revolt as they could not go for collective action. Their self-protests lay in neglect, refusal and separation and sometimes, in sacrifice. Many rich/educated/elite Indian women resisted against the male world/injustice/denials. These were their deeds of resistance. Their writings like autobiography and fiction constituted their writing of resistance. Cornelia Sorabji, Krupabai Sathianadhan, Pandita Ramabai Saraswati, and Begum Hossain wrote for change. Sathianadhan's novels *Saguna* and *Kamala* challenge the oppressive Hindu system. Sorabji's *India Calling* criticises the society for women's problems.

These women were conscious of societal issues, because their conversion to Christianity. Ramabai's motto for woman was 'self-reliance and participation in public life.' She believed that an oppressive society cannot progress. Begum Hossain's literary piece 'Sultana's Dream' is a feminist utopia. She registers woman's resistance against man's restrictive attitude. Her husband called it 'a terrible revenge.' Begum Hossain denounced purdah and condemned man for patriarchy. Toru Dutt's *Bianca* is another such old text. Kamala Markandaya's novel *Silence of Desire* and *Nectar in a Sieve* show woman's resistance. Attia Hossain's *Sunlight on a Broken Column* (1961) shows how the protagonist Laila defies the patriarchal power structure, breaks the rules and creates her own space. Bapsi

Sidhwa's *Ice-Candy Man*, Dina Mehta's *And Some Take a Lover* and Nasrin's *Lajja* show the resistance powerfully.

Anita Desai, Shashi Deshpande and Nayantara Sahgal's fiction depict woman's resistance. Divorce and personal freedom is the ultimate in woman's assertion of the self in Sahgal's early novels. Desai's heroines, for example, Maya commits suicide, Sita quits her home for a while and Nanda Kaul withdraws to the hills. Bim rebels. Deshpande's heroines draw their inner vision to achieve autonomy. Her fiction shows how resistance can be used for bending rather than for breaking and that is for social transformation.

Namita Gokhale's *Paro* is known for resistance. Shobha De presents an outrageous picture of perversions as resistance. Sunita Namjoshi deals with lesbian relationships. The great Indian diasporic writers exhibit resistance in still many more ways. Bharati Mukherjee's Dimple (*Wife*) is far removed from her later heroines who resist being hyphenated Americans. Her Jasmine (*Jasmine*) appears to resist her native culture at every step and with every bold assertion but all her moves and thoughts border on fantasy. This is corroborated by the author's claim that her novel is a 'fantasy' but fantasy itself is a mode of resistance. Resistance can be lived privately or practiced publicly. As Carla Rice points out, "Resistance can be open and confrontational, or quietly subversive; it can be humorous and playful or serious and painful; it can be individually motivational or socially organised in group action."[3]

It is said, "Resistance in fiction falls in the category of the possible rather than real and it may not affect the community of women as such immediately but in the hands of discerning readers—men or women—the fictionalised account may become an agent of change."

Feminism and feminist literary theory provide us tools to recognise literary resistance and determine its history. Yet as Simone de Beauvoir and Virginia Woolf regret, we do not have feminist literary tradition. Understanding feminism is to understand what it means to be a woman. Elaine Showalter, Gilbert and Guber talk of this at length. Showalter's *A Literature of Their Own* (1977) is an account of woman's fiction as a subculture recording female experience. In considering women's writing in terms of 'feminine,' 'feminist' and 'female,' Showalter sees the first period termed as 'feminine' as a period of imitation of the masculine model, 'feminist' phase which lasted from 1880s to 1920s, as a phase of feminist protests and demands, and the third period from 1920 onwards as moving progressively towards self-discovery and the exploration of the inner space. Sandra Gilbert and Susan Gubar's *The Madwoman in the Attic* (1979) is expansive analysis of Victorian women writers in which the authors discuss women's resistance to social and literary constraints in terms of a theory of anxiety of patriarchal influence. Rosemary Jackson thinks subversion is one such kind of resistance.

Indian feminism is slightly different from the Euro-centric, White Christian feminism. It is based upon the Asian social constructs of religion, caste, gender and region. Indian feminism has been studied by scholars such as Radha Kumar, Kumkum Sangari, Suresh Vaid, Kumari Jayawardena and many others. In the field of literature, significant contribution in the shape of theory and analysis have been provided by Jasbir Jain, Amina Amin, Ashis Nandy, Malashri Lal, Gayatri Spivak among others. While Spivak dwells on deconstruction and Bhabha and Nandy on post-colonialism, Sudhir Kakar offers psychological view of the Indian situation. The Indian woman looks back in complacency to Sita-Savitri type.[4] New Indian woman writings show woman's resistance for change. Usha Bande says, "Representation, resistance and resolution are broad areas of contestation that need to be addressed with cultural framework in mind. We seek answer Spivak's questions: Can a subaltern speak? Can the subaltern as female get out of the 'shadow' and come to light? Strategies for social change lie as the heart of many of women's works."[5]

Women resistance to others, after patriarchy, is against matriarchy. This matriarch is patriarchs' agent. Of course, patriarchy is an all inclusive term in feminist studies. Matriarch as the patriarch, oppresses woman—particularly over the daughters and daughters-in-law. She is a female leader in a system in which power passes from the mother to the daughters. Nancy Friday observes, "When a woman, as an agent of patriarchal norms, acts with oppressive power politics and represses her daughter or daughter-in-law, she is resented and feared as a matriarch. She may not be the proverbial 'bad mother' and may act with good intentions for the well-being of the female child, or she may just be as insecure and may want to protect the girl from the patriarchal institutions, but many a time her moves are misinterpreted and as Nancy Friday argues, the girl child who did not get enough symbiotic closeness as a child becomes a problem of juggling security vis. Satisfaction."[6] There are situations in life and in literature in India when the matriarchs are resented, opposed and hated.

In India and, of course, in the third world countries, historically mother is the deity. She is a bringer-up, protector and nurse. She is the first teacher in the family. Mother plays a vital role in all kinds of myths and literature. In Indian history she was an inspirer—Mother India and she was invoked for her maternal strength. Mothers were perceived as the builders and preservers of the culture and the state and hence as the repositories of national identities. The fundamental shift occurred during the second half of the twentieth century when women creative writers started redefining the parameters of what constituted motherhood. It was a process of cultural translations and hybridisations to ascertain speaking positions from which to refer to the concept of modernity.

Here an effort is made to analyse a few novels which portray women's resistance to patriarchy. Arundhati Roy's *The God of Small Things*, Gita Hariharan's *The Thousand Faces of Night* and Shashi Deshpande's *The Dark Holds No Terror* create a complex mother-daughter schism. Daughters' resistance is seen here from two angles - the situation of dissonance and the subsequent reconciliation. Adrienne Rich makes some basic observations about mother-daughter understanding in the transmission of knowledge and experience common to them because of their gender. She observes: "Mothers and daughters have always exchanged with each other—beyond the verbally transmitted lore of female survival—a knowledge that is subliminal, subversive, pre-verbal: the knowledge flowing between two alike bodies, one of which has spent nine months inside the other."[7] Nancy Friday opines, "When one woman gives birth to another, to someone who is like her, they are linked together for life in a very special way."[8] Conversely, mother-daughter conflict is the result as much of socio-cultural factors as of psychological. One of the reasons, Jasbir Jain points out is 'power.' Discussing Shashi Deshpande's novels, Jain categorically remarks, "Motherhood is egocentric, it gives a sense of power, power that women may not necessarily wield in the wider, social world."[9] Since the mother is the first pedagogue of the do's and don't's, she is the source of anger, resentment and emotional pain for the daughter. A quick look at the conversation between Saru and her mother in *The Dark Holds No Terrors* would suffice as an example of the verbal give and take that later augments the mother-daughter bitterness:

> As young Saru and her brother play out in the sun, the mother comes down heavily on Saru:
> 'Don't go out in the sun. You'll get even darker.'
> 'Who cares?'
> 'We have to care if you don't. We have to get you married.'
> 'I don't want to get married.'
> 'Will you live with us all your life?'
> 'Why not?'
> 'You can't.'
> 'And Dhruva.'
> 'He is different. He's a boy.'[10]

Saru, being a girl, faces much trouble. She resents identifying with her mother. The daughter faces the dilemma of the difficult choices of either rejecting the mother or replicating her. She thinks mother's life is worthless. In Manju Kapur's *Difficult Daughters,* the mother as patriarchy's agents clamps social and familial norms on the daughters and create a generate revolt; and in Shobha De's *Socialite Evenings*, the mother's submissiveness and subservience becomes the cause of Karuna's waywardness and search for money power. Mother, often defends *status quo* and act for their husbands. Hence, they play negative roles.

The Dark Holds No Terrors builds a powerful rhetoric of love-hate relationship between Kamala (Saru's mother) and Saru. Saru categorically mentions how she 'detests' her mother, thus sealing the possibility of any future improvement. The narrative throbs with the ominous presence of her spiteful remarks, 'If you are a woman I refuse to be one.' There is so much exchange of bitterness and unkind words that the venom seeps into the life of both. 'I hated her, I wanted to hurt her, wound her, make her suffer. But did not know how?' The mother, in her turn, negates and rejects her, 'What daughter? I have no daughter.' 'Daughter? I don't have any daughter. I had a son and he died. Now I am childless.' When Saru announces that she was marrying Manohar, her mother's words 'you won't be happy with him,' have the sinister effect of a curse. And when Saru is really unhappy with her sadist husband, she blames her mother, 'if you hadn't fought me so bitterly, if you hadn't been so against him, perhaps I would have never married him.'[11] They are in fact, at a point of no return.

Likewise, Kapur's novel *Difficult Daughters* opens with Ida, Virmati's only daughter, categorically denying her mother. "The thing I had wanted was not to be like my mother," and proceeds on with Ida's search, her discovery of her mother's strength, her own resentment, her effort to reconstruct her mother's past till finally with words she forges a connection with her mother.In *The Thousand Faces of Night* mother-daughter relationship is explored from yet another dimension. Sita is a strict disciplinarian, undemonstrative and restrained. Devi craves for her motherly touch but finding her too unapproachable misunderstands her as 'too snobbish to caress freely.' The only memory of her tender touch was when Devi once fell sick and her mother had caressed her while Devi feigned asleep. On close reading, we discover that Sita has covert love and sympathy for her daughter that she conceals to live by her motto of having 'order, reason, progress' in life. Because she herself had to acquiesce in order to be an ideal daughter-in-law and wife. She envisions Devi to be perfect in every way and is quite disappointed to see 'Devi grow into an awkward, thin, ache-ridden stammering adolescent and indulging in flights of fancy with imaginary characters. In *The God of Small Things*, Mammachi is a weak and suffering mother whose shadow falls on the girl's upbringing hindering her healthy development. Ammu has seen her mother being ill-treated, but as a female she is powerless to stop her father's atrocities the way Chako puts an end to the daily battering. The daughters hate mother on her restrictions. This woman-woman hate dyad is built upon restrictive/controlling factors like lack of free behaviour, purdah and zenana practices.

The relationship of mothers-in-law and daughters-in-law is ridded with problems. Vrinda Nabar asks an insightful question: "Why are Indian women so manifestly hostile to one another especially in relationships where they could through mutual bonding achieve so much?"[12] Probably, here it can be interpreted as resistance in the reverse. Anees Jung's query puts it more succinctly, "Does the home continue to be a haven? Or is it a prison where they find their strength and also realise their vulnerability? Do they from being prisoners themselves turn themselves into jailors, repeating a pattern in the invincible image of their mother-in-law?"[13] It is the patriarchal mission the matriarchs undertake at the cost of their femininity

In De's *Socialite Evenings* Karuna and her sisters are terrified of their father and though Karuna records her father's dominating presence, she categorically admits 'in retrospect' that he was not an unkind or cruel man. Contradictions appear to an extent in De's work that depicts (through Anjali) motherhood as a burden but also extols it through Karuna's desire for a child. Another contradiction is visible in the social psyche that expects women to be mothers and also deploy motherhood as a powerful form of social control. Almost all the daughters accept their own motherhood with pleasure. Ida and Kåruna, though new-fangled, feel psychologically and emotionally amputated after their abortions. Conversely, motherhood can be the means of women's autonomy and self-creation. The older generation women do not see motherhood as a marker of women's subjection and self-alienation. But, by and large, mothers—the matriarchs—are projected in contemporary writing at once as victims and perpetrators of the despotic regime.

Children's resistance to the adults can also be seen in Indian English fiction. Bapsi Sidhwa in *Ice-Candy-Man* (1988), Arundhati Roy in *The God of Small Things* (1997), and Mrinal Pande in *Daughter's Daughter* (1993), assign the child narrators the task to look at the adult world with their innocent I [Eye] and de-create the past in order to discover themselves as women. Whereas *Ice-Candy-Man* and *The God of Small Things* work through the larger backdrop of socio-historical and political happenings which the narrators resist, *Daughter's Daughter* highlights women's restricted life, their choicelessness and the strength gained by sisterhood and women's solidarity through the child narrator's perception. Modern Indian English women novelists in English are trying to reverse/re-create their myths for expressing themselves.

Myths, worldwide are male-based and biased. In literature, revisionist mythmaking challenges the canonical texts both at the structural and thematic levels and enriches the literary tradition. Myths are symbols and signs that codify values and beliefs and shape the culture, whereas mythmaking is the action of modifying and renewing those modifications. It is said, "Revisionist mythmaking is the potential of the writer to appropriate the mythic tale or the mythic figure for altered ends, which may ultimately make cultural change possible." [14]

Culture is, as G.C. Pande observes, "part of a consciousness which is self-conscious' and myth is the 'intuitive wisdom' of that culture." [15] But culture as seen here stands for the hegemonic, mainstream value system of which women form a part. The act of 'revision' provides a key to locating and defining women's experience within that hegemonic value system.

Myth as an ideological practice within the feminist literary criticism and feminist theory can be traced to the rise of the second wave feminism in the West. While Northrop Frye in his *Anatomy of Criticism* (1957) and Roland Barthes in his *Mythologies* (1973) were providing the theoretical framework of traditional canonical myths, feminist theorists were inquiring into their structural patterns, and deciphering the politics of foregrounding male experience and beliefs through them, and were exploring the possibility of writing a counter-mythology from a woman-centered point of view. Once feminists discovered the power of myth to define women's experience, they-tried 'to appropriate new definitions' and new meaning to the existing definitions. Adrienne Rich gave a call for 're-visioning' the old pattern and claimed that revision implies remembering and refocusing on the past. Revision is an 'act of survival,' a 'drive to self-knowledge' achieved through 're-writing.' Feminist discourse deploys rewriting to map female-centered myths and to reintegrate them into female experience as a liberating and promising value. "Revision," according to Sankovitch, "is a process of 'recovery and reformation' by which old myths are driven away and revitalised by reinterpretation."[16]

The *Woman's Encyclopedia of Myths and Secrets*, published in 1983 attempted to create counter-mythology to view myths from a woman-centred angle and to displace the traditional dominant mythologies that have devalued and suppressed women. The idea was to recreate a past with a focus on women as vested with power. Kim Chernin's *Reinventing Eve* (1987) and Paula Caplan's *The Myth of Women's Masochism* (1985) reconstruct the Hebrew myth of the 'Fall' and deconstruct the myth that women are masochistic, respectively. Estelle Lauter's *Women as Mythmakers* (1984) examines women writers and artists to find out how they give expression to powerful mythic energy.

Meenakshi Mukherjee's perceptive observation that Indian people are closer to their mythology than the Irish or the British are to Celtic or Greek lore speaks for the hold of mythological and legendary tales on Indians. Mukherjee further asserts: "If a world-view is required to make literature meaningful in terms of shared human experience, then the Indian epics offer a widely accepted basis of such common background, which permeated the collective unconscious of the whole nation."[17]

The position of women vis-a-vis the traditional myth is ambivalent in Indian culture. Sita, Savitri, Damayanti are familiar figures in the Hindu imagination. They are the epitomes of devotion, wifely duties, supreme sacrifice and the begetters of sons which leads to the all-too important position of motherhood. Vedic culture extols the feminine principle in Nature—nature as a mother, loving but unpredictable, bountiful but withholding; and she must be propitiated through a wide variety of rites and rituals. The concepts of *Prakriti* (nature), her *Lila* (activity), *adi shakti* (the primal power) are all feminine. The feminine cult thus 'represents power, an image of resurgent and fearful strength. C.N. Srinath, for example, discusses the presence of myths associated with the Ganga and the ancient city of Kashi. Contemporary Indian women writers stand at a curious intersection - on the one hand, they are the carriers of a culture that is a peculiar blend of victimhood and triumphant strength, on the other, the Western feminist concepts imbibed through the postmodern/ postcolonial encounter, highlighting the drawbacks of their indigenous culture, encourage them to doubt and counter the cultural constructs.

Here an effort is made to examine the revisionist mythmaking in Anita Desai's *Where Shall We Go This Summer*? (1982), and Gita Hariharan's *The Thousand Faces of Night* (1992). In both novels, myths are rewritten in order to articulate the recovery of the female voice. While Gita Hariharan uses the traditional myths to re-vise the past and reconstruct Devi's present, Anita Desai erodes the more personal/social myths associated with the protagonist's father to let Sita break free from her constricting past. Each translates the marginalised and the silenced other into the central figures in the narrative; each seeks to recover the female history lost to the silences of the dominant myths; and each succeeds in creating female spaces for the protagonists with the possibility of their becoming visible subjects.

Resistance against rape is another dimension here. Rape is a form of systemic and systematic violence against women with a vulgar display of social power relation. Resistance to rape is an interesting phenomenon in feminism. Here an effort is made to analyse rape in Shashi Deshpande's *The Dark Holds No Terror* and *The Binding Vine.* Allusions to other works are made. I shall allude to Anita Desai's depiction of the pathetic incident of rape and death in *Fire on the Mountain* (1977), Kamala Markandaya's treatment of it in *A Handful of Rice* (1966), and the manifestation of female violence as a subversive act in Bharati Mukherjee's *Jasmine* (1989) to understand the changing perceptions of Indian women writers. Though the reality of Kalpana's rape is different from Manu's sadistic attacks on his wife (Saru, *The Dark Holds No Terrors*) and Sadashiv's obsessive love which is categorised as rape in marriage (Mira, *The Binding Vine*), what the women resist is the denial of right to their body, the violence done to the woman's person. As a matter of fact, women have been trained to choose silence in such matters, to ignore the indignity of the experience and to feign that all is normal. It is this unmentionable and the unspeakable that these novels are articulating. That women have chosen to 'speak' rape is itself a kind of resistance, a 'measure of liberation.'

Indian English fiction by women though not fierce, has nonetheless, been significant because it has tried to question the commodification of women as bodies and their projection as mindless, mute sex objects that devalue their individuality and violate their dignity as humans. Since the concept of sexuality is based on the paradigms of male supremacy, and on the concept of property rights, the factor like 'force' or 'without consent' appear redundant.

Simply and briefly, rape is an offence of violence. It is also violation of a woman's privacy; and since it is against her will and wish, it falls in the category of oppression and hence humiliation. Rape is a human rights issue. The ultimate violation of the self; and clarifies that "it is a humiliating event in a woman's life which leads to fear of existence and a sense of powerlessness."[18] Feminists call rape 'sexual invasion of the body by force'[19] and 'a violation of pride and dignity.'[20] Carole Sheffield uses a blanket term, "sexual terrorism for all forms of sexual violence - rape, wife battering, incest, pornography and harassment."[21]

Rape predominantly falls in the category of forced and nonconsensual sex. The common factors in these and various other definitions are the rape is not only violence but also violation. In India, there are a number of legislations affording legal protection to women from violence, which include domestic violence and sexual abuse. Under Sections 375-377 IPC (Rape and Sexual Offences) various protective measures and legal actions have been given. "Section 375 defines rape as 'sexual intercourse with a woman under circumstances falling under any of the six following description.' These are, against her will, without her consent, consent obtained by putting her under pressure, with her consent obtained in a state of intoxication, and with or without her consent, when she is under sixteen years of age. This definition excludes sexual intercourse with wife with or without her consent."[22]

The Binding Vine and *The Dark Holds No Terrors* portray almost similar, though not identical problems. In the former, there are two incidents of rape – Mira's rape in marriage and Kalpana's ravishment by her relative—but these are reported in absentia with both the victims missing from the scene: Mira is long dead and Kalpana is nearlydead being in a coma ever since. In *The Dark Holds No Terrors*, sadistic attack is construed as rape in marriage and is recounted from the consciousness of the protagonist-narrator, Saru, and is situated within the narrative so skilfully that it appears alternately as imaginary and real.

The Binding Vine opens with Urmi grieving over the death of her girl child, Anu and ends with the death of a young woman Sulu, traumatised by her husband's inhuman behaviour in raping her niece; in between lies the story of a woman's journey to the past, to the innermost depths of her 'self' and thence to the experiences of women in the traditional patriarchal society.

The case in point is Mira's rape in marriage. Shashi Deshpande's Urmi (the narrator-protagonist), and Mira (the resistant wife) all seem to problematise the question of woman's consent, the importance of saying an effective 'No' to the exploitation of woman's body for man's need, and the traumatic effect of enforced sex on woman's psyche. In *The Dark Holds No Terrors*, Shashi Deshpande looks at rape from a different angle. Here, it is not 'love/lust' that kills as in *The Binding Vine*; it is Manu's sadistic attack that terrorises Saru and kills her 'self.'

Anita Desai's *Fire on the Mountain* has an incident of rape, reported briefly. A marked change in woman's response to rape is discernible in Bharati Mukherjee's *Jasmine*. Similarly, in *the Painter of Signs*, R. K. Narayan presents a comic picture when Daisy climbs up a tamarind tree sensing Raman's wicked intentions.

References

1. Radtke and Stam, *Power Gender*, Sage, London, 1994, p. 53.
2. Usha Bande, *Writing Resistance*, IIAS, Shimla, 2006, p. 4.
3. Carla Rice, "Between Body and Culture," *Gender, Race and Nation*, ed Vanaja Dhruvaraj, Toronto Univ. Press, Toronto, 2002, p. 177.
4. Meena Shirwadkar, *Image of Woman in Indo-Anglian Novel*, Sterling, New Delhi, 1979, p. 154.
5. Usha Bande, op. cit., p. 30.
6. Nancy Friday, *My Mother/Myself*, Bantam Doubleday Dell, New York, 1987, p. 62.
7. Adriana Rich, *Of Woman Born*, Virago, London, 1976, p. 220.
8. Nancy Friday, op. cit., p. 39.
9. Jasbeer Jain, *Gendered Realities*, Rawat, Jaipur, 2003, p. 59-60.
10. Shashi Deshpande, *The Dark Holds No Terrors*, p. 45.
11. Ibid., p. 96.
12. Vrinda Nabar, *Caste as Woman*, Penguin, New Delhi, 1995, p. 185.
13. Anees Jung, *Unveiling India*, Penguin, New Delhi, 1987, p. 49.
14. Elaina Showalter, *The New Feminist Criticism*, Pantheon, New York, 1985, p. 317.
15. G. C. Pande, *Foundations of Indian Culture*, Books and Books Publishers, Allahabad, 1984, p. 189.
16. Tilde Sankovitch, *French Women Writers and the Book*, Syracuse Univ. Press, Syracuse, 1988, p. 146.
17. Meenakshi Mukherjee, *The Twice Born Fiction*, Arnold Heinemann, New Delhi, 1974, p.131.
18. Law Commission Report 1980, p. 1.
19. Susan Brownmiller, *Against Our Will*, Simon Publishers, New York, 1969, p. 376.
20. Gonnie Guberman, *No Safe Place*, The Woman's Press, Toronto, 1985, p. 63.
21. Carole Sheffield, "Sexual Terrorism," *Women: A Feminist Perspective*, ed Jo Freedman, Mayfield Publishers, California, 1989.
22. Jilani Syed, *Women in India*, 2002.

8

The English Language

C.L. Wrenn writes, "Language is an expression of human personality in words whether written or spoken." Language is a medium of expression. And as a twentieth century linguist Prof. Michael Halliday says, it is a semiogenic process, which helps man to understand himself and the world. Language has limitless uses. Its shades of meaning include indicative, emotive and symbolic. Since man is a thinking animal, he is a talking animal too and he has to exploit language to its full possible extent.

English is one such language which because of its multifarious facets and universal features, has, these days, become most useful to the welfare of mankind. The general characteristics of English are that it is extraordinarily receptive and it has an adoptable heterrogeneousness. However English was a pure language when Anglo-Saxons first conquered England in AD fifth century, today it is the most mixed of languages. A second outstanding feature of English is its simplicity of inflexion. Its relatively fixed word-order is its third hallmark. It has roundabout ways of saying due to the loss of inflexions. It uses prepositions. A fifth quality of English is the development of new varieties of intonations for expressing shades of meaning which were formerly indicated by varying the shapes of words. These five features have made English so much popular that today it is spoken by the largest number of people all over the world.

But it does not mean English is a language very easy to speak. To speak in English means one has to learn it with constant care and industry. In Wrenn's words, "English is among the easiest languages to speak badly, but the most difficult one to use well."[1]

A careful study of some elements of world languages drives home the point that at one time in the past, most of these language had shared some common elements. For example, the Sanskrit Pitra and Matra, the English Father and Mother and the Latin Patre and Matre display this element of onetime togetherness. In this light, English and Sanskrit bear certain resemblance. Therefore, English is said to belong to the family of Indo-European languages. This is also called Indo-Germanic or Indo-Aryan. The term Indo-European is used as it covers all the major languages – Eastern and Western. 'Indo-European' world group has eight sub-groups or families such as Balto-Slavic, Indo-Iranian, Armenian, Albanian in the East and Greek, Latin, Celtic and German in the West, and English belongs to the Germanic sub-group. The common features of Indo-European languages share a similar structures (parts of speech) and common roots in vocabulary.

English like Dutch, Scandinavian and German, belongs to the primitive or common Germanic (Teutonic family). These languages have stress system and two-tense system. This stress system makes English words end weak or consonantal.

Well in the fifth century, the German tribes of Angles, Saxons and Jutes invaded the then Romanised Britain and they spoke 'Low Germanic' whose dialects were Dutch, Flemish and English. Bede says English language of the first millennium was known as Saxon. Later king Alfred called it Englise or Angles. The term old English is referred to as Anglo-Saxon English (upto AD 1100). Middle English is from 1100 to the end of Middle Ages (AD 1500.) and therefrom starts the era of Modern (New) English.

Old English was homogenous and inflexional. Its word order was relatively free, while in pronunciation it had no silent syllables. Just at the close of the eleventh century, some Latin and Norse started influencing the language.

The Middle English began with Normal Conquest, which along with Scandinavian invasions, influenced the vocabulary of English language. French scribes, the use of Latin for learned work and of Norman French for aristocratic entertainment reduced English to a set of dialects. So, for some time English became a dialect language. But when London turned into a commercial hub, English gained an upperhand over the French. This period of Middle English ends in AD 1500.

King Alfred who ruled England supremely in the ninth century came from West-Saxon area and made West Saxon the standard language. But the present-day standard English is based upon South-Eastern or East Midland type which we call as RP today, and Alfred's English has become 'Cockney.' Modern English which is greatly affected by Caxton's revolution in printing is divided into Early, Modern and Later Modern English. Later Modern English is characterised by the loss of inflexions, fixation of word-order and greater use of prepositions. Yet the language is constantly fluid, and it needs to be appreciated in relation to thought, feeling and form.

Of all world languages, English is the most copious, heterogeneous and varied, because its vocabulary is highly affected by several sources such as Latin Fathers of the Church, Danish and Norwegian invaders, Renaissance, the Italian artists and men of letters. Certainly the influence of Latin is substantial. Words such as 'street,' 'mill,' 'cheese,' 'minister,' 'mass' and 'bishop' are Latin. Though Aelfric, a Medieval English prose writer tried to keep English homogenous, he did not succeed. The same is true of the nineteenth century Dorset philologist William Barnes. So Latin influenced the grammatical terminology of English. In C.L. Wrenn's words, "English is a Germanic language, belonging therefore to different group of Indo-European family from Latin: yet the ghost of the Latinate tradition still haunts our classes."[2] The difficulties related to the usages of 'It is I' and 'who' and 'whom' are due to Latinate complications. Scientific writes like Francis Bacon and Sir Isaac Newton wrote in Latin thinking that Latin was an everlasting language. Even Thomas More's *Utopia* is in Latin. This made Shakespeare and his men criticise them. However the overuse of Latin by the seventeenth century writers like Milton and Sir Thomas Browne resulted into pedanticity, or 'Un-English,' Latin has helped English formidably. For instance, the so called suffixes like *-ic, - ate* and *–al* are Latin.

What is true of Latin influence of English vocabulary is true of Greek influence on English. It is said that many Greek words entered English trough Latin and French. Greek medical science has given English much terminology.

Likewise, French has heavily influenced English. When the Saxon King Ethelred, the Unready (978-1016) married a Norman princess, the link between England and France promoted. Norman nobles, French culture and fashionable way of life, conquest of William of Normandy in 1066, French legal terms, University of Paris, 100 years of war, literature, social intercourse, loan words in terms of art, letters, textiles and furniture, diplomacy, Renaissance, French revolution, etc. affected the nature of English words and pronunciation. For example, French words like castle, prison, tower, mercy, passion, image, war, lamp, soup, per excellence, brochure-entered English and there are as many as 18 French words in Chaucer's introduction to prologue. In terms of pronunciation, the Norman-French brought into English the sound *c* and *ch* in place of English sound *k*. So we have *Chancellor* and *cancellor* (*wicing* became *viking*). Likewise because of *w* in place of *g*, we have *warden* and *warrant* in place of *guardian* and *guarantee* respectively. Dryden followed the French literary form of drama called 'Comedy of Manners' in literature and made fun of Frenchified English.

Similar is the German influence. We know English is basically a Germanic language. But it is a 'Low Germanic' language like the Dutch, Flemish and Frisian. English acquired words from these other low Germanic languages.

Italian influence on English is more in terms of art and painting. English men liked to live like Italians in the sixteenth century and Shakespeare and Ben Johnson attacked the same. Some Italian words are stanza, canto and studio.

Spanish words potato, renegade; Portuguese words caste, pagoda, ayah Welsh word bard have entered into English. One time Cornish, Scottish, Gaelic, Welsh belonged to the Celtic family of languages, while Czech, Polish, Hungary and Russian belonged to Slavonic family of which have given us words such as intelligentsia, robot and mammot. In C.L.Wrenn's opinion, "In view of the world-wide contacts of speakers of English – through competition with the empires of Spain, Portugal, the Netherlands and France, in Africa and the Far East and the British settlements of the newly discovered continent of Australia in the 18th and early 19th centuries – it is not surprising that the English language has absorbed various and heterogeneous quantity of words from almost everywhere." [3] Many Arabic words from Indian vernaculars, words from China, Japan, Australia, Borneo, Malaya, Africa, Haiti and South Sea Islands have entered the stream of English vocabulary.

Besides, cant, slang and colloquial have gone into the making of literary English. Alfred, the King, William Barnes, and William Morris attempted to add a local colour to English by bringing dialects into use.

Spelling and pronunciation are the two changing facets of English language, because of variations in each. They are like thunderbolt and lightening of the environment. The reformation of English spelling and pronunciation has been attempted in every age. Aelfric, Chaucer, Shakespeare, G.B. Shaw and others have reformed the system. English, once had been a phonetic language, but later, due to different continental influences, became slightly un-phonetic. For example, the word 'cure' became 'church.' Earlier 'y' and 'u', 'u' and 'v' as well as 'f' and 'v' were interchangeable. Due to French influence 'riht' became right and 'gost' became 'ghost' First the suffixes '-s' and '-es' were in the shape of '-th' and '-eth.' But Caxton and Wynken de Worde, the printers and Dr. Samuel Johnson, Dryden and Swift reformed the English spelling system in their own ways. Printing, compulsory education, radio, cinema and computers have furthered linguistic reform. English Academy, Society for Pure English, the ELBS etc. have been set up to make English a living world language. Accordingly Noah Webster in America has updated the spelling system. Stress and intonation have enriched English, and dialects are its great wealth. These components give different shades of meanings. Localities have played an important role in making English vivid and expressive. Homophones (e.g., red-read) and homonyms (lead-lead) have added an extra dimension. Archaism has brought in a romantic atmosphere and effected mystery. Thackeray, Spencer, Keats have made use of this in literature.

In the course of the history of English language some individuals too have contributed to the making of English. These influences are the Bible, William Shakespeare, Chaucer, Dryden, Milton, Pope, Dr. Johnson, Wordsworth and others. The Bible work done by Wyclif, Tyndale, Coverdale, Calvinists, Jesuits and the King James people have brought in diverse elements into English.

English language today has been different because of modern happenings. American speech is one of them. Radio, cinema, TV, newspaper, computer, internet, discoveries and inventions in the fields of science and commerce, pop-culture and the process of globalisation have modernised the language.

We must aim for good English which is clear, intelligible and uniform in spelling, pronunciation, and rhythmic and good in intonation. For maintaining speech standards, the BBC along with its Advisory Committee on spoken English has made the language pleasing and natural. Societies like ELBS, have been set up to train speech habits. Speech therapies make the speakers' use of language clear, natural and extremely effective, So 'proper words in proper places'. Today, we have to make use of linguistic discipline and self controlling. Basic English spelling reform and phonetic spelling is prepared and taught to make English a global language just with 850 words.

References

1. C. L. Wrenn, *The English Language,* Macmillan, London, 1990, p. 32.
2. Ibid., p.45.
3. Ibid., p.770.

9

Foreign Influence on English Language

Many times we do not know the language we speak. Still we must care for it as it plays an important role in projecting our existence in society. Knowledge is power. Simeon Potter argues, "The power of rightly chosen words is very great, whether those words are intended to inform, to entertain, or to move."[1] English is one such language which we must take care of.

English is an Indo-European/Germanic/Aryan language which was spoken in Ukraine and Southern Russia five thousand years ago, between 6000 and 4000 BC. It was a proto language in the Neolithic Age. Lithuania bears many forms of that still.

Indo-European family had eight branches Greek, Latin (French, Spanish, Italian and Portuguese), Germanic (East, West and North Germanic languages), Indo-Iranian (Indian languages relating to Sanskrit family plus Iranian languages like Persian and Arabic), Armenian, Albanian, Celtic (Briton, Cornish, Welsh, Irish and Scottish) and Balto-Slavanic (include Lithuania and Latvia). The unique features of these languages are that western languages, maybe, due to proximity, have a similar structure (ex: parts of speech) and vocabulary (common root forms). Such primitive words like *father, mother, brother, sister* denoting blood relations exist in many Indo-European languages as evidenced below. For example: the helping verb *is*:

Sanskrit	Greek	Latin	German	Russian	Italian
Asti	*esti*	*est*	*ist*	*est*	*e'*
Pitru		pater	fader		

It is believed that Sanskrit must be the oldest Indo-European language.

Another thing is that western languages use *c* or *k* dominantly and they are called *Centum* languages, while eastern languages use *sh* for *k* and they are called *Satam* languages. This is to say those languages that do not have a common structure such as parts of speech or common roots of lexis are not included in the tag Indo-European. Chinese, Dravidian and some European languages like Uralian, Finnish and Hungarian do not have one or the other features of the above family. Some of these are agglutinative.

The sub family Germanic, also called Teutonic or Gothonic, developed three geographic divisions: East Germanic (Burgundian, Vandal and Gothic), North Germanic (Norwegian, Icelandic, Swedish and Danish) and West Germanic (German, Dutch, Flemish, Frisian and English). The proto-Germanic language existed before the Christian era. The unique features of these languages are that they have common stress and intonation patterns, two tense verb system (present and past) and strong and weak verbs (as Grimm's Ablaut series explains. Ex: drive, drove, driven). Tacitus (1st century) speaks of this in his *Germania*. Scandinavian runic inscriptions evidence this. Wulfila (AD 311-83), a bishop of Vasigoths translated the *Bible* into Gothic and this work is the earliest extant proto-Germanic work. Now the question arises why this proto Germanic language vanished? Maybe because of disintegration. If that be what percent of words of that language have come into the present day English?

Certain events like the arrival of Germanic tribes Jutes (from Jutland, the Jute brothers Hengist and Horsa arriving in England in 449 soon after Romans left England in 410), Angles (from Schleswig) and Saxons (from Holstein) to Romanised Britain, England's conversion to Christianity (in 597), Scandinavian invasion, Norman conquest, revival of learning, the English migration to America and colonisation have played an important role in the development of English.

Anglo-Saxons created a sort of history. They helped British kings but they refused to go back. Jutes settled in the present day Kent, Saxons in South West and Angles in mid north. First literature grew in the north which being divided into Northumbria and Marcia. Hilda, Abbess of Whitby, Caedmon, Benedict Bicop (founder of Jarrow monastery) and his pupil Bede (the Venerable), worked there. When Saxon kings became dominant the literature-area was shifted to Wincanster (Winchester), the capital of West Saxons. The Scandinavian or Viking invasions in the seventh, eighth and ninth centuries disrupted all this. But King Alfred (871-99) himself a man of letters stopped them and encouraged the growth of literature. Wulfstan and Alfric created a literary renaissance.

English as a Germanic language has certain position and grandeur. The English spoken by these tribes was nothing but a low Germanic language like Dutch, Flemish and Frisian. In fact, this was common to all low Germanic people. English people called it Saxon or Anglo-Saxon. But King Alfred called his language and nation as *Englisc*. The phrase Old English was used in the thirteenth century. Not to speak of Old English was a pure language with little Latin and Norse.

The unique features of Old English are:

a) Inflections,

b) Free word order,

c) No silent syllables, and

d) Dialectability.

Then came Norman Conquest in the eleventh century leading to the eventual influence of the French. Already Christianity had brought in Latin. The French also brought in Greek indirectly and the Renaissance increased real Greek influence. Likewise, due to trade, there was felt the influence of other Romance languages like Italian, Spanish and Italian. During the Middle English (1100-1500) period, English changed greatly and its unique features were:

ii) Loss of Inflexions,

iii) Leading to Fixed Word Order, and

iv) The Use of Preposition,

v) Creating Spelling Confusion (because of French scribes).

These features continued in modern English as well. The use of French and Latin was heavy. As we know, gradually Chaucer and other writers' effort for strengthening English succeeded. London emerged as the center of learning and of standard English language. The reasons were not far to seek. It was a Norman capital; near it lying Anglia, a wool trade center and Oxford and Cambridge universities. Besides, London had Caxton's printing press. Renaissance and Shakespeare enhanced the prestige of English and during the time of Dryden it reached its highest growth. British colonialism in the next centuries was to expand English further. Modern times are in favour of it. So it is a global language today.

The arrival of Germanic tribes plus Scandinavian and Norman invasions and Latinisation led to the death of many native Celtic languages such as Breton, Cornish and Gaelic, and others Welsh, Irish and Scottish exist weakly.

First, the Anglo-Saxons used Germanic runes as a script. Later they used Roman script from Phoenicians via Greece and Rome. English is not England's native language. It is a Germanic language with Scandinavian, Greek, Latin, French and other influences. Because of heavy influence, its structure, spelling and pronunciation systems changed considerably. As a result, the language fluctuated in its look, and great men did not like heavy changes. Some said it is a wild and chaotic language. Though it attained maturity in Dryden's time, Dryden himself said it had no prosody, no tolerable dictionary and grammar.

English is a West Germanic language. The Scandinavian languages are North Germanic. Racially these people were one living entity in proximity. Once Germanic tribes settled down in England some Scandinavian tribes wished to follow the suit. After sporadic raids (beginning in 787 at Dorset), Alfred and Guthrum had the Treaty of Wedmore in 886 and Scandinavians were permitted to settle down in Danelaw (between London and Chester. That is to the north of Thames). So they had their own rule there. Danes plundered again and defeated Athelred in 991. He ran away to France. Again in 1009, they plunderd Oxford and took Winchester. Athelred came back and sacked them. This provoked Sveinn's son Canute and he arrived in 1015 with forces and defeated the king. In fact, he ruled England from 1016 to 1036. At the same time he was also the ruler of Denmark and Norway. After him his son ruled for another 6 years. The Danes settled down in Anglia, Midlands and the North from 850 and lived there for three centuries. Though they came as plunders (Vikings), after their common originality asserted, they blended with the English. The Icelandic poet Gunnlang would recite his poem to king Athelred effortlessly. A Scandinavian chronicler says, "The language in Norway and England was one and the same when William won England."[2]

As a result of Scandinavian influence, the words of Scandinavian languages like Norse, Danish, Norwegian and Swedish left their marks on manorial organisation, local government and law. Yet this was through spoken media. Words like *law, statue, outlaw, husband, fellow, wrong, walk, want, weak, wing, sky, ski* and, *skull* came into English. Scandinavian influence is still strong in Cumberland, Riding and Anglia. Some people use that language's numerals there. Since Middle Ages Scandinavian influence is occasional. Such new words like *skii, saga* and *tungsten* are rather of Common European stock.

Since Danelaw, a colony between London and York where Scandinavians lived, had not yet developed much writing, Scandinavian influence was not felt in writing immediately. It was to be seen only in Early Middle English. Names of certain parts of human body (*leg, skin, skull*), animals (*calf, bull*), prepositions (*fro, thwart, till* (meaning *to*), *until*), pronouns, (*they, their, them*), pronominal adjectives (*both, same*), verbs (*are*), phrasal verbs (*take, take off*), verbal operator *get*, and —*s* (in *goes*) affix of the third person singular (for English *th*) are Scandinavian.

Scandinavian endings are seen explicitly in place names as:

—*by* means 'village' as in Normanby (Norse men, and, 'by' means village from *byr*= village of the Northmen, Norsemen, Norwegians). Likewise, Derby and Denby.

— *beck* 'brook' in Birkbeck

— *brick* 'slope' in Norbreck

— *fell* 'hill' in Whinfell

— *garth* 'yard' in Applegarth

— *mel* 'sand-dune' in Cartmell

— *rigg* 'ridge' in Lambrigg

— *thwaite* 'clearing' in Braithwaite etc.

Some Scandinavian words remain with their English counterparts as doublets. Of course, they have slight difference in meaning.

English	*Scandinavian*
no	nay
from	fro
rear	raise
shirt	skirt
ditch	dike

There was a competition between English and Scandinavian words for survival and the latter shot to fame: *sister* against English *swester, egg* against *ey*.

John of Trevisa (in 1387) said Scandinavian influence defiled and corrupted English. But 45 per cent of English language is of Germanic in its origin.

Next to Scandinavian Greek influence is felt heavily. The ancient Athens from the sixth century onwards led the world in knowledge. Pericles (95-429 BC), Socratus, Plato, Aristotle and a host of others, particularly writers, created an everlasting corpus of writings.

The seven ancient arts Grammar, Logic, Rhetoric, Arithmetic, Geometry, Astronomy and Music are Greek in origin.

Greek, as an Indo-European language, was mature enough to sustain growth. So it helped European languages like Latin, French and English grow with its word-power.

Therefore, Greek was is taught in all European universities.

Chaucer, Petrarch and Boccaccio regretted to have not learnt Greek.

Greek words either in toto, or in adaptation and assimilation, or in translation came into English abundantly enriching English. But it is difficult to distinguish Greek words as they came through Latin and French. The common words like *phone, atom* and *graph* are Greek. When it comes to Literature basic words like *drama, tragedy, comedy, catastrophe* and *climax* are Greek; and many science words like *psychology* and *neurology* are Greek.

The classical renaissance led to the importance of Greek learning. The rediscovery of ancient classical Greek knowledge brought a new way of looking at life. There was a wealth of thought. Greek brought a new set of ideas and terms for political science, art and literature.

Greek has given us affixes like, *un—*, *—ness*, *—ly*, *post—*, *anti—*, *a—*, *—ology* etc.

Latin is another important Indo-European language that influenced English heavily. Contacts with Roman Empire during several centuries introduced Latin words to the people of England. Roman-Britons had a good number of Latin words like *Chester* appearing in place names like Dorchester. But Latin influence was through written language.

Once Christianity came to England with St Augustine in 597, the English began picking up Latin. Latin words like *street, mill,* and *cheese* became quite common. Words like *minster, monk, mass, church* and *priest* spread immediately. Secondly church fathers created new words and assigned new meanings to English words. For ex: the English festival *Easter* and the rite *Baptism* acquired new meanings.

Latin words came through religion, science and literature. The 9th century Benedictine revival with Dunsten and Alfric, and other trends brought as many as 400 words. One thing is that English then had its own power to create new words and it created words like *Gospel* from Latin *God spellboc*. Alfric wrote a Latin grammar using technical terms like *part taker* for *participle* and *nama* for *noun*.

The Greek borrowing continued in Middle and Modern English too, in areas like technology, law, science and religion. So words like *index, pauper, legitimate, scribe, simile, collect* and *tolerance* came into existence.

Some Latin words like *exit, genius, specimen, album, inertia, alib* and, *extra* were taken into English as they were, and most others were anglicised, acclimatised (e.g.,: tele*phone*), adapted and translated. Latin affixes like *–ment*, *–ation*, *–able*, *–ate*, *–ic* and *–al*, came into English for word creation. Likewise, Latin *–or* was used as *–our* (as in labour) and Latin *–er* as *-re* (ex: *center* as *centre*). Latin words came in legion, sometimes creating synonyms/doublets as *blame-blaspheme, frial-fragile, poor-pauper, reason-ration, respite-respect, sure-secure, equal-egal, adventure-aventure, confer-collate* and *construct-resurrect*. The latter words came through French. *Sin* basically wrongdoing means *crime* now. This is called semantic borrowing.

Latin affected the structure of English. For ex: we say '*It is me*' for '*It is I*.' We use *whom* in place of *who* sometimes. This is because of Latin influence. Secondly some English metrical system is Latinate. Though English is a stressed language, Latin syllabic length decides English stress.

Latin became the first language and useful. It was taught in schools and colleges. It was a religious language upto the 16th century, haunting many intellectuals. Many writers and scientists used it. Roger Ascham, Bacon, More, Harvey and Newton wrote in it. The English intellectuals thought that Latin was a more durable language.

Similarly French is a fundamental (second big) influence on English for dignity and eloquence. This was there even before Norman Conquest as English kings had relations with Normans. Such pre-Norman words include *castle* for the English *burg*, suggesting a new way of life.

Scandinavians as that of Huns were heroic and nomads. Their king Cnut ousted the English king Athelred the Unready

(978-1016) in 1016 and ruled England for 26 years. So the English king who had married a Norman princess took refuge with Norman king William and later his son Edward regained his father's throne. Edward as a mark of gratitude, because of his issuelessness, assured William that he would, on getting back his kingdom and on his death, pass it over to him. Once Cnut's successor son died in 1042, Edward regained his kingdom and ruled for 26 years. But when he died in 1066 his adviser Harold (former minister Godwine's son) who became the king of England refused to pass it over to William. This angered William and the latter defeated the English in 1066 at the battle of Hastings.

Norman conquest was a landmark in the history of Britain. Normans changed the face of earth in England. William with him brought French nobility and culture. The French held all high posts. It is said the king banned English in office. The English kings neither learnt English nor married English women for the next three centuries. French became the first language and its use became common in administration, court, education and social life. Anglo-Norman was the French used in England. It was a written technical language as well as a dialect. In fact, Normans placed all the four Old English dialects on a level. Likewise they shifted the capital from Winchester to London. Bokenham says the French barbarised English. A chronicler Robert wrote 'unless a man knows French one counts of him little.' A lady at Charles II's court was despised if she could not speak fashionable French.

As a result, French words like *arrest, market, rent, justice, prince, duke, duchess* and *baron* came into English. But *king* and *queen* remained English. Those of more elegant occupations are French: *carpenter, draper, mason, painte* and *tailor*, while simple occupations remain of English. Another thing is that French words like *table* and *chair* got assimilated in English but words like *garage* and *amateur* did not. They retained their original spelling, stress and pronunciation. Some English and French words are synonymous. So are *shire, town, home, house, cows, sheep* and *pig* as English, *county, city, palace, mansion, beef, mutton* and *pork* as French. Yet English words are stronger, more physical and more human. Some English words competed with the French: *writ* with *scripture* and *board* with *table* and the latter succeeded.

When Henry II extended his rule in Norman provinces and England's royal contacts with France grew, Paris-French influenced English. This introduced Paris-French soft sounds (*ch* and *w*) for Norman hard sounds (*c* (from Latin *k)* and *g*), creating doublets. For example:

Norman French	*Paris French*
atch	chase
warden	guardian
reward	regard
real	royal
count	compute
colur	colour
dainty	dignity
wile	guile
prisun	prison
warrantee	guarantee
wage	gage
gaol	jail

The Norman-French monks altered the look of English profoundly. The Old English (OE) contained the letters , , , of which the first and the last were abandoned in Middle English and the middle one was used rarely. Some letters like k, q, x and z were seldom used. So Old English 'cyning' became king, cw became quath, cw becoming, qu, and (1) c, (2)-er, (3)-te, (4) sc and (5) c , becoming (1) ch, (2)-re, (3)-ty, (4) sh/sch and (5) gg/dg respectively. There are many French affixes like *–able,* metres and stanza forms, literary genres and syntax being used in English.

The English kings lost their Norman possessions in the thirteenth century and they merged with the nation. In 1362 the English parliament passed a law that English must be used for all purposes. Still the events of Hundred Years War, Restoration and its repercussions in literature, French Revolution, colonisation, world wars and multiculturalism brought enormous contact between the two nations influencing each other.

But too much of French influence was criticised. Mulcaster in his spirited plea asked "Why not all in English?" He said: (1.a) English is needless (but look at the time wasted in the learning of foreign languages!). (b) It is coarse and uncultivated (uncouth) (but look at the state of Latin before Cicero made an effort to polish it!). Dryden made fun of French in his play *Marriage d la Mode*. Dr Johnson said, "English would become a dialect of French if this influence continued."

Germanic languages like German, Austrian, Dutch, Flemish and Frisian affected English. For example: the beginning of a sentence with predicate as in 'said he,' 'came a pause' and 'Down went king royal George' is a German feature. This was predominant in Anglo-Saxon, and half of Alfred's writing is like that. The English 'better' is German 'besser,' the *t* and *s* being interchangeable. Words like *zinc, bismuth, cobalt, quartz* and *nickel* are German. Dutch influenced English with words like *plunder, bear, skipper, deck, excise, guilder, dollar, yacht, tea* and *brandy. Island* from *iegland* is Frisian.

Of the Slavonic languages Russian contacts produced words like *rouble, sable, Czar, steppe* and *mammoth. Intelligentsia* is Polish and *robot* is Czech.

Other European languages like Italian have their share. Italian's main contribution is through French. Italian words in painting *(studio)*, music (*opera, solo, temp* and *gusto*) and architecture *(portico, villa, balcony* and *arcade)* came into English retaining their original spelling and pronunciation. Italians were surprised at Englishmen's visiting Italy and behaving like the natives. They said: "An Italianate Englishman is a devil incarnate."

The English contact with Spanish for trade and war brought in some Spanish words like *renegade, vanilla, cork, banana, sherry, cigar, matador, armada, tornado* and *potato.*

The English contact with the Portuguese brought *marmalade, buffalo, caste, coco, mango, copra, teak* and *apricot.*

C.L. Wren says, "In view of the world-wide contacts of the English speakers—through competition with the empires of Spain, Portugal, the Netherlands and France, in Africa and the East, the Red-Indian languages by way of America, British dominion in India, Africa, and the Far East and the British settlement of the newly discovered continent of Australia in the 18th and 19th centuries—English language absorbed a variety of words from almost every where."

Turkish means Arabic and Persian. First Arabic deserves a special mention, for it was Arabs or Moors of Spain and of Arabic centers that introduced many technical terms into English. Arabic science, renaissance learning and Islamic studies influenced Europe and English language. Words like *algebra, alcohol, zenith, cotton, amber, magazine, fakir, ima* and *harem* are Arabic. Persian words like *azure, jasmine, shawl* and *paradise* came into English through Arabic.

Hebrew words include *cherub, messiah, sabboth, seraph, torah, bethel* and *log. Zebra* and *mumbo jumbo* are African.

From India came Sanskrit, Hindi and other vernacular' words. Religious technical terms like *guru, pundit, nirvana, yoga, karma, maharaj; jute, jungle, sahib, pariah, sahib, cot, rupee, pukka, coolie, nabob, khaki* (Hindi), *mongoose* (Marathi), *bungalow* (Bengali), *juggernaut* (Oriya), *chatni* (Kannada), and *curry* (Tamil).

Tea is Chinese, *rickshaw* is Japanese, *boomerang* is Australian, *bamboo, paddy* and *cockatoo* are Malay, *igloo* is Eskimos and *canoe* is Haiti.

Thus English is a world language as the world has made it over the centuries.

10

English as a Global Language in Higher Education

A headline like "English is a Global Language" may surprise us often. But it is a truth that English is a global language today. Why ? one may ask. The answer is that it is a language of higher education, science and technology, a link-language wherever there is a multi-lingual society. The need of English is acute particularly in the globalisation era. David Crystal argues, "English will put us in touch with more people than any other language of the world."[1] As per the recent statistics, English is the language most widely taught as a main foreign language in over 100 countries, such as China, Russia, Germany, Spain, Egypt and Brazil. English language has been used as the first language, second language, and foreign language and as an official language all over the world. It is said nearly a quarter of the world's population is already fluent or competent in English. That means English speakers are more than 1.5 billion, exceeding the Chinese speakers. (1.1 billion).

What makes a global language is a political hegemony more than the simplicity and internationality of a language. As we know, once Sanskrit was a pan-Indian language in India because of Aryan hegemony. Hindi has replaced Sanskrit today. The ancient Tamil was a south East Asian language for more than 500 years, solely because of Tamils' enterprises. Latin was a leading language because of the hegemony of Roman Empire in the first millennium A.D. Latin remained for a millennium as the international language of education thanks to a different sort of power—the ecclesiastical power of Roman Catholicism. Usually people use the language of their masters, colonialists, or rulers. Once the rulers go the language goes with them or it remains if it is a language as a paragon, on account of its implicit aesthetic qualities, clarity of expression, literary power, or religious standing. Sanskrit, Hebrew, Greek, Latin, Arabic and French are among those which at various times have been landed in high terms and English is no exception. It is said,

A language does not become a global language because of its intrinsic structural properties, or because of the size of its vocabulary or because it was once associated with a great culture or religion. These are all factors, which can motivate someone to learn a language, of course, but none of them alone, or in combination, can ensure a language's world spread. Indeed, such factors cannot even guarantee survival as a living language – as is clear from the case of Latin, learned today as a classical language by only a scholarly and religious few. Correspondingly, inconvenient structural properties (such as awkward spelling) do not stop a language achieving international status either.

A language becomes an international language for one chief reason: the political power of its people – especially their military power. The explanation is the same throughout history. Why did Greek become a language of international communication in the Middle East over 2,000 years ago? Not because of the intellects of Plato and Aristotle: the answer lies in the swords and spears wielded by the armies of Alexander the Great. Why did Latin become known throughout Europe? Ask the legions of the Roman Empire. Why did Arabic come to be spoken so widely across northern Africa and the Middle East? Follow the spread of Islam, carried along by the force of the Moorish armies from the eighth century. Why did Spanish, Portuguese and French find their way into the Americas, Africa and the Far East? Study the colonial policies of the Renaissance kings and queens, and the way these policies were ruthlessly implemented by armies and navies all over the known world. The history of a global language can be traced through the successful expeditions of its soldier\sailor speakers.[2]

Still simplicity and beauty of language is a greater virtue. The reason why many people use English is it has less grammar than other languages. People say English is easy because of its inherent features like parts of speech, fixed word order and loss of inflections. In 1848, a reviewer in the British periodical *The Athenaeum* wrote:

"In its easiness of grammatical construction, in its paucity of inflection, in its almost total disregard of the distinction of gender excepting those of nature, in the simplicity and precision of its terminations and auxiliary verbs, not less than in the majesty, vigor and copiousness of its expression, our mother-tongue seems well adapted by *organisation* to become the language of the world." [3]

It is to admit that English has a cosmopolitan character, which many think is an advantage for it to become a global language.

Why do We need a Global Language?

As we have to live in a global society, we have to depend upon either translation or on a global language. As we know, the work of translation of all knowledge from one language into another is hardly possible. And then learning many languages is a waste of time. In fact, learning many languages is a painful experience. So no other medium than a global language can help the people of the planet to achieve internationality.

However, one fear when we adopt a global language is the fear of the death of thousands of languages and their cultures. For instance, because of the emergence of many languages, for example, Hindi in India, Arabic in Africa and English and French in Europe and the Americas, it is estimated that perhaps 80 per cent of the world's 6,000 living languages will die out within the next century. Indians must notice the death of Pali, Prakrit and hundreds of tribal languages as provincial languages emerged. Linguists feel, if it happens, it will indeed be an intellectual and social tragedy. It is said, "When a language dies, so much is lost. Especially in languages which have never been written down, or which have been written down only recently, language is the repository of the history of a people. It is their identity."[4] Still we cannot help having a global language. And it is indeed true that the culture of perish(ed)ing languages will remain in the global language partly, and partly an effort to save or record it must be done honestly.

Why English as a Global Language? A Historical Context

'Why is English the global language and not some other?' There are two answers to the question: one is geographical—historical; the other is socio-cultural. We know that Europeans, particularly the English explorers explored several lands and settled down there, becoming the conquistadors. Socio-culturally, the western civilisation and culture reached the people of the second and third worlds through the agency of English. The English separatist church people emigrated to America, facilitating English mass emigration to the new continent. A similar story holds true of Canada, Australia, New Zealand, the Caribbean Islands, South Africa, South Asia, particularly India, the African colonies like Sierra Leone, Ghana, Gambia, Nigeria, Cameroon, Liberia, Kenya, Tanzania, Uganda, Malawi, Zambia and Zimbabwe and South-east Asia and the south Pacific, particularly Singapore, Malaysia, Hong Kong and Papua New Guinea. Braj Kachru, the US linguist says English has spread around the world rapidly. He says nearly one third of the world population knows English, though only a proportion of these people have some command of English. It is estimated that the users of English as L1 are 337,407,3000 and the users of English as L2 are 235,351,3000 in 1995.

Why English? The Cultural Foundations

John Wallis says, "Because there is clearly a great demand for it from foreigners, who want to be able to understand the various important works which are written in our tongue." And he goes on: "All kinds of literature are widely available in English editions, and, without boasting, it can be said that there is scarcely any worthwhile body of knowledge which has not been recorded today, adequately at least, in the English language."[5]

If John Wallis wanted English for the English of knowledge it had, Richard Mulkaster wanted it for patriotic reasons. He said in 1582: "I love Rome, but London better. I favour Italy, but England more. I honour the Latin, but I worship the English."[6]

The poet Samuel Daniel speaks of the blessings of his tongue:

> And who in time knows whither we may vent
> The treasure of our tongue, to what strange shores
> This gain of our best glory shall be sent,
> To enrich unknowing nations without stores?
> Which worlds in the yet unformed Occident
> May come refined with the accents that are ours.[7]

The Earl of Chesterfield wrote in 1750 about the rapid growth of English: "I have ...a sensible pleasure in reflecting upon the rapid progress which our language has lately made, and still continues to make all over Europe."[8] Although French was almost a continental language in the eighteenth century David Hume foresaw the rise of English because of its rapid application in America. He wrote:

> Let the French, therefore, triumph in the present diffusion of their tongue. Our solid and increasing establishments in America...promise a superior stability and duration to the e English language.[9]

John Adam agreed to this when he said:

> English is destined to be in the next and succeeding centuries more generally the language of the world than Latin was in the last or French is in the present age.[10]

Jakob Grimm, a leading German philologist of the time commented that "...of all modern languages, not one has acquired such great strength and vigour as the English," and he concluded that it "may be called justly a language of the world...destined to reign in future with still more extensive sway over all parts of the globe."[11]

Indeed a letter published in the *Gentleman's Magazine* in 1829, illustrates this candidly:

> It is evident to all those who have devoted any portion of attention to the subject, that the English language would, if proper care were devoted tc its advancement, stand an excellent chance of becoming more universally diffused, read, and spoken, than any other now is, or ever has been. In Europe, the study of it seems to be gradually spreading. It Germany, Russia, and Scandinavia it is esteemed an essential, in France a highly useful, branch of education; in Africa it is gradually superseding the Dutch, and becoming the medium of valuable information. In Australia it is not only widely spoken, as the only European language known on that vast continent, but written and printed in an almost incredible number of newspapers, magazines, and reviews. In Asia so great is the desire manifested to learn it, that it was thought by Bishop Heber, that, if proper facilities were afforded, it would, in fifty years, supersede Hindoostanee, and become the court and camp language of India. In America, millions already speak, write, and read it, as their mother tongue...Never before did a language look forward to so bright a prospect as this... [12]

Isaac Pitman in the *The Phonetic Journal* states:

> We may esteem on this basis that in the year 2000 the most important language will be spoken by the number of persons as ur.der:

Italian	53,370,000
French	72,571,000
Russian	130,479,800
German	157,480,000
Spanish	505,286,242
English	
a. Europe	178,846,153
b. United States and non-European British dependencies	1,658,440,000
A+b	18,372,8653,13 [13]

Similarly William White said later that "English is the language of the future." It is said English language has found itself "in the right place at the right time." Isaac Pitman observes:

The British Empire covers nearly a third of the earth's surface, and British subjects are nearly a fourth of the population of the world.[14]

What makes English a world language is that it facilitates an access to knowledge.

Why English? The Cultural Legacy

English language is used in the former colonies as a cultural legacy. Those who hated the English ruler then did not mind to retain their tongue. India is an example. In fact, some countries replaced French and other languages by English as they found English to be a better language. In this regard, the statistics of Union of International Associations' Yearbook sounds pleasant. As it repots there were about 12,500 international organisations in the world. A sample of 500 of these showed that 85 per cent (424) made official use of English for more than any other language. French was the only other language to show up strongly, with 49 per cent using it officially. Thirty other languages attracted occasional official status, but only Arabic, Spanish and German achieved over 10 per cent recognition. Of course, other European languages to achieve a satisfactory progress are French and German. It is said, "The overriding impression is that wherever in the world an organisation is based, English is the chief auxiliary language."[15]

In Europe itself English is being increasingly used as an 'interlingua' (intermediary language). No wonder, 42 per cent of Europeans converse in it, while the same figure for German is 31 per cent and for French, 29 per cent. Still the whole world uses English when it is a matter of international concern. For example, when there was an anti-English strike in New Delhi, some banners had the lines "Death to English."

As for the use of English in the media, the press uses it powerfully. According to the data compiled by the Encyclopedia

Britannica in 1994 about a third of the world's newspapers are published in English. *The Book of Lists* (1977) states the top five papers were all in English. The top was *The New York Times* followed by *The Washington Post, The Wall Street Journal*, and the two British papers *The Times* and *The Sunday Times*. Of particular importance are those English-language newspapers intended for a global readership, such as the *International Herald-Times, US Weekly* and *International Guardian*.

Similarly the publication of most of the periodicals and magazines is in English. As we know two-thirds of modern newspapers, especially in the USA are devoted to advertising. Once Dr Johnson commented about the use of English in advertising as holding a 'magnificence of promise.' So is the case with posters, billboards, electric displays, shop signs and others. What a wonder English was the first language to be used in radio transmission, and the BBC has proved it effectively. So is the case with TV. It is true that 505 of the world's TV users are in those countries where English language has a special status. Of the motion pictures, it is said in 1933 of the 2,466 artists listed, only 83 (3%) were making movies in languages other than English. So English language dominates the film world. When T.A. Edison devised the phonograph, the first machine that could both record and reproduce sound, the first words to be recorded were 'What God hath wrought,' followed by the nursery rhyme 'Mary had a little lamb.' Modern pop music was an English scene altogether. English music is so strong that it follows us wherever we go, threatening the life of ethnic musical traditions.

Interestingly English for the younger generations in many counties has become a symbol of freedom, rebellion and modernism. The same for women is a means for their emancipation and empowerment. English being used greatly in the signs, boards, banners, restaurant menus, credit cards, master cards, it is helping international travel. International safety measures are in English. There is a drive by ELBS-kind of language institutions to teach English easily and in time. Teaching packages like 'Emergency speak,' 'Airspeak' and 'Esperanto' are devised.

The use of English in higher education is greatly enhanced as English is the medium of a great deal of world's knowledge. Black South African writer Harry Mashabela puts it thus in 1975:

"Learning and using English will not only give us the much-needed unifying chord but will also land us into the exciting world of ideas; it will enable us to keep company with kings in the world of ideas and also make it possible for us to share of our brothers in the world..." [16]

An Indian Sridath Ramphal wrote an anecdote in 1996:

> ...shortly after I became Secretary-General of the Commonwealth in 1975, I met Prime Minister Sirimavo Bandaranaike in Colombo and we talked of ways in which the Commonwealth Secretariat could help Sri Lanka. Her response was immediate and specific: 'Send us people to train our teachers to teach English as a foreign language.' My amazement must have showed, for the Prime Minister went on to explain that the policies her husband had put in place twenty years earlier to promote Sinhalese as the official language had succeeded so well that in the process Sri Lanka—so long the pearl of the English-speaking world in Asia – had in fact lost English, even as a second language save for the most educated Sri Lankans. Her concern was for development. Farmers in the field, she told me, could not read the instructions on bags of imported fertiliser – and manufacturers in the global market were not likely to print them in Sinhalese. Sri Lanka was losing its access to the world language of English. We did respond. I believe that today English is doing better as the second language in Sri Lanka. [17]

The English Language Teaching (ELT) and The British Council have made it a business to teach English as a language that "English will remain the world's language forever."

The Future of Global English

English as a global language is detested by some, particularly the French, the German, the Hindi Indians and others. Mahatma Gandhi wrote:

> To give millions a knowledge of English is to enslave them...Is it not a painful thing that, if I want to go to a court of justice, I must employ the English language as a medium; that, when I become a Barrister, I may not speak my mother-tongue, and that someone else should have to translate to me from my own language? Is this not absolutely absurd? Is it not a sign of slavery? [18]

The people of local languages usually wish to use their languages. They hate English as and when it holds their languages in contempt. They think to use English means sacrificing their cultural heritage. Some countries like Tanzania, Kenya and Malaysia rejected English. But other countries like Algeria (a former French colony) and parts of Italy (Padania) opted for English. Today some countries think of, and in fact, use bilingual policies draining their resources. America is a leading nation to use English heavily. In fact, it is America which has ensured the position of English as a global language to the discomfiture of Britain. Whereas its Americanisms is worrying those who use British English. To think of following Webster's ghost is still worse!

New Englishes

Salman Rushdie comments, in his essay "Commonwealth literature does not exist," that:

> The English language ceased to be the sole possession of the English some time ago. [19]

David Crystal observes:

> When even the largest English-speaking nation, the USA, turns out to have only about 20 per cent of the world's English speakers, it is plain that no one can now claim sole ownership of the English language. [20]

The problem of pronunciation leads to dialects and the latter to the birth of new languages. For example, due to incomprehensiveness of pronunciation, Latin gave birth to Romance languages like French, Spanish and Italian over a thousand years ago. So is the case with the vernaculars of Sanskrit and Dravidian families of languages in India. In 1877, the British philologist Henry Sweet (a probable model for Shaw's Henry Higgins in *Pygmalion*) thought that a century later,

> England, America, and Australia will be speaking mutually unintelligible languages, owing to their independent changes of pronounciation. [21]

Raja Rao, the Indian novelist looked forward to the development of a new Indian English:

> English is not really an alien language to us. It is the language of our intellectual make-up- like Sanskrit and Persian was before – but not of our emotional make-up...We cannot write like the English. We should not. We can write only as Indians. We have grown to look at the large world as part of us. Our method of expression has to be a dialect which will some day prove to be as distinctive and colourful as the Irish or the American. [22]

The Nigerian novelist Chinua Achebe speaks thus:

> The price a world language must be prepared to pay is submission to many different kinds of use. The African writer should aim to use English in a way that brings out his message best without altering the language to the extent that its value as a medium of international exchange will be lost. He should aim at fashioning out an English, which is at once universal and able to carry the weight of my African experience. But it will have to be a new English, still in full communion with its ancestral home but altered to suit its new African surroundings. [23]

So also we have an English today. The kind of English used in Europe is known as 'Euro-English.' Other varieties include Indian English (General Indian English, GIE for short), Australian English and Caribbean English. Not to speak of in spite of the English of World Standered Spoken English (WSSE), most people have become 'multidialectal' making their language a heady mixture of several dialects.

Finally David crystal concludes his book *English as a Global Language* thus:

> If there is a critical mass, does this mean that the emergence of a global language is a unique event, in evolutionary terms? It may be that English, in some shape or form, will find itself in the service of the world community forever.[24]

References

1. David Crystal, *English as a Global Language*, CUP, Cambridge, 1997.p.
2. Ibid., p.7.
3. *The Athenaeum,* qt by David Crystal, *op.cit.,* p.6.
4. David Crystal, *op.cit.,* p. 17.
5. John Wallis, qt by David Crystal, *op.cit.,* p.64.
6. Richard Mulkaster, qt by David Crystal, *op.cit.,* p.64.
7. Samuel Daniel, qt by David Crystal, *op.cit.,* p.65.
8. The Earl of Chesterfield, qt by David Crystal, *op.cit.,* p.65.
9. David Hume, qt by David Crystal, *op.cit.,* p.66.
10. John Adam, qt by David Crystal, *op.cit.,* p.66.
11. Jakob Grim, qt by David Crystal, *op.cit.,* p.66.
12. *The Gentleman's Magazine* in 1829, qt by David Crystal, *op.cit.,* p.67.
13. Isaac Pitman in the *The Phonetic Journal*, qt by David Crystal, *op.cit.,* p.67-68.
14. Isaac Pitman, qt by David Crystal, *op.cit.,* p.70.
15. David Crystal, *op.cit.,* p. 81.
16. Harry Mashabela, qt by David Crystal, *op.cit.,* p.101.
17. Sridath Ramphal, qt by David Crystal, *op.cit.,* pp.101-102.
18. Mahatma Gandhi, qt by David Crystal, *op.cit.,* p.114.
19. Salman Rushie qt by David Crystal, *op.cit.,* p.130.
20. David Crystal, *op.cit.,* p.130.
21. Henry Sweet, qt by David Crystal, *op.cit.,* p.134.
22. Raja Rao, qt by David Crystal, *op.cit.,* p.135.
23. Chinua Achebe, qt by David Crystal, *op.cit.,* p.136.
24. David Crystal, *op.cit.,* p.140.

11

Evaluation of English Education in India

The British who entered India as traders established their political hegemony for two centuries. Gradually they thought of imparting some sort of English education for the natives with a view to train them as clerks for running their administration. Lord William Bentink, the Governor General of India in the 1830's reserved some funds for the education of the Indians. When the question of which language should be made the medium of such education, arose, Lord Macaulay, as the Law Member of the Governor General's Council, in consultation with the progressive ideas of Indian social reformers like Raja Ram Mohan Roy, approved English as the medium of instruction for Indians. In the words of Lord Curzon, "The cold breath of Macaulay's logic became the language of the rulers, and thus of those who wished to emulate their masters socially and professionally. It became almost exclusively the language of higher education. English was the language of the missionaries who ran a number of outstanding educational institutions in different parts of the sub-continent. English began to assume the position of lingua franca of the multilingual Indian communities."[1]

Macaulay's reasons for making English as the medium of education was that Indian languages were not strong enough (with a complete apparatus) to impart science education. English is considered easier/ more important and conenient than Indian languages. English would bring Indians a lot of knowledge from the West. Then there is the downward filtration of education from English to Indian languages. What

Latin did for the European languages, English would do for Indian languages. More importantly India does not have a proper national/pan-Indian language. Though Hindi as an imperial language would be there to spread the whole country, Southern states do not like its imposition. Some people thought, "Hindi today may return to Hindu tomorrow." Of course, English became almost an Indian language over the years.

The Role of Language in Intellectual Development

K.L. Sharma observes, "Those who are seriously interested in the health and vitality of the intellectual and cultural life of the nation regard language as the soul of the nation."[2] Because language is not merely the medium of instruction. It is the medium of growth, of free and fresh thinking and research. Language helps man for his personality development. It gives him the style of life. It makes the mind imaginative, widens intellectual interests and provides emotional overtones. Speech is mainly a human faculty. It is a complicated phenomenon too. W.S. Tomkinson comments if literature is a communion with the imagined world, language is the means of intercourse with the real world. Today is the age of speech machines and the importance of language is more. Stevenson has rightly said that when a man has not a full possession of language, the most amiable qualities of his nature have to lie fallow and buried. Mastery over one or two languages is a must for the march of the human race.

In view of this, man must learn one or two languages carefully. This is more so in Indian situation. This is truer in our era of globalisation. The German poet Goethe says, "He who knows no foreign language knows nothing of his own." Growth is the characteristic of life. Language is a need of all human and social works. It is a means of social control. Ideas crystallise in mind by means of language. The aim of language-teacher is to seek action—action which gives rise to speech. Language helps not just for acquiring knowledge and information, but for acquiring human sensibilities. The purpose of language-teacher is to train students in speech as well as writing. The teacher teaches the four arts of language called language skills.

Language is a medium of literature. Literature teaches the finer ways of life. It is culture-bound.

Now we need to know why we should learn a foreign language like English. People whose mother tongue is not English ask the question why English should be taught as a second or third language. This is because of the reason that the British left it for us. This is because of the reason that India is a multi-linguistic country. This is because of the reason that English has become an international language. This is because of the reason that English language has complete apparatus to impart science knowledge to anybody. This is because of the reason that most of the people of the world speak or know English. English has substantial literary heritage. It is easy to learn and speak.

Linguistics and Teaching of Language

Linguistics is a science of language. The same helps us to have rapport with social sciences. Linguistics enables us to know the laws, principles and facts about language. If one does not know the science of language he cannot be able to use the language properly. As we know, language is the index of personality. Language mediates and establishes relationships between man and his environment. Linguistics deals with the structure and system of language. Language is subject to change. In fact, it is good for man's progress.

Aims of Teaching English

As we know, mother tongues are taught without any strain, even without any grammar-teaching or awareness of it. They are taught without the help of writing. They are learnt at home and in the company of parents, friends and relatives. But mother tongue alone is not enough for Indians as India is multi-lingual. The Indians need to know our imperial language Hindi and even English for a better life. The second or third language should be taught carefully. The teaching of English should be according to the needs of time and the demands of people. The people who choose to learn English must learn it well if they want to benefit from it. What is more important is to teach language skills more than mere literature. Children must know knowledge, comprehension, its application, analysis, synthesis and evaluation.

Teaching of English in India: A Study of the Problems

English should be taught not as an end in itself, but as a means to other things. Indians need to learn it for making use of the western sciences and technologies. English helps us to know the knowledge-industry of the world. It will help us for four purposes: social purpose, technical purpose, administrative purpose and cultural purpose. Language-learning is an exercise. A combination of direct method, vocabulary method, communication method, inductive-deductive methods, direct and translation methods can help us to teach them the fluency of English. English should be learnt in young age as early as when the child is between five and ten years. At least five years of English teaching is necessary for learning English. Teaching and learning processes must be quite intensive. One cannot learn a foreign language when old (particularly after 40 as such age sets deterioration). In a bi-lingual situation the foreign language (ex-language) may affect the growth of mother tongue (in-language). If English is taught as a third language, it should begin as little late as possible.

Principles of Teaching English

A foreign language must be learnt with a purpose—social, scientific, academic or literary. In India many people do not learn English with a clear-cut purpose. *Chalata hai* attitude is responsible for all this. Language teaching and learning is an art. Palmer says language is a habit-forming activity. It goes in the making of the personality too. Teacher needs to be careful in teaching it, for students copy him greatly. Motivation, stirring, warming, encouragement, help and the like must be there. The classical kind of lecturing method, grammar teaching, composition works, all kinds of methods, conversation, dialogues, debates, the use of play-way, cultural activities, teaching aids are quit necessary. Mass media plays a vital role. English should be taught from concrete to abstract. Accuracy and correction are necessary. Grading may be useful. Learners must achieve linguistic competence and use the language appropriately.

The teacher needs to prepare a fine lesson plan or blue print of what he wants to teach to students. He must provide them learning, reading and writing materials. Speech came to man as a gift from nature. Students must use all the available resources to use it. The English essayist Francis Bacon says, "Reading maketh a full man, conference a ready man and writing an exact man." The business of printing has made writing very important today. Our abilities in language are made perfect in writing. Writing trains both ears and eyes and fixes vocabulary, spelling and patterns in the children's mind.

Teaching of Prose and Poetry

More and more teaching activities help students to learn more and more. More teaching means facilitating students to do intensive study which makes them learn vocabulary, grammar and spoken English. We need to make them read literature too, as it teaches them finer sensibilities of life. The poet Coleridge once said of prose as 'words in their best order,' and of poetry as 'the best words in their best order.' Teacher must visualise poetry and teach it with right association of ideas. Poetry is a powerful stimulus to the aesthetic consciousness. Yet teaching of poetry is different from teaching of prose. Model reading, loud reading, and silent reading are necessary.

Dr Sweet says grammar is the practical analysis of a language. It is its anatomy. Yet as the language depends upon speech, grammar changes from time to time. Grammar is quite necessary for learning a language. 'Grammar first language next' is a saying.

Evaluation of English Teaching

Examination means measuring of students' knowledge. It is weighing the achievements of the learner against a standard weight. The standard weight is the question paper set by the examiner. Those who are intellectually less weighty are put in the category of failures. Now the method of evaluation is more important than examination. It is concerned with the testing of scholastic achievements of students at a particular age or grade. Evaluation goes much beyond the ends of examination and it measures all round progress. It goes on with teaching process. It is based on the objectives of teaching. It is a continuous process. It is mainly internal. It is more reliable and valid. It is a part of teaching and learning process.

On the other hand, the act of examination is only at the end; it is once in a year. It is unreliable. Similarly tests are a small examination at intervals. A test demands short answers. It concerns with a portion of the syllabus.

Examination, test and evaluation are necessary for running the system of education. Though they are boring, we cannot work without them. Such of examination/testing/evaluation must, however, provide a fair sample of the students' attainments, covering a wide range of material taught in the class. This sample should be truly representative of the areas covered and the skills involved. A few essay type questions will not do. Better there must be a large number of questions covering different areas. The teachers should not set difficult questions. There is a saying 'teach, test, reteach and retest.' Your test/ examination should be helpful for the students.

So that your questions should be easy, understandable, cover the main points taught in the class, and provide an adequate sampling. The evaluation should be sound and healthy. The examination must make the results as objective and consistent as possible. As you know, the traditional methods of examination cannot inspire confidence and it cannot test language abilities properly. The questions should not be too difficult or subjective. The examination should be the so called New Type Test.

English language teachers need to examine/test students' command over English. Such an examination must consist of (a) oral tests including Reading and Comprehension of oral expression/spoken English, (b) written test to test their language abilities and grammar. Auditory comprehension is equally important. The English language teacher can make use of students' mother-tongue to test their English language competence.

Some of the reading skills can be:

> Knowing word-meaning/referring to it/understanding passages, answering questions/ recognising literary devices/ drawing information about writers. Students should have a good speed in reading/pronouncing words correctly/ and comprehending the same.

One traditional method for assessing written expression is free composition. But it is subjective and elaborate. It is difficult to mark. Teachers assess such compositions by total impression, depending upon quality, quantity, vocabulary, grammar, punctuation marks, spelling and handwriting. This is called analytical method. Tests for correct usage, word-order, spelling, vocabulary, expression in speech, conversation and debate should be allowed. We shall add new writing skills such as letter-writing, precise, dabating, drama, writing poems and the like. All efforts must be directed for the realisation of noble aims and objectives. It should not be like the poor aims of the Indian Pundit:

> For example, there was a great Pundit in Bengal and he was once visited in his hut by a Rajah. "Can I be of any help to you in case you have any wants?" enquired the Rajah. "Wants?" said the Pundit, "My wife will tell you if there are any." When asked, the Pundit's wife said, "The tamarind tree bears plenty of sour leaves to eat our rice with, what else is there to want?" The Rajah left hanging his head.

So, dear friends, you are wrong to think that you could be as great as anybody if only you had enough fish and mustard oil to brighten your dinner time. There have been great men who did not need these at all.

References

1. Lord Curzon, qt by K. L. Sharma, *Methods of Teaching English in India*, Agraval Publishers, Agra, 2001, p.1.
2. K. L. Sharma, op.cit., p.13.

12

Travel Literature: A Study

The very idea behind the philosophy of travel is noble "Travel is worthwhile," says George Santayana. According to him, "Life is but a form of motion and a journey through a foreign world."[1]Even birds and beasts also have an inclination to travel. In animals the power of locomotion changes all this pale experience into a life of passion wherein intelligence is grafted. Travel lends us a meaning to the images of the eye and mind. Often we owe our intelligence to our feet. According to George Santayana, "Thinking while you walk, on the contrary, keeps you alert; your thoughts, though following some single path through the labyrinth, review real things in their real order; you are keen for discovery, ready for novelties, laughing at very little surprise, even if it is a mishap; you are careful to choose the right road, and if you take the wrong one, you are anxious and able to correct your error."[2]

Migration is the most radical and hard form of travel. Yet migration to a dream town like El Dorado and the Golden Age is worth and heroic where our soul signs away her safety for a blank cheque. Such travel outweighs all sorrows and dangers. In this one can change his moral climate and his inner landscape. Old habits have to change. Here life transforms thoroughly and heartily as both moral and material environments change and memories start afresh. Even mountain climbers, arctic explorers, passionate hunters undergo these experiences. The merchant is another type of traveller on the watery globe. The latest type of traveller is tourist obviously thirsting for facts or for beauty in a strange and remote land. But travelling in any form, any way, any time, anywhere is worth, for, "There is wisdom in turning as often as possible from the familiar to the unfamiliar: it keeps the mind nimble, it kills prejudice, and it fosters humour. I do not think that triviality and dissipation of mind and aversion from one's own birthplace, or the aping of foreign manners and arts are serious diseases: They kill, but they do not kill anybody worth saving."[3] What Wood says of Overbury is appropriate that he travelled for a time, and returned home a most accomplished person. In ancient days people who travelled remote lands, as is now, no doubt, acquired a lot of worldly knowledge, and such people were given key positions in administration. Examples include Inigo Jones, Milton, Hobbes, Bacon, John Taylor. Ibna Batuta, a great medieval traveller travelled a lot. This Moroccan was, by the Delhi Sultan Mahammad Bin Tugluk, made the Mayor of Delhi.

Travel is a basic human instinct. So birds and beasts travel far and wide for food and shelter, but man travels at times and again for quenching his curiosity of knowing the truth and the beauty of unknown. As the 'unheard melodies' looked more interesting to the Romantic poets, the unknown lands interested and mystified human minds. It is said, "the nature of man, by an inward inclination, is always inquisitive of forraine newes; yea, and much more affecteth the sight and knowledge of strange, and unfrequented kingdoms, such is the instinct of his natural affection." This made men trace the unfamiliar and they began to know the remote lands, to hear the mysterious sounds and to write about them. Human's interests lay in the exploration of truth, beauty and nobility and enriching his conscience. According to Aldous Huxley, interested travellers, "love what is unfamiliar for the sake of its unfamiliarity, they take pleasure in every manifestation of beauty." Travel gives man a tremendous knowledge of the places they visit and the people they meet. Out of travellers' experience and observation, arises a rich fragrance of life and personality of the past and the past-present encounter extends the meaning of travelogue. Men tour the places of another land and they get acquainted with people who differ from them in any respects. However, their knowledge of men and matters may be different from the natives of that land in its entirety.

Travellers get much joy and mirth in their wanderings. Of course, the difficulties go together with their moments of happiness. Anyway, as Mark Twain puts it, "Happiness lies in sorrow." So the moments of travellers' sorrows may be turned joyful to them the next time. Whatever difficulties travellers come across or whatever misfortunes befall upon them, they find happiness. For example, when many European travellers came to India, they landed into troubles. But the troubles were of a temporary nature. We know many English and Italian travellers escaped death and disaster. But most of them, as reflected in their travel-accounts found joy, satisfaction and immense knowledge. Besides, some travellers like Sir Thomas Hawkins, Ibn Batuta and Pietra da Valle got immense fame and their travel-accounts are still read. All educated men know the importance of travel-writings written by Hukluyet and Marco Polo. These two travelled all over the world. Similar is the case with navigators. Some navigators like Magellan circumnavigated the globe and they are now eternalised in their writings.

People travel for a variety of reasons. The objectives of travelling may be different in different countries and in different times. It also depends upon the advancement of nation to which the man belongs and also the quality of one's conscience. So several reasons and traits go there in making a best traveller out of hundred persons.

Man travels to see, to hear and to know the unfamiliar, strange and remote. He also travels with a religious mission. Some people go for an adventure. Some go for trade and commerce. Some travel to discover new geographical habitats. Most of the religious people travel either to see holy places and escape from sins or to spread their faith. Still a class of people travels for acquiring knowledge and exercising their wit. The people who travel for getting pleasures are not less significant. Travelling gives man all things—familiarity, experience, followers, wealth, fame, adventure, nobility, joy and happiness. According to *Encyclopaedia Britannica.* "Travel gives the writer the illusion of flight of his wearied self." Travelling is done to avoid frustration and responsibility. When the famous Pietro do Vallė visited Queen Abbakkadevi of Ullal at Manel in Karnataka, she put a variety of questions to him. She asked as to why he came to India. She thought he could have come because of frustration or because of escaping responsibility. But he replied her that he came to see foreign countries just out of his curiosity but not because of his undersatisfaction in life or unruly behaviour.

Most of the travellers who visit other countries do it for the sake of knowing the unfamiliar. Only those who want to see the unknown, strange and remote travel joyously, while those who desire to trade or to spread religion, do not travel with any genuine travellers' zeal. Travellers who merely go to see Gods or to get gold and glory do not attain any substantial knowledge, like the real travellers. Many travel-accounts begin with the introduction I wanted to see foreign lands and know about aliens' 'mode of life.' To them travelling is an urge, a desire to 'walk, watch and report.' It is almost a hobby rather than a well-planned work. They also desire to write accounts of the things that are abnormal, curious, exceptional, funny and odd. They portray alien's strange manners, customs, society, mode of living, style of working, outlook, religion, superstitions and other phenomena. Indeed, to see and to hear and to report is a great thing to genuine travellers.

A traveller, however, must be a systematic person. Good plans, right work out of them, adjustment with aliens etc. go together in making an ideal traveller. 'The best way to travel is to go well heeled' is a common saying. He should adjust with his co-travellers and make it a good company. "Travelling," as Leigh Hunt affirms, "in the company of those we love is a home in motion." Another adage runs 'Travel only with thy equals or thy betters, if there are none, travel alone.' Lin Yutang says, "A good traveller is one who does not know where he is going and a perfect traveller is one who does not know where he came from." Likewise a traveller is supposed to be a kind and wise person. One of the purposes of travelling is to get acquainted with the natives of new land. This expects the travellers to behave with aliens as humanly as possible lest travellers cannot get a cordial relationship with the natives. That is why Clifton

Fadiman writes, "No matter how widely you have travled, you have not seen the world if you have failed to look into the human hearts that inhabit it." It is better to listen to the warning of the same critic that "When you travel, remember that a foreign country is not designed to make you comfortable. It is designed to make its own people comfortable."

The question what is a travelogue is an ever perplexing one. As the art of travel-writing is a recent genre or it is less cultivated and encouraged, it has not yet attained as prestigious a position as that of an epic or a tragedy. Unlike poetry the art of travel-writing has not yet attained a perfect form and reading public. It is still in its immature stage. As the reading public has not yet been ready to read travelogues as they study poetry and novel, the position of the art of travelogues is still in a state of confusion. But it cannot be affirmed that the art of travel-writing is not an old one or useful. Evidences show that travel-writing is an ancient art practised even in the first millennium BC. The ancient Greeks and Romans, the medieval Europeans and the modern writers across the world have written travelogues. Today there is a vast and interested reading public. So travelogues are read as any genre of literature proper. Hence, there are some writers who consider the art of travel writing as a genre of literature. No wonder, like short story or novel, travelogue has found a form and an audience.

Let me answer the definition-eluding question: 'What is a travelogue?' A travelogue is an account of those who travel abroad or in their own countries. It, like a diary, consists of a traveller's accounts of experience, observations and knowledge of the country and its people. A travel-account usually in the form of a diary, or letters or for that matter jottings of outlines, consists of cultural, civilisational and geographical panorama of the travelled land. Some critics consider travelogue just a tourist guide. But travelogue is more than a tourist guide, because it is invariably literary both in style and matter. Nor is it a history? No. Because of its fragmantariness, literary aspects, lack of accuracy and vast outlines, it cannot be a history book. After all, a history book is an accurate and systematic account of the past, whereas a travelogue combines the past history with the present life differing from history. The common works with which a travelogue bears a similarity is a good account or a memoir, a diary or an autobiography. No wonder, usually a travelogue is written in the form of a diary or a memoir but all possible literary aspects are unfadingly enshrined in it. Even because of this, travelogue cannot be a diary or an autobiography. Travelogue, due to its literary aspects cannot be compared with any of these. It can be compared with a novel. Count Keyserling says, "A travelogue must be read as a novel." Travelogue bears a marked resemblance with a novel.

A good travelogue is a literary work. It is more than a tourist guide, a report, a diary, a memoir and an autobiography. Another marked feature of travelogue is its subjectivity grounded in literary quality. For example, a statement about Hukluyt's *Voyages* runs thus: "Maybe read in many ways but it must be read as literature of the creative artist." Another remark on *The Travels* by Marco Polo runs thus: "The book can be enjoyed by the modern reader as it was by the contemporary, for its own sake, as a vivid description of a fantastic world so remote from his own experience." Ujwala Hiremath affirms: "A travelogue is a diary and narrative of travel, sport and adventure...a blend of description, anecdote and personal commentary...a vast mosaic of impressions, responses and images of scenes and atmosphere... . It is a precise delineation of external detail but with a personal and imaginative vision." A similar note is struck in P.E. Dastoor's travel account that his travelogue is an unembellished record of his passing impressions. Even in his post-script to *The Emerald Route*, R.K. Narayan insists upon the point of subjectivity.

A travelogue is a book about varied interests dealt in several ways and forms. It is said a travelgoue is a story in fragments. It is a record of one's experiences, feelings, thoughts and observations of a foreign land (sometimes of one's own land). It is a window to the fascinating world. A travelgoue is said to be a literary 'portmanteau.' However, there must be a personal touch in a travel account. Hence it is subjective in treatment. Accordingly, "A travelogue registers the physical, sensual, emotional and intellectual reactions of the traveller." McFlecknoe says, "I write my travels...but to satisfy the curiosity of some noble friends and make honorable mention of others, to whom I am infinitely obliged."

A good travel account is as interesting as any form of literature. Nehru remarks, "It is good to travel, but if travel is denied then the next best thing is to read on travel." Aldous Huxley writes, "It is delightful to read on the spot impressions and opinions of tourists who visited hundred years ago, in the vehicles and with aesthetic prejudices of the period, the places which you are visiting now." Wit, style, a keen sense of humour, descriptions of the unknown territories and original mind are what delight the readers. Even what the travellers feel and think matter. So a well written travelogue is a work of art.

However, travelogues, like novels and epics, do not have a clear cut formal structure, but outlines and descriptions. A travelogue may be in diverse structures—diaristic, reportorial, journalistic and expository. Sometimes descriptive. Whatever may their formal structure, their language and style are not different from literature. In fact, men of literature write the best of them.

Travelogues were written before tenth century BC. The Italian priest Wenammenn's travel account written in 1130 BC still exists. Harodotus's *History of Persian Wars* is said to be available. Megasthanese's *Indica*, though lost now gives us a fair idea of ancient India. *Periplus and Iterian Sea*, an unknown Greek navigator's account of India is still extant. *Si-Yu-Ki* of Huen Tsang and *Go-Ko-Ki* of Fahien, the Chinese travelogues are useful. Alberunis' *Tehkik-I-Hind* gives us a fair idea of the eleventh 11th century India. In Europe some good accounts have created a name for their authors. Goethe's *Journey to Italy*, Daniel Defoe's *A Tour Through the Whole Island of Great Britain*, Henry Fielding's *A Journal of a Voyage to Lisbon*, Mary Montagu's *Travel Letters*, Hudson's *Far and Long Ago*, Graham Greene's *Journey Without Maps*, Huxley's *Jesting Pilate*, J.B. Priestley's *English Journey*, Doughty's *Arabia Desert* and others are excellent works of art. Man's creative imagination and originality are reflected in them. Marco Polo's *Travels*, Hukluyt's *Voyages and Discoveries* (1582) and Christopher Columbus's *Epistola* (1493) are established classics today. Even Americans and the writers in the commonwealth countries have written valuable travelogues.

Colubus's *Epstola*, Cabeza de Vaca's *Relation* (1542) and Samuel de Champlain's *Voyages* made Americans realize the importance of travel works. So Bayard Taylor, Ralp Waldo Emerson, Hawthorne, Walt Whitman, Melville, Washington Irving and others visited many countries and wrote about them.

William Bartram's *Travels*, Bayard Taylor's *View Afoot*, Walt Whitman's *Diary in Canada*, Mark Twain's *The Innocents Abroad*, Melville's *Typee*, Washington Irving's *A Tour on the Prairies* and John Steinbeck's *Travels with Charley in search of America* are read all over the world. They display local colours and climate of the lands their authors visited. Truly, they give us their authors' illusion of their wearied self. For example, when Hukluyt's travel account was published in 1582, it captured the reading public. Look at the quote: "For, which of the kings of this land before her Majesty, had theyr banners ever seene in the Caspean sea? which of them hath ever dealt with the Emperor of Persia, as her Majesty hath done, and obtained for her merchants large and loving privileges? who ever saw before this regiment, an English Ligier in the stately porch of the Grand Signor at Constantinople? Who ever found English Consuls and Agents at Tripolis in Syria, at Aleppo, at Babylon, at Balsara, and which is more, who ever heard of Englishman at Goa before now? What English shippes did heeretofore ever anker in the mighty river of Plate? Passe and repasse the...straight of Megallan, range along the coast of Chili, Peru, and all the backside of Nova Hispania, further than any Christian ever passed?"

Hukluyt's *Voyages* is still read with curiosity. The information it furnishes and the wide interest it covers make it a great work of human intellect. Sometimes travelogues give themes for literary activities. Bartram's travels helped many writers to expand their intelligence. It inspired Coleridge to write *Kubla Khan* and *The Ancient Mariner*; Wordsworth to write 'Ruth'; Southy to write 'Modoc', Tennyson to write *In Memoriam* and Campbells to write 'Gertrude of Wyoming.' So is the case with Francois Burnier's *Travels in the Mogul India* on which is based Dryden's play *Aurangezeb*. Great travel accounts inspire men of genius to produce works of everlasting beauty and importance.

In America, the art of travel writing has greatly flourished. Bayard Taylor was an early American travel-writer. His *Views Afoot*(1846) about the naïve raptures of a 20 years old boy captivated the nation. Twenty editions of the book were sold in 10 years. He writes, "I am led into these wanderings without my will; it seems to be my destiny." In *Leaves from My Journal*, Lowell writes at length on modern travels. He says, modern travellers see nothing out of sight; they are skeptics and doubters; they are only materialists reporting things for other skeptics to doubt still further upon. He regrets our inheritance of the wonderful is diminished and the world is getting disenchanted. Travelogues written by Americans are widely read. Travel books of Lowell, Curtis, Hay, Warner and Aldrich are greatly enjoyed. But the best of American travelogues in point of time and in obsolete excellence are Emerson's *English Traits* (1856), Hawthorn's *English Notebooks*, Mark Twain's *The Innocents Abroad* (1869), Howell's *Venetian Life* (1866), De Forest's *Oriental Acquaintance* (1856) and Henry James's *A Little Tour in France* (1884).

Americans' views on travelogues are useful. Henry James thinks the greatest problem for a travel writer is how to fuse the past and present, the monuments of unageing intellect and the politics of the moment. However, to James, travel is an immense pleasure. While perpetually going on journey he was willing to permit the scene to take hold of him and speak. "To travel," he says, "is to go to a play or attend a spectacle." To him a great ruin was a great opportunity. Whereas Mark Twain fled from ruins because he did not have the skill to make them speak. But James was impelled to them by a kind of aesthetic hunger. He used to say 'shadow is the artist's thought.' In fact, it was James' quest. It gave him a new proof of most pertinent lesson of art that there is no limit to the amount of substance an artist may put into his work.

Even in Commonwealth countries like India, Australia, South Africa and others, the art of travel writing has been intensified now. V. S. Naipaul's travelogues on India and other countries have captivated readers across the world. R.K. Narayan, Salman Rushdie, Nirad Chauduri, Santa Ram Rau, K.P.S. Menon, Ved Mehta, Dom Moraes and Mallikarjun Patil have written many of them. Although travelogue is not a full-fledged genre of literature, its cultivation has reached a state of modest maturity. However travelogue is not as lofty as an epic and not as profound as a tragedy, it is largely graceful as a lyric and any comic literature.

References

1. George Santayana, "The Philosophy of Travel", ed. by Denial Cory, *The Birth of Reason and Other Essays*, Vokils, Feffer and Simons Pvt., Bombay, 1968, p.180.
2. Ibid., p.8.
3. Ibid., p.14.

13

Literary Translation: Its Importance, Ways and Difficulties

No wonder, man cannot master many languages. Contrarily, if he can, absolutely he cannot write or speak in his second language fluently. Albert Baugh is right when he tells, "Few people ever master a language not their own and writings done in an alien speech rarely rise above the level of school exercises. Now and then some genius may transcend these limitations, but, even so his works usually remain an aesthetic curiosity, of little consequence in the literary scheme of things." If the condition of an average man's linguistic potentiality and diversity is so bleak then translation for our understanding of others is most essential.

Translation is as necessary as our very breathing to understand global relations in terms of arts, science and commerce. Since learning more languages or writing proficiently in an alien tongue, is hardly possible, the work of translation for the rise, promotion and development of literature, art, business, technology, medicine etc is inevitable. Translation promotes experiments and discoveries, it enables inter-linguistic communication in a country like India where multi-linguistic cultures exist. Translation recreates and intensifies the channel of life and diversifies human activities.

It is because of translation, the world's great works like the *Bible,* epics like the *Iliad,* the histories of ancient Greece, Rome, India, Babylonia, Sumeria and China are known to the people living in all the spheres of globe. It is translation that led to the medieval renaissance in Europe, to the spread of education and western culture in the New and Third Worlds. The role of translation in enabling the dissemination of new ideas in the developing countries today is crucial as ever before. Owing to translation, poets like Kalidasa, Shakespeare, Tagore, Eliot, Yeats etc are known to those who can never read each of these poets' mother tongue. Besides, translation for the sake of teaching in one's mother tongue is emphasized. Indeed, translation plays a vital role in a country like India where besides hundred vernaculars, three language tier system at national level works in bringing out a pan-Indian cultural tradition.

Well, translation is indispensable for the welfare of mankind. However, the eternal question that eludes us an answer is 'can the act of translation be possible?' People wonder, since language is god-gifted or wholly emotive, whether one can translate the sensibility of others into his language. Of course, according to certain people, translation of poetry is nearly impossible but not the translation of prose. Dr. Samuel Johnson, Didero and Nebakov subscribe to this view.

However, translation is possible, desirable and essential. For spreading knowledge, to get fame or pecuniary benefits, translation is done every time, everywhere. This is true of lands where multi-languages exist. In his letter to Thomas Carlyle, the German poet Goethe thinks, "Whatever might be people's opinion regarding the inconsistency of translations, for the sake of our worldly business, translation is most indispensable." However people wonder the mysteries of human experience, the shades of sense and sensibilities, ambiguities, language change etc cannot be rendered from one language to another language, human mind has already succeeded in rewording one's mind and heart into another's. Although the use of a word by several writers will not be the same always, sets of meanings in all languages for such words and senses exist and such things can be decoded. Indeed, in this light, translation can be undertaken to deliver the goods.

Oxford English Dictionary defines translation as "an action or process of turning from one language to another," and the *New Standard Encyclopedia*, tells, "translation is rendering of meaning especially in writing, from one language into another." In his work *Translation and Translations,* J.P. Postgate writes, "Translation in literature is the art of rendering the writing of one language into another language. The art of translation lies not merely in translating the literal sense of one language into another but of translating also the feeling, thought and character of the work, so that the finished translation is equal in quality to the original." 'A translation is at best a dislocation' in Collingwood's phrase, and Wilmowitz believes translation to be a metempsychosis.'

The word 'Translation' is derived from the Latin term *tranlsatus.* The prefix 'tran' means passing something, while the stem 'slate' means cover. The generic term translation has several implications such as alteration, change, conversion, interpretation, paraphrase, rendering, rephrasing, rewording, transcription, transformation and transliteration, and the specific meanings of the word are translating, rephrasing, interpretation, rendering, decoding etc.

A brief history of translation can be drawn thus. The discipline of translation first developed in Greece. Later Romans borrowed this. In medieval times, due to translation, all the ancient Greek and Roman classics were published in other European languages. Afterwards translation, through bureau or courtly support, turned oriental knowledge into occidental and vice-verse. This spread the knowledge everywhere. Al-Mansur's (the Kalif of Bagadad) Bureau of Translation and Translation Institute at Toledo, Spain and Queen Elizabeth's support to her court people gave a great boost in the field.

However, owing to printing and paper-back revolution, translation-business flourished everywhere. This is how Plato, Aristotle, Socrates, Aesop, Homer, Dante, Patriarch, Virgil, Tasso, Mantaigne and Ibson are available in English. Chaucer's *Roman de la Rose,* Malore's *Arthur,* Wycliff and Tyndale's *Bible,* Philoman Holland's *Pliny's Natural History,* North's Plutrach's *Lives* (1579), Harrington Ariosto's *Orlando Furioso* (1519) and Tasso's *Jerusalem Delivered,* Chapman's *Homer*, John Florio's *Montaigne's Essays* (1603) and Cervantes' *Don Quixote* (1602) are exquisite translations. Similar are Dryden's *Ovid* and *Virgil,* Pope's *Iliad* and *Odyssey,* Thomas Gray's Icelandic and Celtic verse, Macpherson's Gaelic Legends and Max Muller's Sanskrit classics. Likewise due to scholars' love of the orientalism, works like *Rubaiyat, Arabian Nights, Panchatantra,* Chinese and Russian novels are translated in several European languages today.

Translation should be faithful and idiomatic. Nothing should be added or omitted. Thus translation is like transferring an employee from one office to another but without any promotion or demotion. A translator should accord in all parts, even length, with its original. Through his dynamic encounter between two tongues he should attempt to pursue closely the syntax, cadences and sound of the other languages into his own. The following couplet by Lord Rosecommon insists upon fidelity of tone:

> Your author always will be the best advice
> Fall when he falls, and when he rises, rise.

But it does not mean the process of translation is a mechanic, exact and artificial endeavour. Otherwise the translated work loses its flavour. Therefore Benjamin Jovet observes: "All translation is a compromise the effort to be literal and the effort to be idiomatic." In the task of following the rules of translation, never one should turn a doctrinaire. Indeed, in this regard, the translator should involve not only his mind but also his heart.

A faithful or a good translator is supposed to be fluent in the languages he has involved in. He must be familiar with the structure of the other language and its linguistic diversity. He should understand a sentence usually as a unit of thought and in accordance with the system of his language that thought must be reworded. Always the right meanings of the words for the original should be used to avoid the loss of the sensibility in the transaction. This is more so in the case of idioms, proverbs and imageries. For example, the English proverb 'Every dog has its own day' should be *Attegondue kala sosegondu kal* in Kannada but not 'everyone has a chance.' Likewise the following English sayings should be rendered into

Kannada as put into the brackets. 'Empty vessel makes much noise' (*Alpa vidya maha garvi*); 'Make hay while the sun shines' (*Gali bittaga turiko*); 'Herculean task' (*Bhagirata Yatna*); Wolf in sheep's clothing' (*Gomukha vyagra*) etc. A literal translation of idioms, phrases, proverbs is harmful. In case of dire necessity new words or patterns in usage and expressions can be created in a way reading public welcomes it. But such innovation must not be ambiguous or obscure. Besides, the style should be in conformity to the contemporary usage. Refined usages should be used to carry on the rhythms, bolts of melody and harmony of the original. The exuberance and magniloquence should not be lost. The imprint of tradition and sound and sense must resound in the translated text. If necessary to make the translated look original the translator can spice it. In this regard, "a good translator conveys the fine distinctions of meaning, feeling, tone, sound, style and diction of the original. It is especially difficult to capture the quality of a great work of literature in another language. Literary translators continuously try to improve upon translations of the classics and new versions are published fairly often." However, during the translation nothing should be lost or changed in the rendering. So there should be a 'self-denial.'

Similarly a good translator should be familiar with the subject of translation. He should be familiar with the author. So in his *Essay on Criticism,* Alexander Pope says:

> Know well each ancient's proper character:
> His fable, subject, scope in every page;
> Religion, country, genius of the age...
> Thence form your judgment, thence
> Your maxims bring,
> And trace the Muses upward to their spring.

Indeed, to preserve the original in the reworded version, the process requires the translator's complete involvement in the life and idiom of one's own age. So much care must be taken. Therefore, 'you must not,' Samuel Butler remarks, 'skin him, stuff him and set him up in a case.'

Translator's understanding of the original should be clear, genuine and complete. It is because of failure in translation either in term of language or theme or both, many times in Shelley's view translators are branded as 'traitors.' Indeed owing to this lacunae only a single work is translated many times. Evidently Homer's epics, Indian epics, or great authors' great works are rendered into the same language many times. To avoid translator becoming a free lancer, in 1540 Atini Dole codified the following rules:

a) The translator should clearly know the author and his work while translating,
b) He should have known his language and the language of the work to be translated by him,
c) He must conform to the meaning of a sentence instead to the series of words in the translation,
d) His aim should be translating in a simple language, and
e) He should achieve a rhythm that sooth the ear and heart of his readers.

Translation can be done in several ways. Firstly a distinction should be drawn between the oral translation and the written. The former is called interpretation in which one who knows the languages of both the speaker and hearers, interprets the speaker's speech in the language of the hearers. During this he may commit any mistakes but such errors will be overlooked unless the process is sufficiently comprehensive. Whereas in written translation, there will be no flexibility or excuses for errors. Here everything should be done systematically. The translated text should look like the original, of course, in a different mettle.

Another classification of translation is machine translation or manual translation. Here machine translation is nothing but computer translation. In this process, the translatable text will be coded and decoded with signs, and rendering will be literal however. But so far machines have not yet succeeded in rendering human sensibility faithfully. So the real work of translation is still to be done by man himself.

More familiar modes of translation are literal translation or metaphrasing, free translation or paraphrasing, adaptation and real translation.

In literal translation or metaphrasing or word to word rendering the translator has to follow the original closely. He has little scope in recreating anything in the process. So this can be suitable only for technical matters. In his work *The Art of Translation,* T.H. Savorie observes, "Literal or word for word translation is a primitive type; it is only fit for prosaic matters." Indeed, it does not make a good reading.

Free translation or paraphrasing is another mode. In this type of translation, the original should be retained. Paraphrasing is a 'restatement of the original passage in other words.' Here language is less important than the matter. The aim of the translator is then less to make an accurate rendering than to make the substance of foreign work thoroughly intelligible to the spirit of the desired language. So the character of the translator thus proceeds as much from the mind of the translator as from the mind of the original writer. In this case the translator may add his own and amplify the original. However paraphrasing is good for rewording difficult or obscure texts in plain language. In it there is no scope for linguistic objectivity.

Adaptation is another mode of translation. In this kind, the original text is abridged. It can be called bowdlerisation where for the sake of rending the text, the translator alters it in accordance with the taste of his readers. This is done when an original text looks cumbersome, obscure, big and difficult for reading it in modern times. This is more so in the case of historical, puranical and mythological works like Vedas, Upanishads, or ancient chronicles of history. Max Muller is right when in connection with Indian epics, he observes: "Life seems too short to read such a gigantic poem as a whole." Therefore when he was up against a truly Himalayan task, Romesh Chunder Dutt decided to reduce the 48,000 lines of the *Ramayan* and the 2,00,000 lines of the *Mahabharata* into 4,000 lines each or ℇ,000 lines in all. So seven Kandas of the *Ramayan* and the eighteen Parvas of the *Mahabharata* became alike twelve books. Similarly most of the classics these days are adapted to readable extents. Filming a novel or dramatising a story involves adaptation. Besides, in adapting, the translator can omit much of the cumbersome text or at times add his own to make the resultant look enjoyable. For example, many of the translations made before 1,660 in Europe, especially those in prose, were marked by a super-abundance of words, characteristic of much of English writing in the sixteenth and seventeenth centuries. So the originals were amplified.

More examples of adaptation should be mentioned here. Dryden's *All for Love* is an adaptation of Shakespeare's *Antony and Cleopatra*.

Similarly the Kannada writer Kuvempu's *Raktaksi* is an adaptation of Shakespeare's *Hamlet,* and B.M. Shri's *Ashwathaman* is an adaptation of Sopocles' *Ejax*. Adaptation is useful to preserve the cultural heritage of the ancient world. But adaptations should do justice to the original, lest they will be adulterations.

Translation can be an interchanging process. In other words, translation of a prose work into poetry or vice-verse, or translation of a text from old language into new language can be done. So genre to genre, age to age, medium to medium translation is done ever the linguistic art of writing has begun. Again this kind of translation is undertaken solely with a view to carrying on the knowledge of the ancient times to the modern people.

When one translates the literature of ancient times to modernise it in a same language, he is bound to face numerous hurdles regarding language and theme. Since language changes both horizontally and vertically, the translator cannot render it faithfully. This is more true in the case of a language that grows rapidly owing to heavy borrowings, coinages, etc. For example, as we know the story of English language, the old King's English, through the ages, because of borrowing, has drastically been altered. Even many of the English words have lost their meanings, and many of the remaining have undergone a change. Coinages and borrowings, in translation, require an extensive glossing. For instance, when one translates old English poems like *Beowulf, Widsith, Finn, Maldon,* he finds maximum difficulties in regard to language. Besides, prosody troubles a good deal as in the old English there were on-verse and off-verse lifts as much as time and stress factors. Here is an old English runic poem rendered twice in modern English:

> Fooh by frofur fira gehwylcym;
> Sceal eah manna gehywylc miclun hyt a lan
> Gif he wile for arihtne domnes hleotan

Its modern translation runs thus:

> Valuables are a joy to everyman;
> Yet every man must needs be openhanded with them
> If he is minded to win favour with the Lord.

The following is another version of the same:

> I am a joy to everyman;
> Yet every man must needs be openhanded with me
> If he is minded to win favor with the Lord.

Similar is human experience of translating old Sanskrit into new Sanskrit. So is the case with other languages.

Be it as it may when one undertakes the work of translating literature of one genre into another either in the same language or from one language into another, he is to encounter myriad difficulties. Here the difficulties are of two fold if say an old English poem is to be translated into a different language, again say in prose. Because of linguistic barriers, the work upsets him. For example, *Finn,* an old English poem sung by scops and gleemen, was rendered into prose in English and other European languages. It underwent a considerable metamporphosis. That is why, it is said, poetry cannot be translated. But in Hilleri Belloc's view, poetry can be reclothed into a living prose. Therefore, Matthew Arnold thinks since it has a rhythm, rhyme and metre, poetic exuberance and melody cannot be rendered into another medium. Frost, therefore, defined poetry as an art which cannot be translated.

Medium to medium translation is possible excepting poetry. Since it has uninterruptible emotional shades, poetry is bound to lose its flavour if it is translated into another medium. However, in Arnold's view only the poet can do it. In this regard, one can remember Tagore who himself translated his poems into English under the title *Gitanjali*. For poetry translation, at least, in J.P. Postgate's opinion, one should have poetic sensibility.

Unfortunately the art of translation is a difficult job again for the same reason that one cannot have two mother tongues, or one can hardly learn two or more languages sufficiently to do justice to the original work. Besides, the difficulties of understanding are there. The re-translation of great classics into the same language is a clear evidence for this. Secondly there are no clear-cut rules and regulations in this regard. Even they cannot be. Maybe for this reason, Wilmowiz thinks translation is a mathematical problem. Since it is not a prestigious work, people do not value translation or undertake it willingly.

However, the art of translation is certainly a useful work—helpful, enlightening and remunerative. But it is not as prestigious as the creative writings. So in Cardinal Newman's view translation is only translation.

14

Stylistics: An Overview

Stylistics is a discipline of literature. What linguistics is to language, stylistics is to literature. In fact, stylistics is the 'science of literature.' It is an objective study of its texts, or an interpretation of linguistic embellishments of language used in literature. There is certain inherent rapport between linguistics and stylistics. However, stylistics as a discipline has its own nature and scope. It concerns itself with the linguistic interpretation of literary texts. In the words of Enkvist, the task of stylistics is "to set up inventories and descriptions of stylistic stimuli with the aid of linguistic concepts." The methods of stylistics are clearly objective. As so stylistics stands apart from the discipline of literary criticism.

As mentioned above, the origin and growth of stylistics is not remote to seek. It looks as though recent in growth. In fact, stylistics began as a subject in the 1950's with a series of fresh starts. Even as a separate discipline it has not yet found a place in many universities today. Besides, there are no ready-made textbooks available save a few editions of articles. Even no proper perspective about the strengths and limitations of the subject are seriously attempted so far.

Stylistics, which arose as a handmaid to literary criticism, aims at studying literary texts bjectively. It does not take care of details pertaining to the author, the period, or the other extra-textual data on which traditional criticism so much relied. This way stylistics resembles Russian formalism as much as French structuralism and New Criticism. Linguistics plays a role here in as much as the stylistician analyses the details that are missed or neglected by the literary critic. Yet we need not think stylistics is a discipline created to replace the traditional literary criticism. Stylistics plays a subordinate role. So it is not a superior discipline. Here both the stylistician and the critic have a duty of complementary nature and they need to work together in the interpretation of a text. Stylistics has something concrete to go by in the textual features whereas criticism chooses to ignore the text at hand totally in deference to the author's biography.

Here I have tried to give certain details regarding the origin, growth, nature and scope of stylistics as an individual discipline. This article aims at providing details regarding the historical antecedents of stylistics, a few theories of style, and the current trends. Information regarding the application of stylistics to the teaching of literature is provided. And a few Indian views on style are given too in contrast to the Western views on the matter.

However the growth of stylistics as a new subject was felt in 1960 with the publication of *Style in Language*, it has an ancient origin. Aristotle had, a long ago, said that style is part of rhetoric. According to him vocabulary, syntax and figures of speech are aimed at producing a certain effect on audience. In his work *Institute of Oratory*, Quintillion (AD 1st century) said the same things, which found their effect in European thought till modern times. In his celebrated essay "Discourse on Style," Comte de Buffoon (1707-1788) viewed style as a means to rhetorical end. As a result, it was inferred that style is an ordering process of writing. Later the views of Ferdinand de Saussure (1857-1913), Charles Bally (1865-1947) and Leo Spitzer (1887-1960) gave a fresh impetus to the growth of the subject. Spitzer made a research on literary stylistics and stated that criticism should deal with the work as much without any preconceived notions of *a priori* judgment. According to him, after reading a work many times over, a critic can grasp the 'spiritual etymon' by an intuitive 'click' and thereafter understand its inner order. This hypothesis led him to establish the notion of 'philological circle.' In course of time Saussurean structuralism influenced Roman Jacobson, Jan Mukarovsky and Rene Welleck, the practitioners of Prague School (circle linguistique de prage). These linguists expressed the view that the formal features of creative utterances can be studied objectively to understand their operation in some general way. So the Prague School served as an important link between literary criticism and linguistic stylistics. Afterwards the structuralists like Edward Sapir (1884-1939) and Leonard Bloomfield (1887-1949) thought that their approach to literature "subordinates aspects of surface structure in favour of an investigation of some deeper, more abstract things, which govern the inner form of the work." Stylistics "emphasizes particularity, individuality, concreteness and makes the individual work some recognisable, more discrete, its physiognomy more salient." While Claude Leve-Strauss elaborated the view that literature combines the features of anthropology and linguistics, and the fundamental principle of human thinking is 'binary opposition.'

Practical criticism originated by I.A. Richards in the 1930's was a new step that gave a fresh insight to the growth of stylistics. I.A. Richards reinforced a close reading of the texts and he paid no attention to historical and biographical details of the texts. This paved a way to the New Criticism, which, in turn, brought us to the threshold of modern stylistics.

New Criticism that was begun with John Crowe Ransom's publication of *New Criticism* (1941) expounded the view that the poem is a 'legitimate object of study in itself,' 'a monumental thing in itself' and a unique but highly-ordered 'organism.' The New Critics did not practise description for its own sake. So New Criticism and structuralism emphasised on objective study of the texts. While Rene Welleck and Austin Warren pointed out that literature is a linguistic art and language is its raw material at all levels. Besides, the formulations of Transformational Generative Grammar by Noam Chomsky and the book *Style in Language* (1960) published by the members of social science research council of Indiana University opened up new ways of handling and laying bare the internal working of language.

However, linguistic approach to literature existed side by side. Many linguists felt that since the language was the stuff of which literature was made, linguistics should be able to comment on it in a sensible way, of course, without affecting value judgments. Harold Whitehall went a step further and affirmed that "as no science can go beyond mathematics, no criticism can go beyond its linguistics." These bold studies of stylistics strengthened the linguistic approach to it. Michael Halliday put it effectively that "there is no text without style." Jan Mukarovsky opined, "All literary language is a purposeful distortion of ordinary language." This led Nils Erik Enkvist to express: "the style of text is the aggregate of the contextual probabilities of its linguistic items."

According to the Prague linguists, the central notion of style is called 'foregrounding.' The opposite of foregrounding is automatisation which is a process by which a previously foregrounded expression loses its aesthetic value for later readers. Here foregrounding serves as an attention calling device in a literary passage through the use of repetition, emphasis, lexical collocations, syntactic inversions etc. While the structuralist school of linguistics maintained that style could simply be studied as the difference between synonymous sentences. According to the British school of linguistics of J.R. Firth and M.A.K. Halliday language is presented as a system containing several sub-systems. These linguists emphasize the aspects of register, field, mode, context, unit, structure, class and system. Of the various linguistic descriptions of style, the one based on transformational generative grammar has commanded a great respect over the years. Accordingly surface structure, which represents performance and belongs to the domain of style is given a main consideration. Richard Ohmann with this technique analysed G.B. Shaw's style. He found that frequent use of relativisation, conjunction and comparison characterises Faulkner's style. In Ohmann's view Henry James used good deal of embedding and D.H. Lawrence's style is built on deletion. In all these linguistic approaches to the analysis of texts, style is identified, in the words of Roger Fowler "as the sum of a number of points on several linguistic scales." Even the short utterance can be analysed with respect to a number of linguistic features. An ordinary sentence like 'what a beautiful day!' assumes different kinds of stylistic significance depending upon the tone of the speaker, weather of the day etc. So the situation is much complex in the case of a literary text. A variety of features, for example, in the case of this sentence, the tone, the weather of the day, the stress etc, are called 'convergence.' Similarly Halliday and Hasan use the notion of cohesion in stylistic analysis. Here cohesive features may be either grammatical (e.g. use of determiners, pronouns, demonstratives, certain adverbs) or lexical (e.g. repetition of words, sequential occurrence of items from a given lexical set).

Thus these approaches to the study of stylistics indicate three current trends i.e., (1) Style as a deviation, (2) Style, as convergence of textual patterns, and (3) Style, as a result of particular exploitation of a grammar of possibilities. When we think style as a conceptual deviance, we mean that the poet or writer deviates from the norm even when he conceives something in his mind and later he commits it to the paper. Let it be born in mind that all great literature is a product of conceptual deviance. So the poetry or any form of literature if it really deviates from grammaticality, it may or it may not be acceptable. For example, "anyone lived in a pretty how town" is tolerated in the context of Cumming's poem. But the following lines of conceptual deviance are not accepted:

a) A who the of today (violation of the basic syntactic rule of English).
b) I thermometer you – (use of noun in place of verb).
c) I elapsed the book to her (elapse is unsuitable).
d) The stone snores (no animate noun).

But the following sentence from *Moby Dick*, which shows conceptual deviation, is accepted:

> And heaved and heaved, still untrustingly heaved the black sea, as if its vast tides were a conscience.

In the light of the above analysis, deviance can thus be redefined as the "difference between a text and the overall grammatical norm of the language" and the sum of nongrammaticality and non-acceptability. Besides, conceptual deviance is metaphorical in nature, and it leads to a great creativity. Anyway there are degrees of deviance, which are closely related to the degrees of grammaticality. We can also say that the more grammatical a sentence is the less creative (deviant) it is, with an attendant quantum of banality (alternatives).

When we consider the style of poetry the importance of stylistic study will be known to us. As most of us know the language of poetry is something quite different from the language of prose though William Wordsworth reacted against this. Accordingly the language of poetry is something that arouses aesthetic imagination (Owen Barfield), 'is a special selection' (Josephine Miles, Donald Davie),' is different from the language of age' (Tennyson) etc. The definition of poetic language given by Jan Mukarovsky is excellent: "Poetic language is the distortion of the ordinary language." This is done for the sake of foregrounding, which creates an aesthetic effect and an everlasting impression. Poetic language is a 'separate language,' 'a dialect of the standard' and it has its own way. It has a special vocabulary and different combinations of it's own. Poetic language is different from the prose language mainly for the purpose of foregrounding, which is done for engaging the reader's intellect. So, poetry uses highly patterned and organised mode of expressions. Look at Steven Orien's "Country House:"

"The house is old, too small to contain lives. Furnished with smog, TV, divorce. The trees I drag like errant children from the hills are squandered in the fireplace."

The beginning is direct, but the comparison of trees with errant children. This is done for the purpose of foregrounding. So here the deviance is conceptual. The strong reason as to why distorted language is employed by poets is to achieve an everlasting poetic effect. Paul Valery states:

> The poem, on the other hand, does not die for having lived: it is expressly designed to be born again from its ashes

> and to become endlessly what it has just been. Poetry can be recognised by this property, that it tends to get itself reproduced in its own form: it stimulates us to reconstruct it identically.

Similarly in case of prose passages, there is no need for a complete inventory of linguistic features; just the salient ones will do to account for its effect. Then it is very useful. In M.I. Sastri's view, to what register the passage belongs, is based on the field of discourse (e.g. journalism, advertisement, science, literature, law, etc.) and the style of discourse (e.g. formal, informal, consultative etc). The lexis and syntax provide us the principle clues to this stylistic analysis of prose pieces.

Since stylistics is regarded as applied linguistics, it is used in teaching of literature. This helps teachers to help their students appreciate the artistic use of language and enhance their linguistic competence. In Enkvist's opinion, this is helpful to them in acquiring a sense of style. Stylistic approach enriches students' aesthetic qualities in regard to their understanding. They learn the role of language in understanding a text. In stylistic analysis, literature is presented as a dynamic communication, not mechanically a response to a stimulus, but something triggering a spontaneous interaction between the text and reader. In his work *Stylistics and the Teaching of Literature* (1975), H.G. Widdowson examines the nature of literary communication and stylistics as an exercise in literary understanding.

In regard to the theories of style, though not a profound study is undertaken, sufficient knowledge is unearthed. Broadly speaking there are three theories of style i.e., style as a dress of thought, style as an organism, and style as the man. According to the first theory both the matter and manner can be separated. Here style is an embellishment to the content, hence divisible from the other. Puttenham and Lord Chesterfield supported this view. They observe that a text can have different kinds of styles (dress) for different occasions. Consequently, the concepts of grand, plain and bombastic styles were formed.

But the Romantic poets like Coleridge and Wordsworth did not accept style as a dress of thought. Instead, they expressed the view that style is inseparable from thought. Their theory is known as 'organic theory of style.' Later Herbert Reed and New Critics practised this view. To Romantics, style is more than the dress of thoughts. The mind is the art-making organism. There can be no kind of divorce between language and thought. To Wordsworth the figures of speech or any other stylistic features appeared not as 'billiard balls' but as molecules. These outside features contribute to the total effect. Poetry to Wordsworth was truth "carried alive into the heart of passion." Coleridge affirms, "They (images) become proofs of genius only as far as they are modified by a predominant passion." In the organic view, intuition is nothing but expression. Newman says, "style is thinking out into language," and Archibald MacLeish states, "a poem should not mean but be... It is autonomous."

The third theory is psychologically oriented. It is illustrated in the well-known definition of Buffon that 'style is the man.' In this we try to attribute certain habits of language to certain character traits in the man. But this theory is unacceptable because man writes differently on different occasions. For evidence, a man's talk with others, in the case of his students, wife, children, friends and kindred will be varied. So are his modes of writing.

There are many approaches to style originated both in India and the West. Bhamaha (6th century), a Samkrit poet says poetry is the togetherness of sound and sense which view corroborates the western organic theory of style. Bhamaha defines poetry as *Sabdarthau Sahitau Kavyam* (Kavyalankar), which is similar to Paul Valery's definition of poetry that "In poetry the form and content are indissolubly united in wedlock." However, Bhamaha emphasizes more on sound or embellishment, which has an effect due to its vakrokti or deviance from the normal language. Dandin, a contemporary of Bhamaha, emphasizes both on sound and sense, which together suggest an elegant idea. So Bhamaha and Dandin reinforce more on the body of poetry than on its soul. But

Vaman's emphasis is on the soul of poetry. He says style is the soul of poetry. Anandavardhana (9th century) and Abhinavagupta give much importance to dhvani or suggestion of poetry. The Indian critics of poetics on the basis of *rasa* theory classify poetry into two kinds i.e., poetry, verse and the middle one that is either equal or inferior to the other two. Kantak (19th century) affirms that poetry is *vakrokti* or deviance, which is similar to Makarovasky's view of poetic language. Kshemendra (11th century) says auchitya or propriety is the life of poetry and *rasa* is its soul. Ancitya is nothing but coherence and unity of the theme and treatment of embellishments So Indian approaches to style are as varied as their western counterparts.

The importance of stylistics for the study, judgment and evaluation of a text is very much in consideration of subjective criticism. But stylistics as a discipline is not yet totally self-sufficient. So the fate of stylistics is a declining one. Only people like historicists and feminists best use the discipline to solve their problems, whereas critics do not exploit it to its full extent.

15

Mankind and Sex: A Dialectics

When I bought *Sex in History* by Reay Tannahimm, a book on the history of sex at an old shop at Oxford it compelled me to read it. The book is quite useful for anyone. Accordingly sex plays a vital role in human existence not only in its capacity as a source of procreation, but in its capacity to satiate human rage. Sex has its own history in regard to human attitudes, customs and practices.

Once man became the master of universe, he started to think of ownership and superiority. The concept of my 'my son' led him to tie a woman to himself,—leading to the creation of 'family,'—nearly 1000 BC. It is cited in a scripture that in the year 4000 BC at precisely 9 o'clock on the morning of October 23, "God created man in his image, in the image of God created he him; male and female created he them," whereas Charles Darwin and the book *The Descent of Man* in 1871 refuted it by saying that man is a gradual creation from the anthropoid ape. This led to the concept that man is a product of an ape but not of an angel. However, human origin is still vague and speculative.

Sex in man of any age is found pleasurable as well as instinctually purposeful. But we do not have the issues about Joy of Sex in the first man homosapiens following Ramapithecus. The first ancestors' sex life remains a mystery uptil 3000 BC.

Man's ancestor such as ape, gibbon and chimpanzee had a variety of sounds for sexual ownership. One of gibbon's sound, as scientists understand, means 'stay away from my wife!' That means gibbon sticked to only one partner. Earnest Kaecket, a scientist and Darwin's contemporary discovered that man is a close relative of gibbon and he bears a convenient resemblance with it by having the system of Husband, Wife and Children—the last severing from the family on getting independence.

Incest tabu was the first, before cannibalism, in the Neolithic revolution (BC 10,000). Like Macaque monkey mothers' avoiding mating with their sons, one time man stopped mating with his daughter. As Venus figurines point out, sex life was unerotic in Paleolithic age. But the sex urge was great. As a single ram impregnated 50 ewes, what man could not do? His role in procreation increased when he established his sex and self-respect, and woman became his chattel.

The sin of sex begins unveiling with the deciphering of Sumerian script. One reads, 'He put a hot fish in her navel.' One time in history polygamy was rampant and as back as 1000 BC the King Solomon (955 to 935) BC reigning) had 700 wives, besides 300 concubines. But later monogamy replaced it for economic reasons yet retaining supplementary concubines and slaves. But instances of polyandry are rare. In all cases, domestic harmony seems to have imposed limits. Besides, secondary wives *asshetu* or *esirtu* meaning rivals in Babylon and *sarot* meaning jealous associates in Hebrews were there. This marital relationship continued in all over the world until the tenth century AD.

Dropping womb, virility melting fear, copulation sickness, etc. oppressed both men and women sexually in ancient days. Regarding Near Eastern preoccupation with male son here is a story: "It was recommended to the Egyptian doctor that he put wheat and barley seeds into separate cloth purses and then tell the woman to 'pass her water on it every day....If both sprout she will give birth....If they do not sprout, she will not give birth at all. "Assuming the test was positive, would the child be a boy or a girl? (Wheat was a more valued grain than barley.)"[1] Around 3000 BC was introduced male's circumcision. Both were practised among Mayans, Aztecs, Incas, Egyptians and later in Arabians. Pagan rite is an index of grace. It is said to be a Covenant of God. When one—either male or female—hurt other's sexual organ—the penalty rule, life for life, eye for eye, tooth for tooth was applicable. Abortion was a criminal offense. A woman aborted was not given a burial. The first century Jewish historian Josephus said, "The Law recognises no sexual connections, except the natural union of husband and wife, and that only for the procreation of children, and there were various provisions, positive and negative, to enforce this principle. It was ordained, for example, that a newly married man should be happy with his wife whom he has taken."[2] Married life, for sexual pleasure, was much respected. There was homosexuality. Babylonians allowed it, Israelis did not. They killed those who lay with the same sex as with beast.

Be it as it may, the ancient people were afraid of population explosion. So they used a variety of contraceptive methods such as honey, auytgum, crocodile and elephant dung to prevent conception. Reay Tannahill says, "The early world had nothing to learn as far as general approaches to family limitations were concerned. As well as mechanical and chemical methods of contraception, they practised abortion, infanticide, abstinence, and nonproductive sex, homo-sexuality, zoophilia, and probably heterosexual anal intercourse—tried to depress fertility through prolonged breastfeeding, and used anaprodisics to immobilise the semen at its source by killing the urge. There is no way of estimating the relative popularity of the various methods, but all later history suggests that infanticides was not the last, but the first resort."[3] Or she jumped up and down to expel semen or drank cups of roots.

Onan's case in the *Bible* is interesting. In those days, in certain race, if a woman lost her husband, bearing him no issue, she was to live with his brothers, this being known as Levirate Marriage. Onan, however, rebelled against it. According to the Book of Genesis (38, 8-10), the eldest son of Judah died without issue, and Judah said to Onan, "Go in unto thy brother's wife, and marry her, and raise up seed to thy brother."[4] And Onan knew that the seed should not be his; and it came to pass, when he went in unto his brother's wife, that he spilled it on the ground, lest he should give seed to his brother. And the thing, which he did, displeased the Lord: wherefore he slew him.

This is a brother\sister-in-law marriage. Though they were undesirable, they were inevitable. Sinai ruled out 'uncovering of nakedness of other women except one's wife.' Soon Halizah rules came up and violation of these tabus resulted into burning to death. But in spite of this, Pharaohs were notorious for incest marriages. C.D. Darlington, a British biologist gives the example of Akhenaten whose emotional life was not healthy. He says,"His first wife appears to have been his mother, Tiy, a strong-minded lady from Nubia; they had one daughter. Then he married his maternal cousin, Nefretiti, and fathered three more and there was one son of each marriage, the second of whom was to rule as the boy pharaoh Tutankhamon. Akhenaten's fifth and last marriage was to the third of his daughters by Nefretiti; they had one daughter who died young. Although none of Akhenaten's own marriages was necessary to reinforce his claim to the throne, both his sons found it necessary to marry their half sisters. In the first case there were no children of the marriage, in the second there were two, both of them stillborn."[5] Akhenaten's tragic tale led to the creation of Sophocles's Oedipus concept.

Here is the *Epic of Gilgamesh* another tale of lust as told 4000 years ago. The hero Gilgamesh, is two-thirds god and one-third man, and the tale of his adventures begins with the people of his city, Uruk, muttering complaints against him: "His lust leaves no virgin to her lover, neither the warrior's daughter nor the wife of the nobleman."[6] To take his mind off such undiplomatic activities, the goddess Aruru creates Enkidu, a huge brutish, hairy creature who lives on the steppe lands among the beasts, a symbol of the pastoral nomads and a menace to Gilamesh's subjects. Gilgamesh, nobody's fool, decides force is not the answer to this threat and sends instead a harlot from the temple of love, a child of pleasure to find and tame him.

The harlot, duly encountering Enkidu, made herself naked and welcomed the eager fellow; she incited the savage to love and taught him the woman's art. For six days and seven nights they lay together and afterward Enkidu was grown weak. When he recovered, the harlot described him the wonders of civilisation and led him like another away from the steppes and down to the plains.

Harlotry—both secular and sacred—existed at both temples and taverns in the ancient world of Sumeria. Dancers and musicians maintained a secondary trade. Even male harlot cults existed. In both cases, citizens lost their substance to them. Childless widows and divorced carried the craft. Usually as Herodotus says their language was intemperate and absence. Solomon with 700 wives was, in his *Song of Songs,* to sing as follows: "My beloved is unto me as a cluster of samphire in the vineyards of Engedi. Behold, thou art fair, my love; behold, thou art fair…My beloved speaks and says to me: 'Arise, my love, my fair one, and come away; for lo, the winter is past, the rain is over and gone. The flowers appear on earth, the time of singing has gone, and the voice of the turtle dove is heard in our land….'"[7]

The ancient Greeks possessed not only pure intellect but also a pure beauty. Even sexual vagaries. The works of Homer and Hosiod, Plutarch and Pausanias—are filled with sex details. Aphrodite was their Goddess of sexual intercourse, and her son Eros, the God of love. Cronos, son of earth and heaven, castrated his father with a billhook and hurled his testicles into sea. The result was the birth of Aphrodite.

Greek heroes were as lusty as the gods. Heracles, whom we admire for his strength ravished fifty virgins in a single night besides sleeping with his nephew Iolaus. Theseus seduced almost as many maids as he slaughtered monsters in his raga. Greek gods and heroes were full-blooded and handsome, as models for others. Greeks were known for pederasty, which is an ancient version of homosexuality. Socrates had this affair with his disciple Alcibiades. So did Plato, a bachelor life long. There were boy-brothels. But certain boys who disliked this used to kill the forcing elders. Examples include the death of Archelaus of Macedonia and Alexander of Phelae. Praxiteles, the last and greatest artist of Greece was heterosexualist. Therefore Solon, the lawgiver passed many laws banning man-boy relationships (pederasty).

Woman was totally confined to home in the Greek world. She was just a gyne ('bearer of children'). Though Socrates remarked 'women are by no means inferior to men,' generally Greeks condemned her as irrational because she was denied education, oversexed, because her husband did not sleep with her often, and morally defective because she criticised man as he did not work instead participated in symposium. Domestic harmony was not a feature of Greek life.

Therefore, many of the figures in Greek tragedy were women. Clytemnestra slaughtered her husband, Medea chopped her brother in pieces and later murdered her children, Phaedra followed perjury with suicide and Electra was an accomplice in matricide. Even Greek heroines were flawed. The goddess Aphrodite was beautiful, charming, but a bitch. So was Helen of Troy. The faithful Penelope, by the time she welcomed her rather less faithful husband Odysseus back from his wanderings, had 20 such tough-minded years behind her that no sensible Greek would have given a fig for their chances of conjugal bliss. And the self-sacrificing Alcestis was clearly a doormat.

The Athenian male recognised all this. Alcestis would have intolerably bored him—except as a wife. But if he found a wife with such qualities he counted himself fortunate. Hosiod, the peasant poet who lived in the latter part of the eighth century BC and whom the Greeks revered only slightly less than Homer explained why it was necessary to marry at all. "He who evades, by refusing marriage, the miseries that women bring upon us, will have no support (children) in the wretchedness of his old age.... On the other hand, he whose fate it is to marry may perhaps find a good and sensible wife." The best ages were 30 for the man and 16 for girl, and on the whole it was better to "buy the woman, don't marry her. Then you can make her follow the plough if necessary." The Athenian's view of a good wife was an almost exact echo of the Hebrew's. She was to be chaste and sober-minded, competent at spinning, weaving, and tailoring, able to allocate suitable tasks to the servants, to be economical with her husband's money and property, to bear children, and to govern the household wisely and virtuously.

If it was necessary to beget an heir in a hurry, she was expected to have intercourse with her husband at least three times a month.

Because of Greeks' infrequent sleeping with their women, the latter resorted to masturbation. Dildo was a safety valve for them. Sappho, a tribal is much spoken for her Lesbian poetry. Demosthenes in his *In Neaeram*, writes, "We have heteirai for our pleasure, concubines for our daily needs, and wives to give us legitimate children and look after the housekeeping."[8] This signifies the creation of courtesans as Aphrodite's servants. Popularly known as hetaera, courtesans like Thargelia (who brokered for Cyrus, the Great of Persia), Thais of Athens (Alexander's mistress) and Aspasia (Who started a literary salon in Athens) played a political role in Greekdom. For instance, Lucuan's dialogues of courtesans holds the following:

Dorion	:	First, Sicyonian shoes—two drachmae. Put down two drachmae.
Myrtale	:	But for that you had two nights with me.
Dorion	:	Then when I came back from Syria I bought an alabaster scent bottle for you, which again—ye gods!—cost two drachmae.
Myrtale	:	But before you put out to sea I gave you the most beautiful shirt. The one the second mate left here after he spent the night with me.
Dorion	:	That's true enough...Then I bought you onions from Cyprus, five herrings, and four perch. And eight ship's biscuits in little wicker baskets, and sandals with gold thread, you ungrateful woman. Oh! And a large cheese!
Myrtale	:	About five drachmae altogether maybe...
Dorion	:	But your Bithynian has never bought even a head of garlic for your mother! I'd very much like to know what you've had from him![9]

Philumena, a courtesan said briskly to her lover:

> Why do you bother writing long letters? I want fifty gold pieces, not letters. If you love me, pay up; if you love your money more, then don't bother me any more. Goodbye![10]

Some, in their heyday earned enough to indulge in works. Lamia of Athens rebuilt a ruined picture galley near Corinth and Rhodopis constructed a whole pyramid.

As for Rome, the poet Juvenal observed: "Chastity was a virtue that had scarcely been seen in Rome since the Golden Age—by which, Stoic that he was, he meant that stern and simple era of the long ago when one cold cavern sufficed to house the 'acorn-belching' early Roman, his gods, his flocks, his 'gigantic children,' and his 'rough highland wife.'[11] Traditionally, Romans had three kinds of marriages—the first *confarreatio*, an arranged marriage, costly too; the second, *coemptio*, a relic of bride purchase, generally cheap, and the third, *usus*, marrying a woman after being with her for a year. The last is a trial and try. Later at the war Oppian law barred woman pass in Roman City streets. But woman took to them brazenly to that extent Cato, the Roman senator argued that they would uproot men's lives. Nay Roman women were given freedom soon and they indulged in all sorts of fashion. As a result, due to extravagance as Pliny says Rome declined in its wealth. Marriage in Romans was a problem—partly men in Rome did not satisfy their women, and their women spent a lot on fashion besides demanding divorce. A second century Roman who woman married eight men in five winters made Juvenal exclaim. Cicero divorced his wife Terentia, because amidst his philosophy he could not keep her in good spirit. What a wonder? She demanded the dowry she had given him. Interestingly enough he married another one for repaying it.

Roman women and men were equally difficult to live with. They were known for doing politics. They ran wilde. In Reay Tannahill's view, "Roman history is full of the names of strong-minded women. There was Sempronia, who was said to be involved in the Catiline conspiracy of the first century BC. There was Cornelia, the high-minded wife of Pompey, and the rather less high-minded Praecia, who was thought to be all-powerful by reason of the influence she wielded over her lover. Cornelia, Servilia, Porcia were great ladies. In later times, Augustus' consort, Livia, helped to stabilise a new order which was promptly to be undermined by the activities of other imperial ladies, among them Julia and Julilla, Livilla, Drusilla, Poppaea, and Messalina."[12] Historians attributed Roman men's lack of enough sexuality to their addiction to drink. The next thing is hot water bath, which affected fertility.

Then came the glory of Christianity succeeding Roman splendor. In the wake of disintegration literacy rate declined. Christian fathers took its full use. Saints like Jerome, Paul and Augustine reigned supreme depreciating the beauty of earthly life with the threat of hell fire. St Paul said celibacy is better than married life; St Augustine said 'sexual intercourse is fundamentally disgusting; and Arnobius called it filthy and degrading. Methodius said it was unseemly; Jerome, unclean; Tertullian shameful; and Ambrosia a defilement. In fact, they wished that god should have endowed man with a better way for procreation. The clerical celibacy came into existence in spite of Germans' protest that they would give up their lives but not their wives. Sexual activities were not curtailed. Evidently, Liege, a bishop in the thirteenth century fathered 65 illegitimate children. However, priests thought "One marriage, it claimed, should supply enough companionship for any man; second marriages were adultery, third fornication, and fourth nothing short of 'swinish."[13]

Though not very often some rigid theologians recommended abstention on Thursdays, in memory of Christ's arrest; Fridays, in memory of his death; Saturdays, in honour of the Virgin Mary; Sundays, in honour of the Resurrection and Mondays, in commemoration of the departed. Tuesdays and Wednesdays were largely accounted for by a ban on intercourse during fasts and festivals—the forty days before Easter, Pentecost and Christmas; the seven, five, or three days before Communion; and so on.

Consequently the role of woman in society did not improve. "Woman," St Peter said, "must live spiritually." St Paul said, "she is created for the benefit of man and must defer to him in all things." They thought every seductive woman was a threat to male salvation. Natural beauty was thought to be dangerous.

Clement of Alexandria summed up the attitude of early church when he said that "woman was man's equal in everything, but that men were always better than women at everything."[14]

Even for emission of semen, in proportion to the mode of it, fasting as punishment was imposed. The minor felony of a kiss? Or full-scale sodomy, "a vice so abominable in the sight of God," said Pope Gregory III, "that the cities in which its practitioners dwelt were appointed for destruction by fire and brimstone."[15]

At the same time ban came on anal and oral sex intercourse. Sodomy too. No two priests or nuns were allowed to sleep on a single bed and light burned the whole night. The king added a punishment of castration for those who committed sodomy. Besides:

> Kissing offenders under 20 years of age were to do special fasts,
> Mutual masturbation doers 20 or 40 days' of penance,
> Interfemoral connection doers a penance of two years,
> Fellatio(oral intercourse) doers a penance of four years,
> Sodomy (anal intercourse) doers seven years penance

Sins against nature such as interfemoral connection, fellatio, sodomy, adultery, contraception, abortion, infanticide, zoophilia, homo-hetro sexual and masturbation were dealt with severity.

Other societies had ventured to suggest suitable frequencies for marital intercourse. "Three times a month," said Solon. "Everyday for the unemployed," said the Jewish drivers." The Church said never, unless children were the objects.

In Asia, as in the west, man was dominant. But sex in Asia was a pattern of life. Asiatic gurus advocated more use of sex for greater enlightenment. Chinese held the view that the more women with whom man has intercourse, the greater will be the benefit he derives from the act. The Chinese yin-yang harmony stands for intercourse. They aspired for immortality and immortality for them was in the Taoist programme of regular exercise, balanced diet, good breath control, sun therapy and a full sex life. A good Chine thought sex was a sacred duty and supreme path, the way to Tao.

Since sex was a highway for heaven, man-woman harmony became essential for the Chinese. Even man and woman gave up to each other before wedding. Han Dynasty (200 BC) manuals for bedchamber activity are well-known. These sex handbooks are about how to treat sex and its cosmic significance. These descriptions of the act were a cure for various infirmities including 'hundred sorrows.' Taoism believed that a man's mind grew restive if he were deprived of sex. They wished yin nourishment from many women leading to polygamy. Nay to a Taoist secret cult of promiscuous sex was a highway to eternity. Bisexuality too existed creating hermaphrodites.

The Chines, as their brethren in Greece, Arabia and India, used stimulants like onions, eggs, honey, mussels, crabs and snails. They believed by eating deer horn potion or bald chicken drug three times daily and for 60 days, a man can satisfy 40 women. A medical Chines civil official by doing so sired three sons after the age of 70. Even mechanical aids to sexual satisfaction like that of Rin-no-tama or Burmese Bell, as attested by Nicolo Conti in China refered to bedchamber. Confucius contributed a lot to Chine concept of night pleasure. He advocated a family life and said woman must be 'gentle, sedate, chaste and orderly' (all wifely virtues). Confucians were against women participation in state. Chinese were polygamous and an average Chine lived with at least ten women. When he married one, all came with her, specially her sisters and nurses becoming his wives.

It must be thought that polygamy did not pay way for prostitution to flourish. But it did in China. *Wa-she*, cheap houses: 'wine houses' with cheerful, handsome, well-dressed girls were expensive; and singsong houses were the three types of brothels. Though a middle-class Chine had a provision to have three to thirty women in any category, he went to concubines not for lust but for rest from home rivalry. Or polygamy oppressed him though he tried to maintain harmony and happiness in his women's quarters. But once the Mongolian king Changish Khan invaded China and his soldiers started raping Chine women, Chinese retrained many of their sex activities and had punishments for the sins.

India just like China, enjoyed the same status of sex. *Kamasutra*, written by Vatsyayana, a-man-about-the-town guided people for safer and pleasurable sex. Hindus' Four Aims included *Dharma*, *Artha*, *Kama* and *Moksha*. Sex for Hindu Indian was a religious duty—least taxing. Hindus knew a good deal about human nature and recognised that emotional starvation was a poor foundation for spirituality. *Kamasutra* is a literature of love, but not of bawdy as that of it in Greece, Rome and Egypt. Love, accordingly, is a chemical reaction between man and woman that can obsess the mind and nerves of the lover to the exclusion of all else. Vatsayana says 'one must marry no other but the one whom s\he loves.'

Indian sex is jet set. Gupta time was not only private and personal, but also open and enjoyable. Vatsyayana set a variety of congress for lovers that included bites, kisses, orality, moving, embracing. This sex was more of acrobatic in design and mechanical aids for those whose penis and vagina did not match were duly used as in China, Burma and Siam. Since sex was the Third Aim, Indians did not hide any of it. Honey, ghee, rock salt etc stimulated them for carnality.

Indians married their women before they reached puberty. The reasons were that: unmarried women were liability, they would become libidinous and they were in shortage. Central Asian invasions increased this tendency. Rich and royal practised polygamy, and women in Malabar and Kashmire practised polyandry. A husband who was sterile could do what then men of Sparta had once done, and "transfer his conjugal rights temporarily to one sexually stronger, from which he could expect beautiful and vigorous children, without the marriage thereby being upset."[16] Draupadi of the epic *Mahabharata* is an example.

Indian sexuality in architecture, otherwise known as *maithuna*, is seen in thousands of temples. Go to the temples of Kailashanath, Konark and Khujurao, you will find the depiction of eroticism and sexual mysticism. The very Vedic god Shiva and his consort Parvati are the fertility gods being worshipped as lingam (penis) and vagina.

Sexual cult of Tantra began in the beginning of Christian era whereby besetting sexualists with numerous rites just for joy. Tantra promised bliss and release in a single lifetime. If we call the world an expression of divinity sex may be used fully and *dakinis* and *sadhaks* (Tantricists) did it indeed.

The Arabs not less than their Greek brethren, kept their women at home. Still Arabia is the last bastion of female subservience. As the sixth century Arab historian Ghazali says, 'women were confined to veil and home, did not bring trials, misfortunes and woes to their men. Arabia had its own schools of love. Even love songs. Muslims did know the difference between love that related to mind and sex to the body: 'Pure love' they had. Kings had grand seraglio and chiefs their herems. Eunuchs served at both. Ssu-ma ch'ien (145-c. 90 BC) a grand historian of the Hun court and the great French logician and teacher, Peter Abelard (AD 1079-1142) were two great eunuchs. According to them, in spite of strict guarding, more bastards than legitimate heirs were born. For instance, of the 38 Abbasid Caliphs who ruled Islam in the early medieval period, 35 were the sons of foreign slave girls.

The Arabian concept of pure love through Spain percolated into Europe. This was to blend morality and motherliness into a new image of the 'the angel of the house.' Gradually woman became a lady and joined the human race. Now she was no more the architect of man. Fashions arose in medieval times drab tones giving way to bright, short robes to long, as dull foods to spicy. Tastes, though irrational and erratic, turned attractive. Guilhem, a French sardar and his daughter Eleneor, both in royal positions, argued that "Love was not an abasement but an exaltation, not a sordid sin but a divine mystery, and the lady within whose gift it lay was a goddess to be adored."[17]

Love then understood, as a gift, freely given. This made lower men struggle to become worthy of rich ladies. Jongleur, singers of courtly love allegorised this throughout Europe. Guillaume de Lorris and Jean de Menu's *Roman de la Rose* narrate these intricacies. So lady as so became an icon coloured by man to suit his own aspirations. Prime of this was shown in the sudden expansion of Mariolatry and Magdalene's upgradation. During this time strange things like incubi and succubus got heard. In these cases, some demons came to man or woman and copulated with them nightly without awakening the other spouse in beds. Bernard of Claivaux, a French bishop stopped it however. Thomas Acquinas convinced that demons even impregnated women. No doubt, they had fantasies about these demons as ugly, sharp-tongued, tall spread. The pure love concept was always studded with the chastity belt, mostly to avoid women from lascivious thoughts.

Prostitution existed in Europe all the while. Even St Augustine said that, though the institution was sordid, immodest, and shameful, "yet remove prostitutes from human affairs, and you will pollute all things with lust; set them among honest matrons, and you will dishonour all things with disgrace and turpitude." Thomas Acquinas added his mite by comparing prostitution with "the filth in the sea or the sewer in a palace. Take away the sewer, and you will fill the world, and you will fill it with sodomy." So the Church took out shares in the business and "gathered the girls tidily under its soutane."[18]

What not? Even Asian temple prostitution was introduced at places like Avignon and later in the Eternal City itself. The number of public women in Rome in 1490 was 7,000; 11,654 out of 30,000 were prostitutes in Venice. The famous prostitutes Veronica Franco asked five crowns for a kiss and 50 for sleeping. Tullia d' Aragona took 100 for a client. Their single kiss or sleeping cost as much as what a domestic servant earned for a year.

America—Latin or un-Latin, though separated from Europe not only by 5,000 miles of distance, but also by well over 2,000 years of technical sophistication, vied with its sex ably. The Aztecs in Mexico, Incas in Peru and Mayans of Yucatan, all, in spite of their cannibalism and human sacrifice indulged in all sorts of sex. The Spaniards who migrated there later not only to rule but to settle down, through cross breeding, created a whole race of mestizos (like Mesticos in Gao) in central and southern America. There were even both men and women zoophiliacs—with jaguar, dog, cormorants. Worst still in some cases men married woman officially only after testing them. Like Muslims in East, a widow in Inca married her brother-in-law and many times, eldest sons took care of their father's secondary wive. . They practised polygamy because, because of human sacrifice (700 people a day) population disappeared as fast as water down the drain. It is said one king Texcoco had 2000 concubines, but he begot only 144 children—a low result.

Centuries later when Portuguese came to Goa, they with their crossbreeding and Christian values, ruthlessly changed the face of Hinduism itself. But most of the Europeans, unlike Muslims who came with a one-way ticket and they carried the image of 'home,' came to India as transients—there to fight, to trade and to rule—but not to settle down. Their way of life, cast of thought and the shade of civilisation can be seen in Eurasians—a crossbreed class—almost casteless. They were rough, ruthless and wholly self-seeking.

The Chinese in late modern times, or in the colonial period thought that sex is a means for longevity and wisdom. Accordingly sex became not a sin but a duty, and their Far Eastern brethren in Japan carried Chinese tradition of sex further.

The early modern Europe by means of its discoveries found that sex in desperate forms remained. For example, illegitimate deliveries continued. Footloose workers as well as the rich produced illegitimate. Interestingly 10 per cent of births in Dover of 1975 were illegitimate and 40 per cent of the born in Paris were left at foundlings. Rousseau was not able to upbring his five children.

What more even there are zoophilias. Thomas Granger of Duxbury abused a mare, a cow, two goats, five sheep, two calves and a turkey. Soon came condoms. Initially Fallopius of France discovered an animal's skin safe against syphilis. Improved version of this proved a shelter for ladies against the fear of conception. The whole sex life those days was beset by worries.

Marquis de Sade, a French nobleman who gave his name to the sexual perversion known as sadism, in fact, wrote novels like that of Richardson's. Sade feels virtue leads to misery and ruin and vice to prosperity—the view leftists uphold today. Soon came semen theories and one of them held that semen of man is more instrumental than woman in procreation; and according to another, masturbation led to imbecility.

Sex in modern Europe assured quite a many intricate shapes creating peculiar situations both for men and women. Europeans, these days, did their best with or without the sex capital. So were American cities. In Cincinnati, there were 7,000 prostitutes in a population of 200,000 in 1869. London had 50,000. Demimondaines and dollymops (both part times and ameturists) came into existence. Women like Cora Pearl (earned 5000 Franks a night) and La Paiva (whom even kings approached) throve. Erotic periodicals like *The Exquisite*, or *Pall Mall Gazette* became guidebooks. This trade in sin endowed people with venereal diseases and it was only the godly that triumphed.

An interesting consequence of pre-aids diseases era was an increase in people's demand for virgins. This is recorded as far back as Sumerian times. One episode in the epic of Gilgamesh refers to the annoyance of the people of Uruk over their king's insistence of demanding virgins. They have a common saying 'to be first with the bride, the king to be the first; and the husband to follow.'[19] Virginity is still important. In 1978, continuing to put price tag on it, an Athens court awarded 350,000 drachmae (5,000 pounds) to the parents of a 16-year-old girl who had been seduced by her foreign language teacher. Even in today's India we see politicians using most virgins. Most virgins have a tab membrane and this is cut bleeding when first man sleeps with her. Interestingly, this cut membrane can be undone by an operation. The modern Japani girls first lose that tab for 'a golden guinea' and then they need it for marrying, and 80 per cent of men demand virgins, they get it in an operation. Equally interesting is the fact that male prostitution came into being in Paris and London hubs. They wore women's dress. Oxford and Cambridge boys have homosexuality even today. Not less interesting, even appalling is the on-going of sadism and masochism. Sade, the French created the first, whereas the second, an Austrian psychiatrist, Richard Ebing created it referring to his friend Sacher-Masoch's life and literature. Masochism refers to women's inflicting pain on men. Examples of such ladies include Queen of Sheba. A.C. Swinburne and Oscar Wilde, as much as the French Taine and Thephile Gautier have been associated with these concepts.

No issue is as controversial as that of sex in modern world. It is a matter of great debate even today as men do not want their women take part in their whisky-and-cigar-politics. But owing to feminist efforts made by women like Mrs Humphrey Ward, Catherine Beecher, Emmeline Pankhurst, France Willard and Susan Anthony women got voting and other democratic rights. They thought anything men could do they could do better as it is come true today. By 1920, Britain and America, and many more gave equality to women. Marriage habits with male supremacy of 5,000 years broke down soon. What more the conventional baby boom or man-woman relations for children's sake crumbled. Shock came after shocks.

Eighty per cent of European male against 20 per cent of females started experiencing sex before marriage, and before 19. Today children are rebelling against sexual orthodoxy of their parents. In the 1970s, America witnessed one divorce to every two and now every one is divorcing and remarrying—not only once but many times. Birth control by pills, mensingha diaphragm, IUD (intrauterine device), vasectomy and injections have fecilitated men for making love—ideal, risk-free and foolproof. Even Oneida Communities where one can sleep with any are coming up.

We know the people of medieval Europe had 12 generations during which to adjust to the idea that women were worthy of sex and the Victorians three generations to accept that they were worthy of vote. But modern world took only a decade to acquire sexual independence. Today due to dozen of sex evils people across the globe are getting confusion. Because sex once a concern of bedtime and darkness is openly used now.

References

1. Reay Tannahill, *Sex in History*, Book Club Association, London, 1980, p. 65.
2. Josephus, qt by Reay Tannahill, *op.cit.,* p. 70
3. Reay Tannahill, op.cit., p. 73
4. *Book of Genesis*, qt by Reay Tannahill, *Sex in History*, p. 74
5. Darlington, C. D., *The Evolution of Man and Society*, London, 1969, pp. 118-119.
6. Reay Tannahill, *Sex in History*, p. 79.
7. *The Bible*, The King James' Version, pp. 10-12.
8. Demothenes, *In Neaeram*, p. 122.
9. *Lucian, Dialogues of Courtesans*, p 102.
10. Alciphron, *Letters of Courtesans,* p. 140.
11. Juvenal, *Sixth Satire* 1-11, p. 127.
12. Reay Tannahill, op.cit., pp. 123-124.
13. Ibid., p. 145.
14. Clement of Alexandria, *Paidagogos* I 4.
15. Judicia Greg. *Pap*. III 21.
16. *Reay Tannahill*, op.cit., p. 215
17. *Reay Tannahill*, op.cit., p. 263.
18. *Reay Tannahill*, op.cit., pp. 278-9.
19. *Reay Tannahill*, op.cit., p. 370.

16

Greek Mythologies

Man is a social and rational being. Intellect is the gift of human race. Man has his own aims and objectives in the world. But in the absence of any certainties he feels vulnerable. So he desired to have his own realities. Myth is exactly that which has emerged as man's personal truth. Myth is a man-made narration that informs us about an older order of the world. And there are as many myths as many civilisations. Though myths are *myths* they are not just fairy tales. For example, Greek mythology is a representation of certain far-off periods and it helps us fill in the gap in history, indicating the level of Greek culture. Greek myth tells the life of a certain number of people in the remote corner of the world, many centuries before Christ, that they built cities, subdued natural forces and foreign nations, set off to unknown parts, founded colonies and led art to great heights.

When historians excavated at Troy and Mycenae, they discovered that there lived historical people, with their cultural magnificence, and fought great battles, all before 1200 BC! The Troy of Priam, Mycenaeans with its richness, with its tombs of Atreas and his son Agamemnon, laden with gold came to light. Oh! Such rich Greek mythology has enriched the western world.

The Creation of the Gods

The Greeks deified many abstract concepts, elements of nature and all amazing things. They called Mother Earth as the goddess force, associating it with fertility cult. So out of Chaos arose Erebus and Night. These two created Air, Day, Death, Sleep, Dreams, Fates, Hesperides and Eris. The Mother Earth and Father Sky, as the first divine couple, gave birth to Titans—Oceanus, Tethys, Hyperion, Theia, Coeus, Phoebe, Creius, Iapetus, Cronus and Rhea. Cronus married his sister Rhea and gave birth to Zeus. There was a war between Zeus's forces called Olympians and the older Titans. Zeus won the battle and he punished Atlas by entrusting the task of holding the earth aloft, for he sided with the Titans. The defeat of the Titans pained the Mother Earth and she gave birth to the Giants. So the Titans with the help of Giants led a battle against the Olympian gods. Heracles and Athena (Zeus's daughter) killed the enemies. When there was peace, Zeus ordered Prometheus and Epimetheus, the sons of Titan Iapetus, to endow the creatures of the earth with gifts and powers. Epimetheus bestowed beauty on one animal and strength on another, without keeping anything for man. But Prometheus helped man with fire which he stole from the heaven. So Zeus chained him for this. Only later Heracles released Prometheus from his terrible ordeal.

One day Hephaestus, the smith, the god of fire, sculpted a statue. Zeus loved it and gave it life. So it became Pandora, a beautiful goddess. Zeus gifted her to Epimetheus. Zeus gave her a gift of magical box, asking her not to open it. Yet as a woman of curiosity Pandora opened it. The result: out flew the miseries and misfortunes, which afflict humanity today. Oh! Hopes also flew out. Later man turned evil and Zeus decided to punish him with flood. Yet to help posterity he created Deucalion and Pyrreha who survived the flood. When they started life afresh and began to walk forward, dropping stones, the latter turned into men. Deucalion and Pyrrha also delivered children and of them the first-born was Hellen, the forefather of the Hellenes (Greeks).

The ancient people, just for wish fulfilment involved with gods. Such gods kept a company in their daily lives and sided with their problems. They regulated their fortunes and even punished them for their sins. Of course, some gods were carefree and fun-loving.

After gaining power over the earth and heaven, the twelve gods of Olympus shared out responsibilities and posts amongst themselves in accordance with the wishes of Zeus. They lived on the Mt Olympus, and mingled with human beings and had affairs with them. They ate ambrosia and drank nectar. Such great Olympian gods are Zeus, Hera, Athena, Poseidon, Demeter, Apollo, Artemis, Hermes, Ares, Aphrodite, Hephaestus and Hestia.

Zeus is the lord of heaven and earth, and father of gods and humans. Thunderbolt is his weapon. Hera is his perpetual wife. Are, Hebe, Eliethia and Hephaestus are their offspring. Hera is the patron goddess of the family and married women. She punished infidelity. Zeus is great. He had affairs with others. He married Europa and begot the legendary Minos, the brave Sarpedon and the just Radmanthys. Zeus had a union with Metis, daughter of Oceanus and Thithys. Athena was the first daughter. She did not marry. She is known as the goddess of wisdom. She helped heroes such as Perseus, Achilles and Odysseus. She is the patron of the city of Athens.

Poseidon is the god of the sea. He is known as 'Girder of the World.' He has affairs with goddesses and human beings and had children. They (with their mothers in brackets) were: Triton (Aphrodite), Polyphemus (Thoosa), Antaeus (mother earth) and others.

Apollo (Phoebus) is the god of light, music and prophecy. Apollo and his sister Artemis (who like Athena remained a spinster) belonged to the second generation of Olympian gods. Apollo was handsome; he was a god of war. His sister is a goddess of the hunt. She was a vengeful deity. Zeus's another wife was Demeter known as goddess of agriculture. Persephone was her daughter. Pluto abducted her once and made her his wife. But Demeter when in search of her starved the world. After an agreement she was to stay with Pluto for four months. So the earth remains barren for those four months.

Zeus's love for Dione gave birth to Aphrodite. Aphrodite (Venus) is the goddess of beauty and love. She married the lame god Hephaestus. Her affair with Ares brought four children — Eros, Deimus, Phobus and Harmony. Zeus with his union with

Maia had Hermes. Hermes was the god of commerce and prophecy. He was the herald of gods.

Zeus out of his union with Hera had Ares, the god of war. His union with Aphrodite gave birth to Cycnus, Diomedes of Thrace (the owner of man-eating horses), Lycaons, Melegar, Dryas and Oenomaos. Hephaestus, a son of Zeus and Hera, was the god of fire. He made Achilles's armour. He was lame. Though he was ugly he was found in the company of beautiful women Chare and Aglaea. Hestia, the elder daughter of Cronus and Rhea was the personification of the family home.

Besides the twelve Olympian gods, there were others. The difference between the two is that the other gods were born to gods and mortals and they did not stay in Olympia. They are often identified with man's way of life.

Gods played with the fate of mortals. They fell in love with them or sided with them when in battles. For example Semele, with Zeus gave birth to Dionysus, god of wine and gaiety. Yet he was born in a different way as 'thigh-born.' He spread the culture of wine and gaiety. The Dionysian cult is associated with wine and dance. The orgies included holy works. His company had nymphs, Sileni, Satyrs and Maenads.

Asclepius, the son of Apollo by Cronis, was the god of medicine. His wife was Epione and he had sons like Podaleirus and Machaon, both physicians, and five daughters Aceso, Iaso, Panacea, Aegle and Hygeia. His descendents the Asclepiads (for ex: Hipocrates) continued the art of medicine.

Iris, the descendent of Oceanus, was the messenger of the gods. Helios, the god of light descended from Uranus and Mother Earth. Hades (Pluto), the brother of Zeus, Poseidon and Hera ruled the underworld. He was harsh and ruthless. His servants (devils) like Charon took souls across the river Archeron. Priapus was the god of fertility. He had a large penis like Jokumar in India. Pan is the god of forests. He lived a bucolic life and he was sexy. He was with Dionysus. Eros was the son of Aphrodite. He was the darling of artists. Themis, the goddess of justice looked after moral order among the gods and men. She was the daughter of Uranus and Mother Earth. Her union with Zeus produced Horace, Eunomia, Dice and

Eirene, each representing a virtue. When Cronus mutilated the sky the dripped blood gave birth to the Erinnyes (the Furies) which control man's conscience.

Sea divinities included Nireas, Proteus, Triton and Glaucus. Other lessor gods are the personifications of abstract concepts. Eris (the goddess of discord), Hebe (Heracles's wife), Peitho, Nemesis, Thanatos (Death) whom Sisyphus outwitted), Anagi (Need) and Iacchus did lots of work in Greek mythology.

The Heroes

When bad times or devils harassed man, demi-gods helped him. They protected the heroes. Sometimes they appear as enlightened (Odysseus) and Robust (Heracles, fighting to make sure that the good prevails). They took dangerous expeditions either to protect a prince, or fulfill a moral obligation, and gods protected them. Such heroes are glorified.

Heracles was a demi-god, endowed with supernatural gift (also with weakness). He was born in Thebes to Amphitryon (actually Zeus in disguise) and Alcemene. He married Megara, the daughter of Creon, king of Thebes. He killed his own children, and for the expeation of sin, when he was to serve king Eurystheus he was given 12 labours. So he killed the Lion of Nemea and the Lernaean Hydra; he caught the Hind of Cernyeia, trapped the Boar of Erymanthus, exterminated the Stymphalian birds, cleaned the Augean stables, tamed the Horses of Diomedes, and brought the Cretan Bulls alive. He took Hippolyta's girdle for Admete, brought the Oxen of Geryon, collected the golden apples of the Hesperides and brought the dog of the underworld. All for Eurysthenes. Heracles accomplished many more feats. He died because of his underworld wife Deianeira's fault and joined the immortals on Olympia. He married Hebe, the goddess of eternal youth. The Dorians worship him.

Theseus was the hero of Athens. He was born to Aegeas, the king of Athens and his mother was Aethra, daughter of king Pittheus of Troezen. He was left with his mother when youth. Later he went to his father, killing robbers like Periphetes, Pityocamptes, Sciron and Procrustes on the way. Aegeas recognied him and drove away his another wife Medea, the sorcerer. Later Theseus was sent to Crete to kill Minotaur, a monster bull fed on human body. Minos, the king had kept it. Theseus killed the bull, and sailed home with Minos's daughter Ariadne. He forgot to use white sails, as he was victorious. His father Aegeas misunderstood that his son had died and threw himself in the sea. That part of the ocean is called the Aegean Sea today.

Theseus proved an able king of Athens. He ruled happily. He married Phaedra. He accomplished great feats. Lycomedes killed him at Skyros treacherously. His remains were buried in Athens.

The Voyage of the Argonauts

We know the campaign of the Greeks to Colchis under the leadership of Jason. The background for the campaign is as follows. Athamas, the king of Orchomenos in Boeotia had two children by his wife Nephele: Phrixus and Helle. But Ino seduced the king and remained his beloved. She created famine. She manipulated a Delphi oracle to say that Phrixas must be sacrificed. But Nephele sent a golden ram and it took her two children away. When in journey Helles fell down in the sea and the water area is known as Hellespont. Phrixis reached Colchis and sacrificed the ram. He gave king Aeetes the fleece. Pelias, the king of Iolkos who had usurped the throne from his half-brother Aeson, told Aeson's son Jason to bring the Golden Fleece if he wanted his father's throne. Jason's ship (Argos meaning quick) had great youths of his time called Argonauts. They do many adventures before they reach Aeetes. In spite of Aeetes' mischief Jason returned with the Golden Fleece. Despite Pelias' callousness Jason ruled in his land. Goddess Media helped him.

Perseus, the son of Zeus and Danae did many adventures. He brought king Polydectes, the head of Medusa, the Gorgon. With this head he turned Polydectes into stone, married Andromedia, and returned to Argos, his native island.

Bellerophon, the son of Sisyphus (actually of god Poseidon and Eurynome) killed tyrant Bellerus, Chimera and fought

Solymi and Amazons. So Iobates, the brother of Proetus who risked his life married his daughter to him and left him his kingdom.

Daedalus was a great craftsman belonging to the royal family of Cecrops, the first king of Athens. He did a crime and exiled to king Minos of Crete where he had to work. He constructed the Labyrinth where Minos kept Minotaur which Theseus killed. The king who knew Daedalus's breach of secracy that he told Theseus, the secret of the monster kept Daedalus and his son Icarious in the Labyrinth. The architects made wings of wax for them and flew out to Crete. But Icarious flew high and the sunlight melted his wings. So he fell down into sea. That sea is known as Icarian Sea.

Orpheus was well-known as a musician. He was the son of Ocagrus and Calliope. He loved Eurydice and when she died of snakebite, he went to Hades to bring her back. As his music charmed, Hades and Persephone agreed to send her with him with a condition that he should not look back till he reached the earth. But he looked back and lost his beloved. Since then Orpheus scorned women, living on music. He discovered Cithara, the ancient guitar.

Oedipus belonged to the royal house of Labdacids. Liaus, the king of Thebes, married Jocasta and had no sons. The oracle said that he would have a son but the latter would kill him. Yet Jocasta slept with him and had a son. Liaus fierced his leg, chained him and sent him for discarding. The guards, because of pity, gave the child to traders who took it to their king Polybus of Corinth. Queen Merope named it Oedipus (swollen footed) and reared.

So fate had it that Oedipus lived. He grew strong. Once he was insulted when somebody said he was not Polybus's son. His parents did not tell him anything about it. So he set to learn the truth of it from Delpic oracles. The oracles said that he would kill his father, marry his mother and his descendents would suffer. Still he believed Polybus to be his father and to stay away from the calamity, he stayed away from Corinth. He wandered making feats. Once he travelled in Phocis and met a royal entourage in which king Liaus was going to Delphi to know about his son. A silly encounter made Oedipus kill all of them except a soldier who slipped away.

At Thebes, Creon, Jocasta's brother, ruled afterwards. But before they could begin searching for the murderer, the terror of the Sphinx engulfed the city. This monster sat on a rock at the edge of Thebes and asked passersby a riddle and since none of them could solve it, the Sphinx devoured them. Creon announced that anyone who could solve the riddle and rid Thebes of the terrible monster would become the king and marry the queen. Oedipus met the Sphinx and the riddle was as follows. The monster's question was: "What creature of earth is it which has four legs, three legs and two legs, and is weaker the more legs it has?" Oedipus solved the problem, replying that the creature is man, who crawls on all fours as a baby, walks on two legs when he is grown, and rests on a third leg – a walking-stick—when he becomes old.

This made Oedipus the king of Thebes. He married Jocasta. He produced four children; Eteocles, Polynices, Antigone and Ismane. He rued in peace. But an epidemic broke and oracle said it would not go until Laius's murderer is driven out. Tiresius revealed the truth that Oedipus killed his father. So Oedipus left his kingdom entrusting it to Creon. The latter looked after his daughters.

Pelopides—The Family of the Atreids

Pelops and Hippodameia were the parents of Atreus, Thyestes, Pleisthenes, Pittheus (grandfather of Theseus) and Niceppe (mother of Eurystheus, uncle of Heracles). After the death of Eurystheus, who had succeeded to the throne of his father Sthenelus, the Pelopids became much more powerful and ruled in Mycenae, Tiryns, Argos and the Argolid. According to one version of the story, Pelops passed on the sceptre of power to Atreus, his first-born. After their father's death, Atreus's sons Agamemnon and Menelaus took refuge in Sikyon. At some later date, Tyndareus, father of Castor and Pollux, Clytemnestra and Helen, helped Agamemnon to regain the throne which was his by right. Thyestes who reigned during that period and his son Aegisthus were exiled, and Agamemnon took Clytemnestra as his wife—after she had killed Tantalus, her first husband (who was also a son of Thyestes). Agamemnon and Clytemnestra had three daughters—Iphigenia, Electra and Chysothemis—and one son, Orestes. Menelaus married the beautiful Helen and ruled in Sparta.

The Iliad

The Trojan campaign which complicated Greek history lasted for ten years, culminating in the death of great heroes. The Achaeans and the Aeolians, Greeks from continental Greece, laid siege to and defeated the Trojans (Greeks from Asia Minor). Myth relates that the war was fought for the sake of Helen. Yet it is not myth as Troy is discovered. The Achaeans with Aeolians had an army of 1,00,000 soldiers and a fleet of 2000 ships, while the Trojans had their own allies. Achilles was the dominant figure of *The Iliad* and others are Agamemnon, Odysseus, Hector, Paris and Menelaus. Historians believe the Greeks spread far and wide as they had shortage of lands in 1100 BC. The war began from the wedding feast of Pelius (king of Phthia) and Thetis (sea goddess). One goddess Eris who did not attend the occasion, in anger tossed a golden apple in front of Hera, Athena and Aphrodite, all goddesses. All claimed it. While far away stood Troy's king Priam's son Paris tending his flocks. Zeus asked Paris to judge which goddess should get it. Then all the goddesses tempted him: Hera, with rule over Asia and Europe, Athena with heroism and victory; and Aphrodite with love, in the person of comely Helen. Paris, who aspired for Helen awarded the apple to Aphrodite. The other goddesses as they were angry supported the Achaeans against the Trojans. Aphrodite advised Paris to get Helen. The union of Pelius and Thetis produced Achilles. Thetis desired to make her son become strong and she dipped him into Styx, holding him from heel. So his heel became weak as known in the phrase 'Achilles' heel.'

The fort of Troy stood on Mt Ida, ruled by its founder Laomedon's son Priam (Paris's father). Priam's wife was Hacuba. Priam's sister Hessione had two sons Teucrus and Ajax, both fought in the war of Troy. Priam had 50 sons and countless daughters. His first-born son was Hector, followed by Paris, Deiphobus, Helen, Polydorus and Troilus; the best-known of his daughters were Creousa, Laodice, Polyxene and Cassandra, who was gifted with the power of divination.

As we know Agamemnon was the king of Mycenae and his brother Menelaus of Sparta. Paris visited him and even tempted Helen. He had a power to tempt her in disguise. So they eloped to Troy and got married. Messenger Iris briefed it to Menelaus. So all Greek heroes, as a matter of honor, united to fight for Helen. Thus the insult which Paris offered Menelaus had to be taken as a personal affront. Odysseus, son of Laertes and king of Ithaca, was one of the men who participated in the campaign, along with Achilles, the king of Phthia, the wise Nestor, king of Pylos, Diomedes, the hero of Aetolia, Ajax, the Telamonian, Ajax the Lorcian, Idas, king of Crete, the wise Palamides and Idomeneus. Once Iphigenia was sacrificed at Aulis, the Achaeans sailed to Troy.

The Trojan War began as is narrated in Homer's *Iliad.* Soon the first Achaean hero Protesilans died in the battle of Ilim (Troy). During the first nine years, Achilles, the greatest Greek hero, killed lots of Trojans and presented their women to Agamemnon, the commander-in-chief. He kept slaves like Breseis and Diomede for himself. He offered Chryseida to Agamemnon. But Chryseida's father, the priest of Apollo came to buy her back. Agamemnon refused the idea. So Apollo troubled the Achaeans. Finally Agamemnon gave up Chryseida and seized Achilles' beloved Breseis as compensation. Now sad Achilles with his Myrmidons stopped fighting while the Trojans decimated them. After a heavy loss Achilles' friend Patrocles in Achilles' disguise fought the Trojans. Apollo told it to Hector and the latter killed Patroclus. So Achilles scornful about Patroclus's death began taking revenge against the Trojans. He killed Hector. However, Apollo told the secret of Achilles' heel and Paris aimed at him. That was a fatal blow. So Achilles fell. Thetis and Nereids undertook the funeral ceremony. He was buried honorably. Paris did not enjoy the fruits of his feat for long. Death overtook him at the hands of Philoctetes, who thus avenged the death of Achilles and the insult which the rape of Helen had meant for the Greeks.

Afterwards, because of Odysseus's tricks, a wooden horse was taken to the gate of Troy. The Trojans feared of it. Still they mistook it for Athena's gift and towed it inside. Once it was night Odysseus and his crew got out, opened the gate of Troy. The Achaean army decimated the Trojans to death. Odysseus slew Priam. All of his kin fell down. Meanwhile, Helen had married to Priam's brother Demophobus whom Menelaus killed. Menelaus and Helen united again.

Once the war was over Menelaus and Helen returned to Sparta. Agamemnon returned to Mycenae where his bloody wife Clytemnestra, already in love with his cousin Aegisthus, killed him. Thereafter, her son Orestes killed both Aegisthus and Clytemnestra. Ajax of Locris met his end in a shipwreck, and Diomedes and Idomeneus spent years in exile in southern Italy.

The Odyssey

After *Iliad* it is *Odyssey*, very popular as an epic. It has a complex plot compared to *Iliad*. Once the war was over, Odyssey(Ulysseus or Ulixis as the Romans called him) set asail for Ithaca. But he took ten years to reach his home as he encountered setbacks. Once he set asail, due to storms, his ship was wrecked and he landed at Thrace where the Cicones lived. As they were the allies of Trojans, he looted their city Ismarus. Then he visited an island off the coast of Africa (the Land of Lotus-eaters) where some of his crew got intoxicated. Then Odyssey sailed to Sicily where the Cyclopses lived. Odyssey met their giant Polyphemus and tortured the cannibalistic monster. Then he came to the island of Aelus where he was gifted with a bag of wind. But one of his men opened it at night and they had to face troubles. The island of Circe was mysterious where Odyssey's crew experienced a transformation into swine. But when Odyssey intervened she helped him with his men, and suggested him to seek Tiresius's advice for a safe return. The Sirens were the next threat. Odyssey dealt with the Clashing Rocks and the Channel Scylla and Charybdis. The island of Thrinacia was Odyssey's next stop where his people ate the meat of forbidden oxen of the sun god. So there was, as punishment, Zeus's thunderbolt and the ensuing shipwreckage. Still Odyssey who did not eat the meat was saved and he landed the shores of Ogygia, the island of Calypso. Odyssey spent an enchanted time with Calypso (Atlas's daughter). She wanted him and did anything to keep him with her. She promised him immortality. Only due to Zeus's intervention and Hermes' help, he landed on the island of Phaeacia (Corfu). The king Alcinous gave him a royal shelter. He said he could marry his daughter Nausica. They helped him a ship for his return to Ithaca. Once he met his servant Eumeaus and son Telemachus, he planned the death of his wife's suitors. They killed the suitors. Finally there was Odyssey's reunion with his wife Penelope. *The Odyssey* is the oldest and the most reliable version of the narrative. Such an Odyssey is a mortal, everyday figure—any one—anywhere—going forward. Homer, the immortal poet from Smyrna, lived in the ninth century BC. His two epics are the finest works of literature.

17

Bijapur Sufis

In 1880 an English archeologist for the Government of India, Henry Cousens described his trip to Bijapur:

> Not many years ago the way was not altogether free from Maratha freebooters; and when the city was reached it was found a lonely and deserted extent of ruins, the haunt of the jackal, the wolf, and the hyaena and an Elysium of bats and owls. Very few families lived within the walls: it had remained a desolate waste from the time of its fall to within the last half century.[1]

Once Bijapur was the second largest and most important state of the Indian subcontinent. What strikes the visitors is the extraordinary number of tombs (around 300) scattered everywhere. As for the dargahs, they are the popular living religion. Urs ('marriage with God') are conducted there yearly and Sufis, as missionaries, are remembered.

Great scholars like A.J. Arberry, L. Miassignon and R.A. Nicholson say a Sufi is a mystic, within the framework of Islam, attempting to achieve direct communion with God. So a 'Sufi' means any person integrated into the organisational structure of the Islamic mystical tradition. This involves a spiritual allegiance going back to the Prophet Muhammad himself. Sufism as such has, as Sir T.S. Trimmingham says, three stages: *Khanaqah* stage, the *Tariqa* stage and the *Tarifa* stage. The first stage Sufis were ascetics until the twelfth century. The second stage Sufis were doctrinals, creating schools like Qadiri order founded by Abd-al-Qadir Jilani (d. 1166), the Rifai order founded by Ahmed al-Rifai (d. 1182) and the Yasavi order founded by Ahmed al-Yasai (d. 1166). *Tariqa* phase introduced specialisation and initiation. In the third phase *taifa*, *pirs* (teachers) became worshipful as if the agents between God and disciples. The *pir* cult became *pirzadas* (a hereditary privilege). Sufis power was attached to *dargahs*, their philosophy becoming devotional. Sufis turned into a popular movement, relieving people's fear and anxiety. The last phase witnessed the introduction of astrology, magic, belief in talismans and charms and other forms of superstitions. Accordingly Indian Sufism belongs to the second and third phases, of course, with some variables.

Ira Lapidaus distinguishes three types of Sufis: those who were well integrated into the social and religious world of the 'Ulama,' those who represented a fanatically puritanical element waging personal wars on vice, and their opposite, and those who represented the 'low life' of the cities.

Bijapur as a Muslim state had many facilities for the accommodation of the sufis. Although the region was a 'shatter zone,' for partly it was (is) linguistically a border and partly it was a barren land, Islam attracted the foreigners.

As for the spread of spiritualism in the region, Hindu bhakti cult rose in Tamil Nadu in the sixth century. It was the growth of an intense theism with a fervid devotion to a personal god. This contrasts with the Vedic aim of merging in the unconsciousness of the Absolute. The bhakti of the *Bhagavata Puran* focused on the deity Krishna or Rama. Its manifestations, the Vithobha cult arose (its preachers were Jnanadev and Namdev) in Maharashtra, while the Virasaivism cult arose in Karnataka. Basavanna (11th c) is credited with having opposed the Hindu caste system, Brahmin supremacy, Vedic polytheism and even authority of Vedic texts. He established Lingayat creed, opening it to all persons according absolute devotion to Shiva. This bhakti cult is Saivite. The unique feature of this is the deity is represented in the emblem of linga. Hence, the sect's name Lingayatism. The linga is the moving deity or the abode of Shiva, often serving as a social laveller, enabling the wearer, to achieve social equality. If

Marathi Vaishnavite cult used abhang for achieving religious integrity, Lingayats used vacana. Richard Maxwell Eaton calls this a 'virtual Kannada phenomenon.'[2] Unfortunately gradually older Lingayat converts began claiming superiority over the never converts, while the priestly Jangams started defining Lingayat orthodoxy. So Lingayats passed from a sect to a caste.[3] Pontiffs of the sect say this occurred in the fifteenth century. Though Jangamas achieved their superiority in the seventeenth century, Maths (monasteries) that gave spiritual guidance achieved it quite earlier. Since the sect made it compulsory that a follower must have a guru and be affiliated to a math, maths achieved prominence in all villages. So from the point of religion, Bijapur was in a fault zone as Pandarpur, the seat of Vaishnavite lay just 65 miles northwest of it and the seat of Virasaiv Kudal Sangam, thirty miles southwest of Bijapur. Sufism settled in Bijapur as a third force.

Politically Bijapur was the provincial seat of Chalukya administration first, and then of Devgiri Yadavas and the Delhi Sultans. Muslims first came to the Malabar Coast in the ninth century. An Arab traveller Masudi writes in 916 that the Arabs established a colony there soon afterwards. Ibna Batuta attested it in 1342. Naturally the Delhi Sultanate invaded Bijapur from 1296 onwards. In the next century Bijapur became a provincial seat of Delhi sultans under Karim al-Din (a mosque for him exists there). Devgiri warriors, unhappy of their loss, found a Hindu state at Kampli. Vijayanagar Empire rose up at Hampi in 1336. Bahmani Empire started at Gulbarga in 1346, allowing the Sufis settle down there.

Sufis as warriors: Sufis came to the Deccan as militant champions waging Jihad (holy wars). Md Ibrahim Zubairi's Basatin al-Salatin (1825) includes an account of the Deccan Sufis. Zubairi was a Nizam's Collector for Raichur district. Later another historian Abd al-Jabbar Mulkapuri wrote Tazkira-yi Auliya-i-Dakan in 1912. This is about Sufis lives.

The first warrior Sufi Shaikh Sufi Sarmast (d. 1281) came to Bijapur from Arabia, defeated Kumaran, a Hindu king of Sagar, seventy miles east of Bijapur in Sholapur and spread Islam. This was Islam as a religion of the sword. Md Zumairi's

Rauzat al-Auliya says Mabor Khandayat of Tamil coast accompanied Malik Kafur to Bijapur on his back home journey and remained here, spreading Islam. The *Bombay Gazetteer* says he converted to Islam a large number of Jains. Shaikh Alik Pahlavan, Sarmast's companion went to Karnool, fought a jihad and died. Shaikh Shahid (d. 1272-73) again Sarmast's follower fought at Talikot and got slain. His burial place is known as 'Gunj-i-shuhadu' ("Treasure of Martyrs'). Pir Junma (d. 1304) fought such a war but the Hindus killed him with his 50 followers. No doubt, these warrior Sufis adopted militant titles such as 'Shahid' (Martyr), 'asad al-auliya' (lion of the saints) and 'tigh barahna' (naked sword). As Sir Hamilton Gibb thinks the early Sufis warred against non-Muslims quite fanatically. This lead to the conflict between Arab Islam which is ardent, dogmatic and austere and Hinduism which is reflective, syncretic and sentimental.

The Deccanis who gave a lease of life to Sufism were of four groups: (1) the descendents of Arab traders, (2) settlers from north India, (3) the Abyssinians (Habashes), black slaves of Africa and (4) the Hindu coverts. While those recruits whom the Muslim kings brought from the Middle East became Foreigners. The Deccanis (who were Sunnis) identified with the natives and evolved a new kind of language called Dakhani, while Foreigners (who were Shia) retained their Persian. Naturally a bitter elite- non-elite cleavage persisted between the two so as to weaken the Muslim states in India. Wolsely Haig adds, "The feud thus began was not confined to intrigues for place and power, but frequently found expression in pitched battles and bloody massacres of which last the Foreigners were usually the victims."[4]

Naturally the orders of the Chishti, the Qadiri and the Shattari percolated to Bijapur as to the rest of India. Muin al-Din Chishti (d. 1236) initiated the Chishti order and, after the spread of Islam, he died at Ajmer in Rajasthan. Ajmer is the holy center of the Chishtis today. Chishtis were ascetics. One of the followers says, "I have two doors. If the Sultan comes through one door, I will leave by the other." Chishtis used to have music and dance for spiritual ecstasy. They said, "All is

He," clashing with Koranic theology "all is from Him." So they had conflicts with the Ulama. They, in accordance with Spanish Sufi Ibn Arabi, remained isolated devoting to "spiritual splendour and concentration on the individual soul."[5] Md bin-Tughlaq did not like the Chishtis and in the name of shifting his capital from Delhi to Devgiri ordered them to move to the south. So their khanaqah were destroyed.

True Delhi's loss was Deccan's gain. When the Bahmani Empire started at Gulbarga, many Sufis migrated there befriending the men in power. The first Sufi in Bahmani then was Shaikh Siraj al-Din Junaidi (d. 1380) who settled down in Bijapur in 1330. Saiyad Muhammad Husaini Bandanawaz Gisudaraz (d. 1422) was the next prominent Sufi in Gulbarga. He came to Devgiri with Md Tughlaq and went back to Delhi again, but when Timur's invasion became sure, he left for Gulbarga. He played a key role in the Bahmani court. Whereas as he gained courtly support, he became orthodoxical, launching his tirade against Ibn Arab, Persian Sufis Farid al-Din Attar and Jalal al-Din Rumi calling them the enemies of Islam. No Sufis succeeded Bande Nawaz and when Gulbarga kings shifted their capital to Bidar, Sultan Ahmad built a dargah over the grave of Gisudaraz. Shortly as Trimmingham says, the institution of the Sufis (*Tariqa*) were replaced by the institutions of the dargahs (*Taifa* phase). This is the end of living Sufism in Gulbarga. Whereas Sufis in Bijapur maintained safe physical distance from state politics. The Qadiri Sufi order came to the Deccan in the fifteenth century. It was a pan-Islamic order, its center being Baghad, where its founder Abd al-Qadir Jilani taught and died (d.1166). If Ajmer was the holy land for the Chishtis, Qadiris' interest lay in the Arab world for spiritual nourishment. Secondly the Qadiris followed orthodoxical Islam. Thirdly they had an urban orientation.

The change of capital also meant the change of Sufi order in the Bahmani empire. Gisudaraz died in the year 1422 when the Bahmanis changed their capital. The Bahmanis wanted to uphold foreigners' cause and concern and they looked for foreign Sufi order for religious legitimacy and piety.

The earliest Qadiri Sufis from Baghad were Shah Zain al-Din Ganj Nishin (d. 1457), Shah Ismail Qadiri (d. 1457) and Shaik Md Multani (d.1529). Then came an exalted Seven Sufis and whose descendents were the Bijapur Sufis.

The Shattari is the third order of the Sufis that lived in Bijapur. The order arose in Iran and brought to India by Shaik Abdul Allah Shattar (d. 1485) in the mid fifteenth century. Shaikh Bayazid Bistani (d. 845) was an intoxicated Sufi. Arberry writes, Bayazid "transported upon the wings of mystical fervour found God within his own soul and scandalised the orthodox by ejaculating, 'Glory to Me! How great is my Majesty!'[6] This was anti-Koranic. Mahammad Ghaus of Gwalior (d. 1563) was a scholar Shattari Sufi. He says, "See the One, know the One, say the One, seek the One; and whatever you see regard as Him."[7] Mahammad Ghaus made Gujarat the center of the Shattari Sufis.

Another follower of the order was Wajah al-Din of Ahmednagar. In fact, Ghaus and Wajah's disciples came to the Bahmani Empire later. Interestingly Shias opposed the Sufis because the latter did not believe in Shia belief that one could not get salvation by way of devoting to an Imam of the house of Ali (Prophet Muhammad's son-in-law). As is known, because of an external threat and infighting due to religious and social differences, Bijapur sultanate could not encourage foreign Sufis for settlement. Only Ibrahim II made Sunni as the state religion. He did not even like Islamic bigotry though he made Bijapur a center of Islamic culture. As Richard Eaton says, the king considered Jami mosques as a physical embodiment of Islamic orthodoxy. Bijapur, due to its diplomatic relations with the Mughal kings like Akbar in Delhi and Ottoman sultans like Sulaiman and the Safawi Shah Tahmasp, became known as Dar al-Islam. Sultan Ibrahim II even facilitated a sort of religious syncretism. Maulana Malik Qumi and Nur al-Din Md Zuhari Firishta (d. 1623) were writers on Bijapur during this time. Firishta wrote an authoritative history of Bijapur *Gulshan-I-Ibrahim* and Zuhuri (d. 1615) wrote the lyrical *Saqinama*. Ibrahim II was a poet and musician and he constructed the famous *Kitab i-Nauras*. He was tolerant of the other faiths, even allowing Christian missionaries. The king was a mystic. Art historian Moti Chandra says the *Kitab-i-Nauras* "reveals a mystic tinge in the character of Ibrahim and he often begins speaking in the language of the Nathpanthic saints who wandered all over the Deccan in the 16th century preaching the mystic yearning of the soul for God. It is possible that Ibrahim came into contact with them."[8] It is assumed Akbar's eclecticism influenced Ibrahim II.

Ibrahim Roza on its walls has Arabic couplets from the Koran extolling the piety and right conduct of Abrahim, father of Isaac. The following verse is inscribed on the pediment over the mausoleum's western doorway:

> No; Abraham in truth was not a Jew
> Neither a Christian; but he was a Muslim
> And one pure of faith; certainly he was never
> Of the idolaters.[9]

Sufi as reformers played an important role in Indian society. No doubt, Chishtis continued to stay in the rural, and Qadiris and Shattari stayed in the urban. Richard Eaton says, "The rustic Litarati and the urban reformist thus represented two Sufi responses to the Muslim city in its Hindu environment."[10] Sufi response was one of a reformist later. For ex: Abdul Hasan did this even by producing miracles. As Naqsabandis opposed Akbar Sufis opposed the kings in the Deccan. Shah Sibghat Allah (d. 1606) from Gujarat stayed at Bijapur, for criticising Ibrahim II of his Hindu attitude. Hashim Pir (d. 1646) was another great Sufi and when Ibrahim II fell ill in 1646, Hashim Pir gave the sultan ten years of his life in return for a favour extended to him twenty years earlier. Md Adil Shah built his tomb Gol Gumbaz just behind Hashim Pir's dargah and died exactly ten years later. Hashim Pir was a social reformer. Shah Allah was a reformer and he built a mosque in Ibrahimpur. Md Muhibbi (d. 1699) records all this in his *Khulasat al-Asar*. Shaikh Abd Allah was sultan's adviser.

The Sufis hated the Hindus. They did not learn Dakhni. They tried to Arabaze the Deccan courts. And once they died or left, their tombs became venerated which they themselves would have scorned.

Chishti Sufis' (who resided at Shahapur Hillock) espoused their own distinctive school of mystical thoughts. They had a role in developing Dakhni and Urdu literature and they diffused popular Islam in the Deccan. Shah Sham al-Ushshaq (d. 1499) and his son Burhan Janam (d. 1597), and Md Dahan (d. 1617) wrote literature. Burhan al-Din wrote *Irshad-nama*. These people revived the Chishti order in Bijapur. They said a man must be a genuine Muslim and seek salvation at the pir. He must cross four stages Shariat (Law), Tariqat (Way), Haqiqat (truth) and Marifat (an esoteric knowledge). Shah Ushshaq's verse makes it succinct.

> One who hears (Shariat) does (Tariqat);
> One who does, sees (Haqiqat);
> And one who sees, enjoys (Marifat).
> At this place, if God is kind, what good fortune comes.[11]

Shaikh Md Khush Dahan's work *Marifat al-Sulik* is an elaborate work on Bijapur Chishtis. The goal of the Chishti was to transcend all of these four stages and attain *maqam-i-qurb*, the place of nearness to God. Burhan al-Din writes:

> The worshipper and the worshipped are now the same,
> And there is no place for dualism.

So because of their popular literature, the Deccan Sufis interacted ably with the non-Muslim populace.

Sufis as Landed Elites

As Sir J.S. Trimmingham says Sufis entered the third stage *tariqa* in the seventeenth century. First the Sufis used to stay at khanaqah, a humble hospice where pirs taught their murids. Dargahs replaced khanaqahs in the phase of *tiriqa*. A dargah was the tomb of a departed pir, typically a structure about twenty feet in height having a square or octagonal base supporting a nearly spherical dome. A Sajjada-nishin looked after the dargahs. Magic and superstitions crept into the system later. The state interfered with the Sufis, granting them imams. Richard Eaton says this totally negated the doctrine of mystical standards and merit. For ex: when Hashim Pir

Alawi died, his son did not continue teaching in the khanaqah. He built a tomb over his father's grave. There, Hushim Pir's grandson Shah Burhan al-Din Alawi (d. 1674) established himself as the first Sajjada-nishin, receiving contributions from the devotees. The same thing happened at the dargahs of Qasim Qadiri, Habib Allah, Hamid Qadiri and Abd al-Razzaq in Bijapur as at Bandanawaz's in Gulbarga.

Not all Sufis got into jagirs or merged into the orthodox religion. Some of them — the dervishes — adopted new life-styles defying the establishment. In J. S. Trimmingham's view dervishes gave importance to practice, while Sufis, to theory. "The Sufi follows a mystical theory or doctrine," he writes, "the darwish practices the mystical way."[12] But some were both. Bijapur dervishes were called majzub (attracted to God). They used wine and opium, associating with the non-elite. Such majzubs lived with the Chishtis at Shahapur Hillocks. Shah Amin-al-Din Ala (d. 1675) and Muhammad Mahmud Bahri (d. 1717) were great critics of the faith. One account of Amin al-Din says that he meditated for twelve years and the other years, he spent his first youth brooding at his father's tomb until finally he emerged from his reflections to declare his union with God. So he became a living object of worship. According to Amin al-Din, a revolutionary, a mosque is not an exclusive house of God. He says:

> Some great people say that prayers to God consist of construction of a mosque and praying in it. They would pray day and night to God in the house of God. (But) the first mosque is the whole creation; the body is the mihrab (a mosque's niche) and the heart is the spiritual light which, when filled and illuminated, prepares a man to offer prayers.[13]

Amin-al-Din was an advaita as Hindus said. He writes:

> When I saw that this is the place of God
> I saw that two names signify one thing.
> You should know and accept that in reality
> God and Man are one.
> The extremity (siwat) of Man is God,

And the extremity of God is Man.
There is only one place of both God and Man
And they both have one sign.[14]

Amin-al-Din's followers believed in his divinity thinking that he would become a Mahdi. One disciple wrote:

The public all agreed that Amin was a majzub,
A salik, a friend of God.
For it is true that Amin has dissolved himself with God
And in truth has become immortal.[15]

No doubt, lakhs of people—Muslims and Hindus—visited him. This attests the fact that Lingayats followed Amin-al-Din. However, the Ulema under Muhammad Bukhari accused Amin-al-Din of heresy and questioned him. Mir Md Sadiq of the Qadiri order by his poetic invectives attacked Amin-al-Din. The main cause of all this was that Amin-al-Din's vision of life was based on Hindu philosophy.

Mahamud Bahri (d. 1717) of Gogi has recorded the lives of many Sufis. He himself was a Sufi recluse affiliated to the Chishti order. He wrote *Bangab-nama* and *Man Lagan*, explicating Sufis' use of wine and opium for 'self-annihilation.' He writes:

Drink your *bhangab* and be happy—
Be a dervish and put your heart at peace
Lose all your life in drinking this exhilaration,
And not in sewing shabby clothes.[16]

Mahamud Bahri spoke of music as an inducement. He says there are many ways to reach God. Islamic law says music is harmful for a divine cause. But Bahri refuted it by writing:

Do not drink *bhangab* without music;
It you are sick with no love (of God)
You should not hear music

Some people say that music must not be allowed
And that it drives away Islamic Law.
But such people do not understand the time, conditions,
And the rapture of those who use music.
They are only boys who do not know rapture.[17]

Mahamud Bahri says a Sufi is a mystic and he need not follow Islam:

> He who trods the path of mystic knowledge
> Bows to no religion
> Whatever comes to his attention contents him,
> And he speaks not of why.[18]

Mahamud Bahri says Bijapur ulam hated Sufis as Mansur al-Hallaj, a majzub of the tenth century Baghad, for his identification with God, hanged to death. No doubt, Mahamud Bahri as well as Amin-al-Din violated the pillars of Islam. Yet Amin-al-Din was a mystic of the high order, and Mahamud Bahri, such sect's spokesman critic. John Fryer however, writes of dervishes in low order. He calls them dissolute, licentious and propane, which, of course, is wrong. The sufis' deviation into dervishes is attributed to the social conditions of the time. First a cholera took a heavy toll of 1,50,000 population; then 1686's Mughal conquest of Bijapur for three years destroying crops; then 1696's Bhima floods wasting a year's crop and finally 1717 famine. These calamities destroyed half of Bijapur population. Richard Eaton says politically the Mughal conquest of Bijapur was an outright failure; and culturally, the dakhni was replaced by the northern Hindustani. This is well reflected in a folk work *Chakki-nama*. Indeed, ulama criticised the Sufis for their using wine, music and opium, for their using prophesying, trickery and magic and for their pantheistic theosophy.

References

1. Henry Cousens, *Notes on the Buildings and Other Antiquarian Remains at Bijapur,* Govt Central Press, Bombay, 1890, p. 1.
2. Richard Maxwell Eaton, *Sufis of Bijapur 1300–1700*, M.M. Publishers, New Delhi, 1996, p. 10.
3. Ibid., p. 11.
4. Wolsely Haig, qt by Richard Maxwell Eaton, op.cit., p. 43.
5. Aziz Ahmed, "The Sufi and the Sultan," qt by Richard Maxwell Eaton, op.cit., p. 48.
6. A.J. Arberry, *Sufism,* Allen and Unwin Ltd, London, 1919, p. 54.
7. Mahammad Ghaus, qt by Richard Maxwell Eaton, op.cit., p. 59.

8. Moti Chandra, qt by Richard Maxwell Eaton, op.cit., p. 101.
9. A. J. Arberry, trans. *The Koran Interpreted,* Macmillan, New York, 1970, p. 83.
10. Moti Chandea, qt by Richard Maxwell Eaton, op.cit., p. 101
11. A.J. Arberry, op.cit., p. 83
12. J. S. Trimmingham, *Sufi Orders in Islam*, OUP, Oxford, 1971, p. 264.
13. Amin-al-Din Ala, *Risala-yi Tasawwuf*, Dakhni MS, Hyderabad, Salar Jung Museum, Urdu MSS, Tasawwuf and Akhlaq No 60.
14. Ibid., p. 60.
15. M.A. Siddiqi, *The Dakani Inscriptions*, Epigraphia India, 1968, pp. 79-92.
16. Mahamud Bahri, qt by Richard Maxwell Eaton, op.cit., p. 260.
17. Ibid., p. 261.
18. Ibid., p. 262.

18

Existentialism: A Way of Life

People experiment with their ways of life as ever before. One such experimentation gave way to a philosophy of existence or existentialism in Europe. This was rather a reaction against Hegelian idealism. Actually the origin and development of existentialism is quite old. Socrates (469-399 BC) asserted for self-understanding. Plato (427-347 BC) and Aristotle (383-322 BC) propounded the theory of 'Being and Becoming.' Here 'being' is existence and 'becoming' essence. They think that 'being' is to be considered in relation to 'becoming.' They concluded that 'being' is a synthesis of 'being and non-being' and 'becoming,' a perpetual transformation of one phase into another.

The medieval thinkers thought that 'being' is either a collective name of all the individuals or a realm of properties and 'becoming' a temporal change. St Thomas Aquinas (1225-1274) said 'being' is a genus or property whereas George Berkeley (1685-1753) rejected this saying that 'being' is a percipient or the perceived. Yet they agreed that 'becoming' is a change in time. In modern times, philosophers like George Berkeley, A.N. Whitehead (1861-1947), John Dewey (1859-1952), Benedetto Croce (1866-1952), William James (1824-1910) and Henry Bergson (1859-1941) supported the Aristotelian theory of 'being' in relation to 'becoming.' They think that 'becoming' is related to time. They think that 'duration' or time introduces an element of novelty. But Immanuel Kant (1724-1804) and G.W. Leibniz (1646-1716) rejected this view saying that time flows unrelated to change.

Existentialists accept the view of Aristotle that 'being' is existence and 'becoming' is transcendence. So they are interrelated. They reject Aristotle's view of pre-determination, which curbs man's freedom of action. They think 'being' is superior to 'becoming' as it precedes 'becoming.' They reject Hegelian concept, which attempts to idealise human existence. Existentialism proposes a subjective interpretation of life. It focuses on the problems of human existence with a view to provide solutions. So existentialism is concerned with a subjective interpretation of life.

Existentialism is not something irrational or absurd of life. It is a new attitude or approach arisen in France and Germany to provide man stability. Man needs to have duty and responsibility for a happy life. Existentialism is a philosophy of freedom and responsibility, which has beset the people of the twentieth century in all aspects of its culture and civilisation. It is a way of life enabling man to lead an authentic life. It is an ethic for human action and involvement for self-realisation. Karl Jasper defines Existentialism as "a way of thought by means of which man seeks to become himself." [1] Jean-Paul Sartre says, "By existentialism we mean a doctrine that every truth and every action implies a human subjectivity." [2] Soren Kierkegaard exhorts man not to follow any useless tradition. Friedrich Nietzsche thinks that there is no God and religion. Human existence should be in relation with transcendence. They think man is just a sum of his choice, action and responsibility. So man must know what he should be or become and how.

The basic tenets of existentialism are right choice, right thought, heroic action and honest responsibility. For this, it stresses on atheism or agnosticism and humanism for a purposeful life in the purposeless universe. It aims at making human existence possible and endurable.

Existentialists think man is a unique being. They think that man is free to think and act. He will be responsible for his commitments. Though man's life is full of uncertainties the new philosophy guides him for progress. There are two branches of existentialism— theistic and atheistic. The first was developed by the 19the century Danish thinker Soren Kierkegaard (1813-1885). In fact, Kierkegaard coined the term 'Existentialism,' to emphasise on man's authentic mode of life. He tried to liberate man from Hegelian idealism. He believed in the existence and benevolence of God but not in the existence and benevolence of religion. He said man, for better life, must pursue either 'aesthetic life' devoting himself to art, music and drama, or 'ethical life' seeking happiness in family, business and profession. He advised people to face life. The German thinkers Gabriel Marcel (1889-1973) and Karl Jaspers developed this line of thought later. The German thinker Nietzsche developed the atheistic branch of existentialism. Jean-Paul Sartre (1905-1980) and Merleau-Ponty (1908-1961) of France, Martin Heidegger (1889-1976) of Germany, Nicholev Berdyayev (1874-1948) of Russia, J. O. Gasset (1883-1955) and Miguel de Unamuno (1874-1948) of Spain and Nicholas Abbagnano (b 1901) of Italy followed atheistic existentialism. They deny the existence of soul and god. They think these cannot be proved by reason. They think that man is all in all.

Both lines of thinkers uphold the idea that man is the master of his biological and material environment. Still man's life is interrelated with his self (*Eigenwelt*), society (*Mitwelt*) and biological surrounding (*Umwelt*). If he adjusts with all the spheres he will become a superman. As for man's relationship with the biological environment, Nature is a source of man's existence. So his love of Nature leads to his love of fellow human beings. That is why thinkers advise man to live amidst Nature with good will. Of course, Aristotle said Nature is blind and imperfect. Existentialist thinkers hold different views about Nature's benevolence to man. Jasper thinks Nature is benevolent to man. So man's relationship with Nature must be ideal and endurable. It should be 'I—Thou' relationship.

But in reality man, due to his science and technology, has become extremely materialistic. He sees everything in terms of utility. He is dishonest. He has mastered Nature and has started exploiting it. There is both misuse and abuse. Albert Camus (1913-1960) feels this strongly. He says modern man, by destroying Nature, has deprived himself of the means of meditation; for, "When Nature ceases to be an object of the means of contemplation and admiration, it can be nothing more than material for an action which aims at transferring it."[3] Man's industrialisation, urbanisation and materialism have disturbed his relations with Nature. So existentialist thinkers criticise science, for it presupposes everything. Unlike Jasper who thinks that Nature is benevolent to man, Sartre thinks Nature is malevolent to him. He thinks Nature appears 'a disorganised mass' of the purposeless universe. Nietzsche supports Sartre's view. He thinks nature is imperfect and lacks a coherent system of its own. So a harmonious man-nature relationship cannot be established. This is why man alienates from society and tries to find out his peace with society. Of course, this leads to his unrest.

Man, after his alienation from Nature, tries to establish his bond with Society. He will base his affinity with Society on the tenets of liberty, equality and fraternity. Jasper thinks man's relationship with Society is inevitable. Ponty says, "We are involved in the world and with others in an inextricable tangle."[4] Jaspers says, "Being-there, being-oneself and being-in-itself, these three realms of being are in no sense reducible to one another." These three spheres — the subjective man, the objective world and the transcending society are inseparable from one another. Jasper calls this 'communication.' This means man has two responsibilities—one he should take care of himself, and two, he should care for his society. For this he should have love, sacrifice and goodwill. Accordingly, man must be aware of the world, which he immediately and intuitively discovers and experiences, and he must be conscious of his existence in point of time and space. So man-society relationship must be based on understanding, goodwill, help, cooperation and sacrifice. Kierkegaard says, "The task is not to exalt the one at the expense of the other, but to give them an equal status, to unify them in simultananeity; the medium in which they are unified is existence."[5] Sartre thinks if man is aware of himself he is aware of others. He says, "In order to get any truth about myself, I must have contact with another person. The other is indispensable to my own existence, as well as to my knowledge about myself. This being so, in discovering my inner being I discover the other person at the same time. This is the world in which man decides what he is and what others are."[6] Even man-woman relationship must be based on these prime virtues like equality and mutual love and fidelity and respect. The writer Hardy says 'Love withers under constraint: its very essence is liberty.' Such a relationship must be 'I-Thou.' But Sartre is of the opinion that man's nature is unpredictable and he does not maintain his good relations with others. His sense of domination and possession mar his goodness. Man thinks 'I' is primarily more important than 'You.' He thinks the 'Other' is just a 'subtilised object.' Kierkegaard thinks society is a crowd and trampling geese. He thinks crowd is untruth. This devaluation of Others causes disaster in human relationships. So to avoid this Sartre advocates life in isolation. This is man's alienation from society.

Man, after his estrangement from society, stands in solitude as a forlorn consciousness striving for higher phases of life. In this Crusoe-like existence he is consoled by his intuition and intelligence. What matters is his goodness, action and responsibility. Still he can be confident and bold enough to live alone. As Sri Aurobindo says the world can be understood through consciousness. It is considered as of born of meditation of the soul. But western thinkers find consciousness as a creative of reality for being and becoming. Then man needs to be resourceful with his reasoning and feelings. Some say passions play a vital role, as they are the motive power in stirring man. Jean Wahl says, "Existence is becoming. Passion and decision are movements. Life is made in the heat of passions."[7] Thus man remains in a state of dread and angst. He is covered with nothingness. This leads to self-alienation.

The term 'alienation' is most discussed in modern times. It includes an extraordinary variety of psychological disorders like ambiguity, dread, despair, loneliness, nothingness, pessimism, absurd, and loss of faith. Kierkegaard thinks alienation is necessary for human destiny. Marcel says man is condemned to be free for his self-realisation. He says man must maintain stoic-resignation. Camus thinks man needs to face life. Hemingway once said, 'man must maintain grace under pressure.' So he must create his own order of life. Sartre observes, "Man is nothing else but his plan; he exists only to the extent that he fulfills himself; he is therefore nothing else than the ensemble of his acts, nothing else than his life."[8]

Man has no prior values like thought and destiny but only existence and attainment of essence. Thought is neither superior to, nor a substitute to existence. Now man has to exalt and excel himself just to conquer his nothingness. He must be prepared to rise above the herd. Existentialists deny the help of God, religion, society and magic for man. So "No one gives man his qualities neither God, nor society, nor his parents and ancestors."[9] He can win the triumph if he is true to himself. Such a man who is good, hardworking, helpful to others, heroic in action and responsible for his acts is an authentic man. He is the hero of the world. Such a man exerts himself. As Ibson says "The strongest man in the world is he who stands most alone."[10] Existentialism is just like Buddhism.

Existentialism in Literature

After the World War I man's existentialistic attitude grew admirably. The new times produced several existentialist thinkers in the west. Kierkegaard in Denmark, Sartre, Marcel, Camus and Ponty in France, Nietzsche, Jaspers, Heidegger and Wahl in Germany, Berdyaev in Russia, Gasset Jose and Martin Buber in Spain and Nicholas Abbagnano in Italy. Likewise, the philosophy of existence was quite pervading in the post 1970s. It influenced many writers like Franz Kafka, Andre Gide, Thomas Hardy, Graham Greene, Irish Murdoch, Samuel Beckett, Eugene Ionesco and Norman Mailer. Sartre's works such as *Nause, The Flies* and *Existentialism Means Humanism*, Nietzsche's *Thus Spoke Zaratustra*, Heidegger's *Being and Time* and Jasper's *Man in the Modern Age* reflect all this. Though the new philosophy has its origin in the thoughts of Blaise Pascal, St Augustine and Socrates, its immediate sources are Buddhism, Edmund Husserl's Phenomenology and the French Revolution.

Existentialism spread to all fields. European writers attempted to create a new order of life based on science. Nietzsche, Tolstoy, Bentham and Mill suggested that man's life must be free and comfortable. Kierkegaard reacted against Hegelian idealism and tradition. Nietzsche declared God's death. Jeremy Bentham pleaded for the greater good of the greater number. Mill sought for the liberty of man and woman. Darwin's discovery of species helped man understand his origin in a better way.

Existentialism influenced literature. People understand that they are destined to live with difficulty. They think that God is indifferent to man's wishes whatever. They have lost their faith in religion. Writers like Camus, Kafka, Gide, Sartre, Berdyaev, Hardy, Greene, Murdoch, Beckett, Pinter and Ionesco wrote about man's life in a purposeless universe. This reminds them Tennyson's lines,

> Self reverence, self-knowledge, self-control
> These three alone lead to sovereign power.

A. C. Swinburne wrote of God's uselessness to mankind. The English fiction of Charles Dickens, George Meredith, George Eliot, Graham Greene and Thomas Hardy is replete with theistic practices. The writers think that man can live in perfect harmony with his biological surrounding, society and his inner self. Yet they agree that society has its own codes to hinder man's path of peace, progress and happiness. They write about man's relationship with Nature, Society and his Self and his existentialistic concerns. Likewise existentialism is closely associated with the Theatre of the Absurd. Existentialist writers are mainly realists. They write about man's struggle for existence in relation with transcendence. They defy traditions and authority. So they think of man as a free individual.

References

1. Karl Jaspers, *Man in the Modern Age,* tr. Eden and Cidar Pail, Routledge and Kegan Paul Ltd, Lonodn, 1951, p. 159.

2. J. P. Sartre, *Existentialism*, tr. Bernard Frechtman, Rider and Co., Hutchinson House, London, 1955, p. 12.
3. Albert Camus, *The Rebel*, tr. Anthony Bower, Penguin, London, 1984, p. 263.
4. Merleu-Ponty, qt by R. C. Soloman, From *Rationalism to Existentialism*, Humanities Press, New York, 1978, p. 307.
5. Soren Kierkegaard, qt by H. J. Blackman, *Six Existentialist Thinkers*, Routledge and Kegan Paul Ltd, London, 1952. p. 11.
6. Sartre, op.cit., p. 44.
7. Jean Wahl, *Philosophies of Existence*, tr. by F. M. Lorry, Routledge and Kegan Paul Ltd, London, 1969, p. 31.
8. Sartre, op.cit., p. 37.
9. Nietzsche, *The Portable Nietzsche*, tr. Walter Kaufman, The Viking Press, London, 1954, p. 500.
10. Ibson, *An Enemy of the People*, p. 247.

19

The Luke of the *Bible*: A Note

The Luke part of the *Bible* has as many as twenty-three chapters. This part is the story of Jesus Christ and his message to mankind. It is about God's ways for man. The work is in simple and chaste prose. It is even interesting to read for other religionists.

Luke Part begins thus: "Several biographies of Christ have already been written using as their source material, the reports circulating among us from the early disciples and other eyewitnesses."[1] Luke tells us that his story begins with a Jewish priest Zachariah. The latter is a priest of the temple service and a member of the Abijah. Elizabeth was his wife. Both are quite old. They have no issues. One day when the priest is in temple, an angel Gabriel arrives and meets him and tells him he will have a child. The priest asks how he can when he is too old. Gabriel punishes him to have been disobedient. He makes him dumb untill he gets his son and asks him to name him as John. The new boy John (known as the Baptist) was to declare to the world about the Messiah's arrival.

The next month the God sends Gabriel to Nazareth, a village in Galilee and the latter tells Mary, the unmarried but engaged to Joseph, the descendent of David and Adam and God, that she will bear the Son of God. Such Son will reign over Israel and all over the world. A few days later Mary visits Elizabeth in Judea and hears about her pregnancy. All are happy.

Elizabeth gives birth to a boy and the father says he should be named 'John.' Immediately his speech power is restored. All are amazed of God's powers and praise is to God there. About this time, Caesar Augustus, the Roman Emperor decreed that a census should be taken throughout the nation. Now Joseph who was a member of the royal family goes to Bethlehem in Judea, king David's ancient home. There Mary bears the divine child and shepherds declare it to the world. Mary takes the child to the temple in Jerusalem and its priest Someon is very happy to die as he has seen the divine child. The priest also says this man is going to be rejected by Israelites. Anna, a prophetesses proclaims the divine Christ's arrival to the world. Then Mary returns to Nazareth in Galilee. Thus pass 12 years.

In the 15th year when Emperor Tiberius Caesar (at this time, Pilate was ruling Judea; Herod, over Galilee, his brother Philip, over Iturea and Lysanias; and Annas and Caiaphas were the Jewish high priests) was ruling. God sends a message to John that he should ask people to get baptized. Accordingly they should declare to become pious people. Then John goes from place to place asking people to get baptised. He says people must stop evil-doing. He criticises Herod's marrying of his bother's wife Herodias. Jesus is also baptised by John and the heavens say: "You are my much loved Son, yes, my Delight."

Jesus is 30 year old now. When he begins his public ministry he is known as the son of Joseph and Joseph is the son of Heli; Heli, of Matthat; Matthat, of Levi; and so on so forth. The author enlists the whole progeny which stretches to Isaac and his father Abraham and then to Noah and then to Adam and then to God Himself. This is interesting.

When Jesus starts preaching, the Satan comes to him and says, 'If you are God's son, tell this stone to become a loaf of bread.' Jesus replies, "It is written in the scriptures, 'Other things in life are much more important than bread.' Satan says that he would give him all splendid kingdoms does he follow him. Jesus refuses all that. Jesus says all extremes may anger God's patience. Everyone praises his sermons in the Jewish synagogue. He says, 'The spirit of the Lord is upon me; he has appointed me to preach good news to the poor; he has sent me to announce that captives shall be released and the blind shall be healed, that the downtrodden shall be freed from their oppressors, and that god is ready to give blessings to all who come to Him.' Jesus returns to Capernaum, a city in Galilee. Jesus is a sort of healer and miracle man. Once a demon requests him, 'Please heal me.' He heals her. When he preaches on Lake Gennesaret the whole crowd listens to him. There a fisherman tells him that he is not getting any catch. Jesus sits in his boat and Simon gets a load of fish. So do others, surprising all. Jesus touches a man suffering from leprosy and the latter becomes a fine man. Jesus says, 'My friend, your sins are forgiven!'

'Who does this fellow think he is?' the Pharisees and teachers of the law exclaim among themselves. 'This is blasphemy! Who but God can forgive sins?' Jesus refuses it. He forgives a man suffering form paralysis. He says, 'My purpose is to invite sinners to turn from their sins, not to spend my time with those who think themselves already good enough.'

One Sabbath as Jesus is in a grainfield he finds a cripple. He says 'You will get it right,' and the man becomes good. He would say to the poor 'that the kingdom of god is theirs.' Jesus would say people:

'Listen all of you. Love your enemies. Do well to those who hate you.

'If someone slaps you on one cheek, let him slap the other too! If someone demands your coat, give him your shirt besides.

'Love your enemies! Do good to them. Lend to them. And do not be concerned about the fact that they don't repay.

'Never criticise others or condemn... For if you give you will get!

'What good is it for one blind man to lead another? He will fall into a ditch and pull the other down with him.

'And why quibble about the speck in someone else's eye—his little fault—when a board is in your own?

'A tree from good stock doesn't produce scrub fruit nor do trees from poor stock produce choice fruit.

'A good man produces good deeds from a good heart. And an evil man produces evil deeds from his hidden wickedness. Whatever is in the heart overflows into speech?'

When Jesus finishes his speech he goes back to Capernaum. He heals a captain's good slave, Liddie, there. Jesus speaks of John highly that he is there to prepare a way for him.

One day one Pharisees take him home. A prostitute arrives there with tears. Jesus forgives her for her sins. Chapter 8 is very eventful in Jesus's life. Jesus begins a tour of cities and villages to announce the coming of the kingdom of god. He takes his twelve disciples (apostles or missionaries). Even some followers – Mary Magdalene (Jesus had cast devil from her), Chuza's wife (Chuza was Herod's manager's wife) and Susanna—follow him. He gives the people an illustration. He speaks of seeds that fall on footpath, that fall on shallow soil, that fall on thistle patches and that fall on fertile soil. This is a very fine parable. Jesus saves a dead boy. This is a great miracle. Jesus asks his apostles to follow him. He asks them to reform people. He says people will respect them and respect him by that way. They work and one day they cannot have enough food and he multiplies five breads and two fishes into large food enough for 5,000 people. Jesus shows his presence with Moses and Elijah to Peter and some other apostles. Once a law expert on Moses asks Jesus what one must do to go to heaven. Jesus says: 'Moses says that one must love the lord with all our heart, strength and mind for going to heaven.' When they are going towards Jerusalem Martha meets him. Jesus seems to despise Pharisees for they are great hurdles for people's uplift. He often speaks of the gifts of heaven. He says, 'Every man is a fool who gets rich on earth but not in heaven.'

About this time, Pilate, the governor of Jerusalem butchers many people who are anti-national. Once 18 men die when the Tower of Siloam collapses. People ask why they die. Jesus says all men will suffer in one way or another. Jesus goes from village to village and city to city preaching people for their good. Now he hears that Herod is after him. One Sabbath he helps patients and Pharisees object to it. He says them all days are equally good. He says: 'Which of you doesn't work on the Sabbath?' He asked, 'If your cow falls into a pit, don't you proceed at once to get it out?' One must be humbled. He stresses on self-reliance. For example, 'And no one can be My disciple who does not carry his own cross and follow me.' He says if we want to build a house we should have enough money and materials. When he even teaches tax collectors, some people who detest them, ask him why he likes such people. Jesus says we have to accommodate all people. Both the lost and found are important. Jesus asks us not to get tempted by worldly things. He says, 'The kingdom of god is within us.' He says constant prayers are important for our well being. When a Jewish leader asks him what he must do to go to heaven, Jesus says he must follow ten commandments. Charity is the key word in Jesus's preaching. The example of Zacchaeus is there. He is a tax collector and Jesus forgives him for his greed and that he becomes a gentleman.

Jesus at the end of his life is found teaching in the temple at Jerusalem. There are frequent clashes between him and the Jewish Pharisees. They often blame him and complain to Pilate against him. Everyday he preachs there and at the end of the day he retires to the Mount of Olives. Then Satan enters into Judas Iscariot who betrays him to Jewish leaders after the Passover Ceremony. Jesus knows when his suffering would begin. The leaders catch hold of him and take him to Pilate. Pilate refers to Herod as the latter is the governor of Galilee to which Jesus' village Nazareth belongs. That day Herod is in Jerusalem and he enquirs Jesus. Pilate too. Both, however find that Jesus is not wrong. Still due to their pressure, Pilate passes the verdict that he should die as they demand. He releases their leader Barabbas. The Jews demand his death by crucifixion. Simon of Cryene bears Jesus's cross. Great crowd trails behind. Jesus is crucified along with two criminals. One of the two is a good fellow and shows sympathy for Christ. Thus Jesus after forgiving them all dies. Joseph claims the body of the Christ and he buries the body in a cave. The next day when some women –Mary Magdalene, Joanna and Mary, the mother of James (an apostle)—go to see Jesus, two angels appear to them. Besides, Jesus's body is not there. That day Jesus's two followers are walking to the village of Emmaus and they find a stranger who is Jesus himself. He goes with them to the village and reveals them his presence and disappears. The third day of his burial Jesus is seen again. He appears to Peter. This is called resurrection. He tells people: 'When I was with you before, don't you remember My telling you that everything about me by Moses and the prophets and in the psalms must all come true?'

The Luke Part ends thus: "And that this message of salvation should be taken from Jerusalem to all the nations: There is forgiveness of sins for all who turn to Me. And they worshipped Him. And were continually in the Temple, praising God."

Reference

1. All the textual references are from Luke from the *Bible*.

20
Cultural Studies

Culture studies involve a host of severl things like name, caste, class, creed, race, religion, sex, ethnicity and media.

The Concept of Culture through the History

The word culture comes from the Latin word 'Kulture.' It is complicated word in English language. In Roman antiquity, culture referred to cultivation of farming, like sericulture or fishi-culture today. Later it was associated with religious faith. In the fifteenth century renaissance, culture meant mental cultivation, refinement. So the words cultured and uncultured were used. The term stood for all human beings, and for their progress. The Germans in the eighteenth century used the word for enlightenment. The word was used to refer to the development of the individual as a refined person. Culture meant to be moral education, or culture as marking the progress of a people or nation.

In France, the word culture was to compete with another similar and smaller word civilisation. In fact, both were understood as one and the same sometimes. The Germans took it for *Bildung* (referring to pedagogical process of the spiritual or moral formation of the individual and by extension to the whole society). But intellectuals differentiated the two words. They said that culture is the way man lived, and the civilisation is the things man used. The former refers to mental or moral state of refinement and the latter to his material progress. Sir Edward Taylor, the English thinker used the word culture for "complex whole." The German thinker Herder said culture differentiates man from animals. He listed as culture's elements: "The language of a people; the means and objects of subsistence; the instruments and ways of communication and commerce; all forms of art, science, political and legal institutions; the forms of religious service and belief; and a people's diversity of customs and mores in their entirety. Thus culture applied to all people, 'enlightened' and 'unenlightened,' signaling a strong comparative interest entailed by the term to this day."

Culture was thought to be a coherent unit governed by a systematic logic and orderly relationships among many parts. The French philosopher Jean Jack Rousseau discussed culture in his work *Social Contract*. The Victorian poet-critic Matthew Arnold wrote about culture in his book *Culture and Anarchy*. He says culture is 'sweetness and light.' The generic notion of culture holds that all peoples and nations have their own cultures. Culture that way helps man to realise his humanness. Then there are notions of high culture and low culture. The word culture is used as a complex and systematic property by which people can be described.

Culture is something which all people possess uniformly. Modern theories of culture have four factors. First, there are many cultures or sub-cultures. This helps us to understand multiculturalism. Secondly, all cultures are relatively good. Thirdly, all cultures are shaped by complex world historical processes. Fourthly, modern cultures are in interaction and contact with other cultures.

Race

Some scientists have divided human beings into different races by looking at things like size, skin colour and other physical differences. Unfortunately this also led many people to hold racist ideas. They decided that some racial groups were superior to others, and this allowed 'superior' races to ill-treat and discriminate against 'inferior' races. European settlers in Africa, Asia and South America took over the land belonging to the original inhabitants. In Australia and New Zealand, Aborigine and Maori people were massacred when they tried to resist the new settlers. Nazi Germany was ruled on racist lines. Jews and Gypsies, and anyone else that Adolf Hitler decided was 'inferior' were persecuted and put into concentration camps. Eventually this led to the Holocaust, in which millions of people were systematically put to death.

Religion

Many people ask 'Where was I before I was born?,' 'Where will I go when I die?,' and 'Why do people suffer?' These are all questions that religions try to answer. They teach that the meaning of life is not only in our friends and families, our interests and work, but in something that will not die or change and is beyond, as well as related to, our world. This might be called God, or an eternal state of peacefulness called *nirvana*. Believing in God, or following the teachings of great leaders like the Buddha, might change the way we behave. It does not mean that we take the world less seriously but that we see deeper meanings in things. Religions are also organisations of people who share the same beliefs or way of life. You may be born into a religion or you can join one from choice.

Nation/ Region

The so called concept of nation came into existence in the Middle Ages. The Renaissance gave birth to it. Industrialisation fostered it. City states led to its base. The theory of nationhood based on language created havoc often. Now the ideals of globalisations are weakening it. This is a good sign for a happy world order.

Class

Class struggle is an old problem in human societies. There are many kinds of class struggles in the name of wealth, position and power. It is differentiation among men. The class struggle has led to several kinds of popular rebellions like the ones in France, Russia and other communist countries. Karl Marx was the first to study class theory. He said the class concept is inherent in the owners of wealth and production. The German sociologist Max Weber said class is operated on the basis of wealth, position and power. He said each of them is independent though interacting. This holds that men in every society are evaluated by their fellow men on a number of different structural bases. Class is understood in terms of job, power to control others, membership, religious and ritual purity, knowledge and education. Class is understood in the form of social stratification. This is gazed for knowing people's style of life. Cultural critics point out that there is some kind of social mobility from one class to another, depending upon people's overall progress. Scholars think that modern societies have greater mobility. May be it is just 10 percent, but it is quite significant for a society's welfare.

Class struggle magazines *The Difesa* of Florence and *The Grido* of Turin in Europe were the most rigid of cultural exponents of the doctrine of intransigence (i.e. refusal to collaborate with a bourgeois government). In the nineteenth century Europe, Fourier, Owen and Cabet tried to build up a classless society. Yet Marx and Engel remarked on them in their *Communist Manifesto.* They said, "They still dream of experimental realisation of their social utopias, of founding little phalansteres, of establishing home colonies, of setting up a little Icaria – duodecimo editions of the new Jerusalem – and to realise all these castles in the air, they are compelled to appeal to the feelings and purses of the bourgeois." Compillo Prampolini (1859-1930) in this *La Giustizia* tried to be a reformist socialist. Indeed, Prampolini concluded his article, "It would be hard to achieve greater proletarian clarity." So Prampolini has a cheap irony about the interpreters of the proletariat who cannot make themselves understood by the proletarians. Because Prampolini, with all his good sense and rule of thumb, thinks in abstractions. The proletarians are more or less educated, more or less equipped by the class struggle to understand the most refined socialist concepts. The socialist weeklies adapt themselves to the average level of the regional strata they address. Yet the tone of the articles and the propaganda must always be just above this average level, so that there is stimulus to intellectual progress; so that at least a number of workers can emerge from the generic blur in higher critical perception of history and the world in which they live and struggle.

On the other hand, one of the most persistent leitmotivs in liberalism's ideological arsenal, one of the most effective anti-Marxist arguments developed by the rhetoric of liberalism and anti-communism, is the notion of the disappearance of class.

The contrast is between the older industrial system and what now comes to be called post-industrial society. Usually in modern countries like the USA where European type of classical aristocracy is absent, there is no class struggle. Modern democracy, globalisation and Americanism are responsible for a new kind of egalitarian society. This is seen in many third world countries too.

Caste

Caste the blot on Hinduism and the greatest nagator of unity, rationality and the emerging growth and change, is its real destroyer in India. On the other hand, China has no caste, no class. It is democratic, secular and human. These two –religion and caste—are the mother vices, encouraging Indians—ignorance, overpopulation and corruption. Man is never the measure of things in India and then how can India be human? Westerners say Indian religion is 'inhuman' compared to Christianity. Indian art is symbolical and never utilitarian. Indians view nature as a means of innumerable gods, without knowing that God is one. We never understand the time process as the real process. Indians are known for inefficiency, dishonesty, laziness, unscientific temperament, unsociability and what not? They do not treat all as equal, nor treat their own women with fairness in society.

Consumption

It is said, 'shopping malls are of cathedrals of consumption.' It is true though shop is a glib word, shop is a metaphor of consumption as religion, in which commodities become the icons of worship and the rituals exchange money for goods. The aspects of consumption expose the evils of limitations of bourgeois materialism and cruelty. And yet the metaphor is both attractive and common precisely because it does convey and construct knowledge of consumerism; it does point to one set of truths however carefully selected as a set. Truths compete in a political arena, and the truths that the consumerism-as–contemporary religion strives to suppress are those that deny the difference between the tenor and vehicle of the metaphor.

The general movement aimed at regulating the products and services of manufactures, sellers and advertisers to serve the interest of buyers is knows as consumerism. However, with steady increases in the volume of consumption by households worldwide from about the 1970s, the term *consumerism* has also come to refer to a preoccupation with obtaining various consumer goods or participation in a consumer culture. A related term *consumption* is used by economists to identify the utilisation of economic goods.

Modern areas of consumer concerns are quality and safety, labeling and pricing, selling and credit, advertising and like. There are many continuing problems too.

Strictly speaking consumption in economics, is the end, utilisation or final use of goods and services. Individual, or private, consumption is direct, as in eating food, wearing clothes, or living in a house. Social consumption is indirect, as when governments or nonprofit groups make expenditures for equipments for weapons, roads and schools. In democracy, social consumption is made, in theory, at least, on the basis of 'one person, one vote,' while individual is made on the basis of 'one dollar, one vote.'

Politics

Culture politics is a big thing. As Cornel West assumes, it is a culture politics of difference. Culture politics hinges on aspects like racism, sexism and non-culturalism. To escape such simplifications and to begin to provide an ethics for cultural workers, West turns to history. He presents a brief genealogy of the decline of eurocentricism and white suprematism — the genealogy being a word refering to Michel Foucault. He argues that the task of demystification can only be carried out by those whose confidence and sense of the contemporary cultural political structures is supported by a knowledge of eurocentrism's history. Here cultural studies and history become indivisible. He says, "In the few years of the 20th century, there is emerging a significant shift in the sensibilities and outlooks of critics and artists. In fact, I would go so far as to claim that a new kind of cultural worker is in the making associated with a new political difference."

The distinctive features of the new cultural politics are to trash the monolithic and homogeneous in the name of diversity, multiplicity and heterogeneity; and to reject the abstract, general, and universal in the light of the concrete, specific, and particular; and to historicise, contextualise, and pluralise by highlighting the contingent, provisional, variable, tentative, shifting and changing things. The new politics is associated with the black, feminist, gay, Jew, dalit, tribal and the third world.

The new cultural politics of difference are neither of adjusting with the mainstream or violating it. They are distinct articulations designed to be with the demoralised, demobilised, depoliticised and disorganised people in order to empower and enable social action and to enlist collective insurgency for the expansion of freedom, democracy and individuality. West says this new cultural politics faces three challenges- intellectual, existential and political.

a) *The Intellectual Challenge*: Cornel West says that the age of Europe began in 1642 and ended in 1945. During this time, Europe, due to its renaissance and industrial revolution flourished. Its colonialism flourished too. So Europe achieved what may be called its grandeur. It had the feelings that the white, the Western and the Christian civilisation was superior. At the same time, the European hegemony was questioned in many ways. There were clashes and wars between the Catholics and the Protestants, between the whites and blacks, between the Europeans and the Eastern, may be the Muslims, and between the patriarchy and feminists lately. The dalits clashed with the Brahmins in the Indian subcontinent. European colonialism proved that Europe was quite powerful. Yet European civilisation was rotting. Matthew Arnold, the celebrated English culture critic in his books like *Culture and Anarchy* argues that the upper class people are devilish. He says, "He felt some sense of 'wandering between two worlds, one dead/the other powerless to be born." He meant that Europe was dead and the non-Europe was weak enough not to be born. The second important thing after the Ago of Europe is that America emerged as a great civilisation. The marginalised groups like the Jews and blacks and the third world people became powerful. This is due to education, humanism and democracy. Lionel Trilling, one of the American Jewish beneficiaries tells that the university education often quiets and domesticates radical and subversive styles of life, art and literature. The word art means culture. He thinks today literature alone cannot be able to educate and culturise the masses. The third thing is the end of colonialism. As we know, most of the third world countries have become free now. One fine example is India. They are self-sufficient. World organisations like WHO and UNO are helpful. Yet Frantz Fanon says, "This decolonisation, which sets out to change the order of the world, is obviously a program of complete disorder." Cornell West says after the 1950s in America began many movements for a true democracy and better life. Movements such as Black peoples' human rights movements, Feminist movements, gay and lesbian and the like achieved much needed liberty. First is the appropriation of the theories of postwar Europe- especially the work of the Frankfurt School, French/ Italian Marxism, Structuralism, and post-structuralism. The theories occupied with keeping alive radical projects after the end of the Age of Europe. Another is the impact of forms of popular culture such as TV, film, electronic media — all liberated culture. American preeminence and decolonisation are there. Critics feel that the blacks and the whites are alike. There is demystification all around. This is called 'prophetic criticism.'

b) *The Existential Challenge:* The existential challenge to the new cultural politics of difference can be stated simply. The widespread modern European denial of the intelligence, ability, beauty and character of people of colour puts a tremendous burden on critics and artists of colour to prove themselves in the light of norms and models set by white elites whose own heritage devalued and dehumanised them. So the people of colour are guilty until proven innocent. There is the Booker T. Temptation's preoccupation with the mainstream and its legitimising power. Then there is the talented tenth seduction, a move toward arrogant group insularity. This alternative has a limited function to preserve one's sanity and sense of self as one copes with the mainstream. The next thing is the go-it-alone option. This is an extreme perspective that shuns the mainstream and group insularity. West says the new cultural politics of difference can thrive only if there are communities, groups, organisations institutions, subcultures, and networks of people of colour who cultivate critical sensibilities and personal accountability—without inhibiting individual expressions, curiosities and idiosyncrasies.

c) *The Political Challenge:* Adequately rejoined intellectual and existential challenges equip the reactionaries of the new cultural politics of difference to meet the political ones.

Cornel West says, "The time has come for critics and artists of the new cultural politics of difference to cast their nets widely, flex their muscles broadly, and there by refuse to limit their vision, analysis, and praxis to their particular terrains. The aim is to dare to recast, redefine and revise the very notions of modernity, mainstream, margins, difference and otherness. We have now reached a new stage in the perennial struggle for freedom and dignity. And while much of the first world intelligentsia adopts retrospective and conservative outlooks that defend the crisis-ridden present, we promote a prospective and prophetic vision with a sense of possibility and potential, especially for those who bear the social coats of the present. We look to the past for strength, not solace, we look at the present and see people perishing, not profits mounting, we look towards the future and how to make it different and better."

> Then we shall consider Indian (Asian) political situation here. As we know Indian politics is based on feudal values like casteism. The Muslims and the British complicated the matter still.

Mass Media

Mass media plays an important role in the birth and growth of popular culture. There are mass media and there is culture. Mass media changes from place to place and from time to time, depending upon the advancement of civilisation. The ancient people used art and literature as mass media. Later on, new discourses were made. Since the nineteenth century, mass media like newspapers, magazines, journals, radio, TV, video and today the so called electronic items like mobile phones, e-mail, website have modernised and globalised our way of life and style of functioning. It is through these media, we try to live together, communicate and come to know what is happening elsewhere. Arts and sciences, pleasures and wisdom are carried through all these.

Radio is a means of communication and of knowledge and of entertainment. Radio can be used to transmit music and speech to listeners scattered over a vast area, as in broadcasting or it can be used for point-to-point communication, as between a control center and a spacecraft. Radio also does a lot of advertising. It is still one of the best and cheapest of means of spreading means of mass communication. Britain, America and Japan improved John Bard's invention of the visual aid. TV is a tremendous force for political persuasion, for education, culturalisation and advertisement. TV has become modern man's eyes and ears on the world.

Today TV has hundreds of channels with distinct programmes in every language of the world. Mass and popular culture programmes are broadcast. Cables provide interesting learning activities. Satellites help TV programmes for interest and diversity. People spend much of their time in watching TV programmes. TV viewing is a pervasive social activity. It dominates all other mass media. TV provides all sorts of knowledge, sports, music, fine arts, news, folk arts, games, cartoons, comics, information of several things, education and weather forecasting. It is a wonder (idiot) box.

Journalism is the collection and periodical dissemination of current news and events, or, more, strictly, the business of managing, editing, or writing for journals or newspapers. The usage of the term has broadened to include to news reporting and commentaries on radio and TV, and to a lesser extent motion pictures. In general, newspapers emphasize current news while magazines deal more with background materials. Newspapers traditionally have not only reported the news but have carried on their investigations. The first prototype of modern newspaper was *Acta Diurna* of the Roman Empire. Later the Venice based *Gazzetta* worked. Johann Gutenberg's invention of the printing press was a great help in printing. With the spread of learning came a heavy demand for a regular and accurate supply of news.

In 1660, there were 20 English newspapers in the form of gazettes, courantes and news books. *Mercurius Gallobelgicus* (1594) was perhaps the earliest magazine published in Cologne. In the early eighteenth century, journalism was more a business. Along with the gifted literary wits were many printers and hacks who also used newspapers and periodicals as mouthpieces for their personal views.

By 1776 there were more than 50 newspapers published in London, the USA, and a growing number in continental countries. These great editors succeeded in lifting a profession once held in ill repute to a new level of dignity and independence.

Journalism took on all characteristics of big business-impersonality, departmentalisation and standardisation. In 1849 Paul Julius Reuter started the foreign news agency that still bears his name. There are two distinct trends in new journalism. It caters to the needs of news and views. The later include lots of things about murder, sensation and scandals. Today the press is very much a legalised institution being called as the fourth estate. It can report good things, or the editor will be held responsible for bad things. He may be sued in a court of law. There is much specialisation.

Globalisation

Globalisation refers to the increasing global connectivity, integration and interdependence in the economic, social, technological, cultural, political and ecological spheres. It is an umbrella term and perhaps best understood as a unitary process inclusive of many sub-process that are increasingly binding people and the biosphere more tightly into one global system with one destiny. Globalisation in short is how our world is becoming more and more like one country each and every day. There are several definitions and all usually mention the increasing connectivity of economies and ways of life across the world. The *Encyclopedia Britannia* says that globalisation is the process by which the experience of everyday life is becoming of production and consumption and a resulting homogenisation of culture. Others add that globalisation has the potential to take diverse forms.

As for the cultural aspect of globalisation, there is growth of cross-cultural contacts; advent of new categories of consciousness and identities such as globalism-which embodies cultural diffusion, the desire to consume and enjoy foreign product and ideas, adopt new technology and practices, and participate in a word culture.

Some of greater international cultural exchanges include: (1) Spreading of multiculturalism and better individual access to cultural diversity. However, the imported culture can easily supplant the culture, causing reduction in diversity through hybridisation or even assimilation. The most prominent form of this is westernisation, (2) Greater international travel and tourism, (3) Spread of local consumer products, (4)Worldwide fads and pop culture, (5) Worldwide sporting events, (6) Formation or development of a set of universal values, and (7) Many technical and legal data flows.

The term 'globalisation' was used in the latter part of the nineteenth century. Mongol empire, later on, the Portuguese and Spanish, then the British colonialism used the term vastly. Liberalisation in the nineteenth century is called 'The first Era of Globalisation,' a period characterised by rapid growth of international trade and investment between the Western countries and the third world. The global problems like global warming and international terrorism are also there. And the future course of global world is unpredictable and uncertain. In fact, there are many pro- and anti-global feelings worldwide.

21

Feminism: An Understanding

Jane Freedman says there are many feminisms of concerns with women's inferior position in society and with discrimination encountered by women because of their sex. Feminists call for changes in the social, economic, political or cultural order, to reduce and eventually overcome this discrimination against women.

The term feminism is relatively a modern one. It was first used in 1871 in a French medical text to describe a cessation of development of the sexual organs and characteristics in male patients, who were perceived as thus suffering from feminisation of their bodies. The French writer-republican and anti-feminist Alexandre Dumas used the term 'feminism' on the subject of adultery to describe women behaving in a supposedly masculine way. G. Fraise thinks the term was used in medicine to signify feminisation of men, while the same in politics for describing the virilisation of women. It is a clear gender confusion prevailing in regard to differences between men and women even today. The term feminism was used for claiming liberty and equality when American Declaration was expedited in 1776 and when Elizabeth Cady Stanton and Susan B. Anthony founded the National Women Suffrage Association. The same reflected in the mid-nineteenth century Britain. It is said even before this, Olympe de Gouges and Theroighe de Mericourt in France and Mary Wollstonecraft (in her work *A Vindication of the Rights of Women*) tried to argue for liberty and justice for women. Ironically, the women organisations did not call themselves as feminists. Delmer observes 'feminist' does not mean a woman working for her social emancipation and empowerment essentially. Accordingly a man can also be a feminist.That is to say feminism is a field itself with its own *locus standi* (ideas, history and practice).

In another way, feminism refers to feminists' movements that took place in the late nineteenth and the early twentieth centuries which being called the 'First Wave.' The 'Second-Wave' feminism refers to the resurgence of feminist activity in the late 1960s and 1970s. Jane Freedman argues that feminism is also a continuum of thought and action. Some theorists divide feminism as liberal feminism, Marxist (social) feminism and radical feminism. Liberal feminists think of social injustice based on man-woman divide basing their thought on capitalism; and radical theorists think of women's depending as a result of patriarchy. Recent classifications include psycho-analytical feminism, postmodern and post-structuralist feminism, black feminism, Western feminism and Eastern feminism.

What makes feminist theme is 'equality-difference' debate over the divide between the two. Women's biological difference mattered most. Sherry Ortner argues man-woman difference is a matter of pan-cultural fact. She says, "Man is closer to culture,' while woman is 'closer to nature.' It is true 'equality-defference' debate is one that has remained central to feminism. Feminists argue, 'women can be equal to men.' Some of them even say, 'they are better than men.' This group reasons are not biological but soci-cultural: as outsiders and nurturers, women do things differently from, and better than, men."[1] The central factor for 'equality-difference' debate is the question of the relevance of biological differences between men and women. Most men argue, even many women admit, that women because of mothering and breast-feeding have lesser physical strength. They cannot equal men in many spheres. Woman is judged to be less reasonable than man, more ruled by emotion, and thus incapable of higher and tougher decisions. Even biologists attest this. Robert Wights is of the opinion that "women lack men's genes for competitiveness and risk-taking behaviour."[2] This led feminists to question man's superiority and for formulating ways for overcoming biological problems.

As a result, concepts like 'biological sex' (female) and 'social gender'(feminine) came into being. But Simone de Beauvoir's *Le Deuxieme Sexe* (*The Second Sex*) published in 1949 exerted a lot of influence on feminism. She said, "one is not born a woman: one becomes one."[3] Jane Freedman says of Simone de Beauvoir that "One may be born as a 'female' of the human race but it is civilisation which creates 'woman,' which defines what is 'feminine,' and proscribes how women should and do behave. And what is important is that this social construction of 'woman,' has meant a continued oppression of women. The social roles and modes have kept them in an inferior position to that of men."[4]Jane says the gender inequality or saying that woman is 'an eternal feminine' is a social construct. Ann Oakley speaks of sex and gender, the latter just as an attribute. She writes, "'Sex' is a word that refers to the biological differences between male and female: the visible differenc in genitalia, the related difference in procreative function. 'Gender,' however, is a matter of culture: it refers to the social classification into 'masculine' and 'feminie.'"[5] Delphy talks of gender and sex difference, saying the former is the constant (variable) and the latter, container (invariable). Even sex is thought of as a construct. Thomas Laqueur says people did not distinguish men from women, just because, women bore children but because, she had different sex organs. Delphy says gender precedes sex.

Interestingly Freud argued that man's morality is higher than women's. Because man's morality is based on notions of justice, while women's on the notion of care.

Feminists are trying to get full socio-political citizenship for women. As W. Brown argues politics is viewed more as a man's domain world-wide. Political philosophers like Plato, Aristotle down to Hobbes, Locke and Rousseau argued that woman is not as rational as man for decisionmaking. As for the public and private domains of life, man belongs to the former and woman, to the latter. This 'public-private divide' is a traditional view. Fraisse argues that democratically woman is not given citizenship from the point of republican thought, she is denied representation, and feudally, it is said, political power is masculine.

Olyme de Gouges, a French revolutionary published her *Declaration of the Rights of Woman and Citizen* in response to *Declaration of the Rights of Man and Citizen* in 1789. She said, since women were men's equal, they must get all that men get. But Olyme de Gouges was guillotined for her radicalism. The pressure for women's right took an air with the nineteenth century Suffrage Movement, in Europe and America. Jane Freedman says this was not the question of women's right but the question of human rights. Stacey and Price think, "If women wish to make changes in the societies they live in, they must seek and achieve power positions. It is essential that women should enter the political arena since the societies are all male dominated, for men certainly cannot be relied upon to initiate or carry through the necessary changes."[6]

Women organisations such as Emily's List in the USA and UK supported women by financing them for the sake of participation in politics. Women got a quota in Scandinavian countries. The French women went to the court in 2000 for ensuring gender parity. Today India is also debating legislation on women's equal representation in elected assemblies. Feminists argue that equal representation for women is a matter of justice. Secondly they say only women can represent women's interests. Thirdly though less important is that women can make the process of governing smooth. Anne Phillips calls the second reason as 'politics of presence.' As for citizenship T.H. Marshall speaks of three groups of rights granted to individuals by the state, these rights being civil, political and social. Jane Freedman says, "Civil rights are those 'necessary for individual freedom–liberty of the person, freedom of speech and thought and faith, the right to own property and to conclude valid contracts, and the right to justice.' Political rights are the rights to elect and take part in the bodies invested with political power. Social rights comprise the whole range from the right to a modicum of economic welfare and security to the right to share to the full in the social heritage and to live the life of civilised being according to the standards prevailing in the society."[7] Marshall adds that women have been struggling for these rights from time immemorial.

Employment and the Global Economy

Many French feminists fought for gender-parity in wages. What more? As Rowbotham explains, "Women workers did not simply say homework should be banned. It was a vital means by which women with children could support themselves. Instead, they proposed that homework be paid the same rate as work in the workshops. They also demanded state child-care, laundries, and restaurants, along with training for women workers. they began to form their own cooperative associations to secure employment, improve conditions, and enable them to run their work-places democratically. These cooperative associations extended beyond the workplace. They provided housing and welfare services and they imagined communal housing with gardens and schools and health services for workers on a large scale."[8] What a wonder, even Marx could not think of women's problems wholeheartedly. He said the struggle for women's emancipation was subsumed within the class struggle. German Socialist Clara Zetkin spoke of protective legislation for women. Others thought of women's unpaid work within the family. Today Globalisation has given an international colouring to the feminist problems.

Job-segregation and sexual harassment explain the low status of women as ever before. Hartman argues that capitalism and patriarchy ('dual-system theory') have done much harm to women. Jane Freedman speaks of men's control of women's access to well-paid jobs. There is an argument that women should not continue doing household work for the sake of paid work on parity with men. Dalla Costa suggests if women do not get recognition for domestic work, childbearing and caring, they should go on strike. But Marxists find this idea as theoretically untenable. Jane Freedman thinks Globalisation, in its way, has oppressed women as did colonialism. Interestingly some feminists like Vandana Shiv argue for eco-feminism. Shiv says, the western colonialism and science have destroyed man's harmonious relations with the natural world. Women say natural environment must be cared for and used carefully. Women's knowledge is vital to the maintenance of biodiversity.

Sexuality and Power

Feminists have hotly thought over sexuality. In 1918, a US feminist Crystal Eastman wrote, "Feminist are not nuns. That should be established. We want love and to be loved, and most of us want children, one or two at least. but we want our love to be joyous and free – not clouded with ignorance and fear. And we want our children to be deliberately, eagerly called into being, when we are at our best, not crowded upon us in times of poverty and weakness. We want this precious sex knowledge not just for ourselves, the conscious feminists; we want it for all the millions of unconscious feminists that swarm the earth, - we want it for women."[9]

Feminists want women control their sex and mothering. So the use of abortion and contraception came into being. Catharine Mackinnon argues sexuality constitutes gender, allowing men dominate women. Walby adds women need a great control over their bodies. This leads to heterosexuality. Feminists blame men for thinking of their own satisfaction in intercourse. Some suggest women must go for lesbianism or think of some mutual sexual enjoyment. Bunch says women then cannot be true sexualists without being lesbians, as "the very essence, definition and nature of heterosexuality is men first."[10] Leeds Revolutionary Feminist Group states heterosexuality proves male superiority. By the bye Robin Morgan who says pornography also contributes to women's misery argues, "Pornography is the theory and rape is the practice."[11] Jane Freedman says, " Feminist have argued against pornography on three counts: first that it encourages sexual violence and rape against women, second that in its humiliation of women it is itself a form of sexual violence, and third that women are hurt and economically and sexually exploited in the production of pornography."[12] Accordingly as pornography arouses desire in men, the latter humiliate women. In Andrea Dworkin's view men colonilise women by way of using institutions like law, marriage, prostitution, pornography, health care, the economy, organised religion and systematic aggression against women (for instance rape). Mackinnon even went to the extent of opposing or banning pornography, while the other feminists want it for sexual expression.

Susan Brownmiller says all women are victims of rape or the threat of it which finally makes women subordinate to men. She compares rape to Myrmidons who served Achilles with loyalty. It is an 'anonymous agent of terror.' So it is a system of male control of women. Some feminists think that reproduction and mothering are a burden on women, part of the oppression which must be lifted; these feminists see new technology that will take the burden of reproduction away from women as the key to women's liberation, whereas the same is a great pleasure for many women and other feminists.

Ethnicity and Identity

It is commonly known that the so called feminism is represented by a dominant white, middle-class, often, understanding the differences of race, class, ability and sexual orientation of others. Jane Freedman says there are many feminisms. For example the popular Eurocentric feminsim has overlooked the working classes and negros and the women living in the Third World. Black women are called 'fallen women, wares and prostitutes.' Black feminists, for ex, think that family for many of them is not a site of oppression but a site of protection from racism. They think white women suppress black women. The popular feminists think that feminism is a Western Ideology, whereas Kumari Jayawardena says feminism was born in the Third World. Uma Narayan argues that Third World feminism is a response to particular problems in Third World countries. She writes, "Issues that feminist group in India have politically engaged with include problems of dowry-murder and dowry-related harassment of women, police rape of women in custody; issues relating to women's poverty, health and reproduction; and issues of ecology and communalism that affect women's lives. Indian feminist political activities clearly make feminists and feminism part of the national political landscape of many Third World countries. I am arguing that Third World feminism is not a mindless mimicking of 'Western agendas' in one clear and simple sense—that, for instance, Indian feminsim is clealry a response to issues specifically confronting many indian women."[13] Cynthia Enloe thinks colonisation made women subservient to the west.

Now we have the so called post-modernist and post-structuralist theories of feminism. These two concepts being the same in the context of feminism, focus upon specific aspects of sex in terms of race, geography, culture and the like. Jane Flax challenges the natural, fixed and universal definitions of gender relations. Chris Weedon writes, "A post-structuralist feminism, on the other hand, committed as it is to the principle of difference and deferral never fixes meaning once and for all. For post-strucuralism femininity and masculinity are constantly in process and subjectivity, which most discourses seek to fix, is constantly subject to dispersal."[14] In sum, Jane Freedman argues for a feminism for some kind of collective identity of women, while at the same time acknowledging differences.

References

1. Hester Eisenstein and Alice Jordine, *The Future of Difference*, Rutgers University Press, New Brunswick, NJ, 1988, p. xxv,
2. Robert Wights qt by Jane Freedman, *Feminism*, Viva Books, New Delhi, 2002, p.13.
3. Simone de Beauvoir's Le Deuxieme Sexe qt by Jane Freedma, op.cit., p.14.
4. Jane Freedman, op.cit., p 14.
5. Ann Oakley, *Sex, Gender and Society*, Temple Smith, London, 1972, p. 16.
6. Stacey and Price, *Women, Power and Politics*, Tavistock, London, 1981, p. 35.
7. T.H. Marshall, *Citizenship and Social Class*, CUP., Cambridge, 1950, pp.10-11.
8. Rowbotham, *Women in Movement: Feminism and Social Action*, Routledge, New York, 1992, p. 61.
9. Crystal Eastman, qt by Rowbotham, *Women in Movement: Feminism and Social Action*, Routledge, New York, 1992, p. 224.
10. C. Bunch, Lesbians in revolt, in Marshall (ed.) *Women and Values*, Wadsworth, Belmont CA, 1986, p. 131.

11. Robin Morgan, "Theory and Practice: Pornography and Rape, in Lederer,"(ed.) *Take Back The Night: Women on Pornography*, William Morrow, New York, 1980, p.139.
12. Jane Freedman, op.cit., p. 64.
13. Uma Narayan, *Dilocating Cultures: Identities, Traditions and Third World Feminism*, Routledge, New York, 1997, p. 13.
14. Chris Weedon, *Feminist Practice and Poststructuralist Theory*, Blackwell, Oxford, 1987, p.99.

Index